For all those committed to the pursuit of democratic
community engagement, solidarity and social justice,
including many of our own former students.

CLASS, INEQUALITY AND COMMUNITY DEVELOPMENT

Edited by
Mae Shaw and Marjorie Mayo

Rethinking
Community
Development

First published in Great Britain in 2016 by

Policy Press
University of Bristol
1-9 Old Park Hill
Bristol
BS2 8BB
UK
t: +44 (0)117 954 5940
pp-info@bristol.ac.uk
www.policypress.co.uk

North America office:
Policy Press
c/o The University of Chicago Press
1427 East 60th Street
Chicago, IL 60637, USA
t: +1 773 702 7700
f: +1 773-702-9756
sales@press.uchicago.edu
www.press.uchicago.edu

British Library Cataloguing in Publication Data
A catalogue record for this book is available from the British Library

Library of Congress Cataloging-in-Publication Data
A catalog record for this book has been requested

ISBN 978-1-4473-2245-0 hardback
ISBN 978-1-4473-2246-7 paperback
ISBN 978-1-4473-2249-8 ePub
ISBN 978-1-4473-2250-4 Mobi

Cover design by Policy Press
Front cover image: Ian Martin
Printed and bound in Great Britain by Clays Ltd, St Ives plc
Policy Press uses environmentally responsible print partners

Table of contents

PART 3: Reconnecting class and inequality through community development

Rethinking Community Development

Communities are a continuing focus of public policy and citizen action worldwide. The purposes and functions of work with communities of place, interest and identity vary between and within contexts and change over time. Nevertheless, community development – as both an occupation and as a democratic practice concerned with the demands and aspirations of people in communities – has been extraordinarily enduring.

This book series aims to provide a critical re-evaluation of community development in theory and practice, in the light of new challenges posed by the complex interplay of emancipatory, democratic, self-help and managerial imperatives in different parts of the world. Through a series of edited and authored volumes, Rethinking Community Development will draw together international, cross-generational and cross-disciplinary perspectives, using contextual specificity as a lens through which to explore the localised consequences of global processes. Each text in the series will:

- *promote critical thinking,* through examining the contradictory position of community development, including the tensions between policy imperatives and the interests and demands of communities;
- *include a range of international examples,* in order to explore the localised consequences of global processes;
- include contributions from established and up-and-coming new voices, from a range of geographical contexts;
- *offer topical and timely perspectives,* drawing on historical and theoretical resources in a generative and enlivening way;
- *inform and engage a new generation of practitioners,* bringing new and established voices together to stimulate diverse and innovative perspectives on community development.

If you have a broad or particular interest in community development that could be expanded into an authored or edited collection for this book series, contact:

Mae Shaw	Rosie R. Meade	Sarah Banks
mae.shaw@ed.ac.uk	r.meade@ucc.ie	s.j.banks@durham.ac.uk

Acknowledgements

We are very grateful to all the contributors to the book for their commitment to the project and for working in such a timely and cooperative way. We would like to thank Ian Martin who generously offered one of his original paintings for the front cover. We also wish to acknowledge the support and advice of Oga Steve Abah, Tom O'Connell, Andrea Cornwall and Gary Craig, who offered very helpful suggestions regarding the development of the book series as a whole. Finally, we would like to thank the staff of Policy Press, particularly Isobel Bainton, and the anonymous referees for their helpful advice and encouragement.

Notes on contributors

Anindita Adhikari is a PhD student in Sociology at Brown University. Her research looks at state capacity and citizenship in contexts of deep democratic contestation. Before this she worked with the Indian government at the state and national levels. She has extensive experience in research and implementation of India's social protection programmes and is also associated with the people's movement on the Right to Work. She received her Master's in Development Studies from the Institute of Development Studies, University of Sussex.

Stefania Barca is Senior Researcher at the Center for Social Studies of the University of Coimbra (CES/UC), Portugal. Her research interests span across environmental history and political ecology, with a special focus on industrialisation and deindustrialisation processes, environmental justice and the commons. Her book, *Enclosing water: Nature and political economy in a Mediterranean valley* (Cambridge, UK: White Horse Press, 2010), was awarded the Turku Prize for best research monograph in environmental history in 2011. She is now working on a global history of working-class environmentalism.

Anna Bilon works at the University of Lower Silesia, Poland. She graduated in pedagogy and philosophy from University of Zielona Gora. Now, she deals with sociocultural animation, career counselling (as a social phenomenon) and neoliberal policies' impact on social services analyses. Her research interests also include social and educational policies. Her latest interests are the effects of political transformation on local communities and social services in Poland.

Gary Craig is Emeritus Professor of Social Justice at the Wilberforce Institute for the Study of Slavery and Emancipation, University of Hull, UK, and has been Professor or Visiting Professor at six other universities. His research interests include community development, 'race' and ethnicity, modern slavery and local governance. He is a former editor of the *Community Development Journal* and has written widely on community development issues. He was a community development worker for 20 years.

Frederico Daia Firmiano is Assistant Professor at Fundação de Ensino Superior de Passos/Universidade do Estado de Minas Gerais (FESP/UEMG) in Brazil, and author of the book *A formação cultural dos jovens* *do MST: A experiência do assentamento Mário Lago, em Ribeirão Preto (SP)* (Cultura Acadêmica, 2009). His research focuses on the expansion of agribusiness in Brazil and the forms of resistance employed by landless rural workers.

Mat Danaher works for UNISON, UK, and has been responsible for working with communities.

Sekou Franklin is an Associate Professor in the Department of Political Science and the Coordinator of Urban Studies Minor Program at Middle Tennessee State University (MTSU). He has published works on urban politics; social movements; juvenile justice; the anti death penalty movement; youth activism, Venezuelan politics and state and local politics. He is also the author of *After the rebellion: Black youth, social movement activism, and the post-civil rights generation* (New York: New York University Press, 2014) and is currently working on a book on racial polarization and Tennessee politics.

Kwok-kin Fung is an Assistant Professor of the Department of Social Work, Hong Kong Baptist University. He is also a board member of the International Association for Community Development and an international advisor for the *Community Development Journal*. His areas of interests include community development, social policy, globalisation, gender and welfare.

Mike Geddes is an Honorary Professor and Associate in the School of Comparative American Studies, Warwick University, UK. His research has spanned a range of issues in local politics and public policy, with particular interests in theories of the state and cross-national comparative analysis of patterns of local governance under neoliberalism. His current research focuses on aspects of contemporary politics and policy in Latin America, especially those countries with more progressive political regimes, such as Bolivia. Specific research topics include radical initiatives in local politics and governance, political and policy programmes that claim to challenge the hegemony of neoliberalism and projects to 'refound' the neocolonialist and neoliberal state.

Janine Hicks has served as a Commissioner since 2007 with the Commission for Gender Equality, an independent statutory body tasked by the constitution with promoting and protecting gender equality in South Africa. Her experience is in civil society activism and advocacy on rural access to justice and human rights and participatory democracy. Janine holds an LLB from the former University of Natal, Durban, and an MA from the Institute for Development Studies at the University of Sussex, UK. Janine is Chairperson of local non-profits The Valley Trust, Agenda Feminist Media and the Community Law and Rural Development Centre. Janine is Honorary Research Associate (HRA) with the Durban University of Technology.

Manish K. Jha is Professor and Dean, School of Social Work, Tata Institute of Social Sciences, Mumbai. His research interests include marginalities and justice; development and governance; poverty and migration; social exclusion, human rights and human security. He teaches social policy and planning, social action and movement, and community organisation and development practice. He has been a recipient of a Commonwealth Academic Fellowship (2009) at the School of Oriental and African Studies, London, UK, an Erasmus Mundus Fellowship (2011) at University College Dublin, Ireland and a UKIERI Visiting Fellowship (2013) at Durham University, UK.

Ewa Kurantowicz is a Professor at the University of Lower Silesia, Wroclaw, Poland. Her research interests include community learning and development, local citizenship and educational biographies of adult learners and non-traditional students in higher education. As a member of the European Society for Research on the Education of Adults, she has been a co-convenor of the network 'Between global and local: adult learning and development'. She is currently a member of the editorial board of *European Journal for Research on the Education of Adults (RELA)*.

Emanuele Leonardi is a Postdoctoral Researcher at the Center for Social Studies of the University of Coimbra (CES/UC). His research interests include the intersection between the Foucauldian notion of biopolitics and the field of political ecology; financialisation of the environmental crisis, carbon trading and climate justice movements; job blackmail, and working-class environmentalism. Among his most recent publications is Foucault in the Susa Valley: the No TAV movement and Processes of subjectification in *Capitalism Nature Socialism*, (2013) 24, 2, 27–40.

María Elena Martínez-Torres is a researcher and Professor at the Center for Research and Graduate Studies in Social Anthropology (CIESAS) where she serves as chair of Graduate Programs. She is faculty in the Society and Environment program at CIESAS Southeast Campus (CIESASSureste) in Chiapas, Mexico. She has published several articles and book chapters on issues of community development and rural social movements and is author of the book *Organic coffee: Sustainable development by Mayan farmers* (Athens, OH: Ohio University Press, 2006).

Marjorie Mayo is Emeritus Professor of Community Development at Goldsmiths, University of London where her research has included a focus upon community action and development, learning for active citizenship, and access to justice in disadvantaged communities. Recent publications include *Access to justice for disadvantaged communities* (2014) (with G. Koessl, M. Scott and I. Slater) Bristol: Policy Press. Previous publications include *Global citizens* (2005), London: Zed and *Cultures, communities, identities* (2000), Basingstoke: Palgrave Macmillan.

Lorraine C. Minnite is Associate Professor of Public Policy at Rutgers University-Camden, where she serves as Director of Urban Studies and mentors doctoral students in the Public Affairs / Community Development program. She is the author and co-author of two books on electoral rules and racial and class politics in the US: *The myth of voter fraud* (Ithaca, NY: Cornell University Press, 2010), and with Frances Fox Piven and Margaret Groarke, *Keeping down the Black vote: Race and the demobilization of American voters* (New York: The New Press, 2009).

Sithembiso Myeni is a Lecturer in Housing Discipline and a Research Associate at SARChI Chair in Applied Poverty Reduction Assessment in the School of Built Environment & Development Studies at University of KwaZulu-Natal. His main research interests are party politics, local governance, gender and politics, state reform and service delivery. Previously, he worked as a principal investigator in a collaborative research project on women and political parties for the Commission for Gender Equality (CGE) and National Democratic Institute for International Affairs – SA (NDA –SA). He has a Diploma in Public Management and a BTech in Public Management from Durban University of Technology, KwaZulu-Natal, a Master's in Development Studies from the University of KwaZulu-Natal and a PhD in Development Policy and Management from the University of Manchester, UK.

Kate Newman has spent the last 20 years working in international development, primarily in the international NGO sector. She is passionately committed to tackling inequality and fighting for social justice. She is currently head of the Centre of Excellence for Research, Evidence and Learning at Christian Aid. Prior to this, she was an associate lecturer at the Open University, teaching international development. She spent 10 years working for ActionAid, supporting participatory approaches and human rights-based approaches to education. In 2012, she completed her PhD, which explored the challenges and dilemmas experienced by ActionAid International in integrating rights-based and participatory approaches to development.

Monika Noworolnik–Mastalska is a PhD student at the University of Lower Silesia, Poland and Roskilde University, Denmark. Her current research focuses on adults' learning and global social responsibility as a sociocultural, economic and political phenomenon. She is also interested in sustainable development and learning, community learning and participation in social innovations. Her recent publications have concerned workplace learning and professional practice development.

Frances Fox Piven is Distinguished Professor of Political Science and Sociology at the Graduate School and University Center of the City University of New York. She is the author or co-author of more than two hundred articles on social movements, the welfare state and social policy, and more than a dozen books, most notably (with Richard A. Cloward) *Regulating the poor: The functions of public welfare*, 2nd Ed. (New York: Vintage, 1993) and *Poor people's movements: Why they succeed, how they fail* (New York: Vintage, 1979).

Mohd. Shahid is Professor of Social Work, Maulana Azad National Urdu University, Hyderabad, India. His research interests include social work education, reproductive health, community development, marginalized groups and the politics of development. He has authored *Beyond contraceptives* (New Delhi: AlterNotes Press, 2010) and co-authored *Muslims and development deficit* (New Delhi: Serials Publication, 2012) and published research papers in national and international journals and in edited volumes on development, disability, minorities and social work pedagogy. Currently, he is experimenting with the theoretical frames of hegemony, common sense and structural violence.

Mae Shaw is Senior Lecturer in Community Education at the University of Edinburgh, Scotland. She has worked as a community development practitioner in a variety of settings and now teaches and publishes extensively on the history, policy, politics and practice of community development. She is a longstanding member of the editorial board of the *Community Development Journal* and co-founder of *Concept*, the online practice / theory journal. She is a member of the international Popular Education Network. Her co-edited publications include *The community development reader: History, themes and issues* (Bristol, Policy Press: 2011) and *Politics, power and community development* (Bristol, Policy Press: 2016).

Marilyn Taylor is Visiting Research Fellow at the Institute for Voluntary Action Research and Visiting Professor at Birkbeck, University of London. She has been involved as an activist and researcher in community development for over 40 years and has published widely on community development and participation (including *Public policy in the community*, the second edition of which was published by Palgrave Macmillan in 2011 and, with Alison Gilchrist, *The short guide to community development*, whose second edition was published in 2016 by Policy Press). She is a member of the editorial boards of the *Community Development Journal* and *Voluntas*. She was a learning advisor to the Community Organisers Programme in England and continues to work with its successor body, COLtd.

Peter Taylor is Associate Director for Think Tank Initiatives at the International Development Research Centre (IDRC), Canada. Previously, he led the Participation, Power and Social Change Team at the Institute of Development Studies, University of Sussex, UK, worked as a technical advisor for the Swiss development cooperation NGO, Helvetas, and was a lecturer at the University of Reading, UK. He has a background and doctorate in agricultural education and interests in organisational learning and development, participatory methodologies, transformative education and social change. He has lived and worked in many regions of the world including Africa, Asia and Latin America.

Pilgrim Tucker is Community Coordinator at UNITE the Union, UK. She has previous experience working with communities.

Mandy Wilson is a practitioner, researcher and facilitator in the fields of community development and public policy and programmes. She has worked in and with communities since the early 1980s, for local, regional, national and international organisations. For four years, she was a learning advisor to the Community Organisers Programme, managed by Locality. She has contributed to several publications that have been published by the Community Development Foundation, Policy Press and the Joseph Rowntree Foundation (including *Building practitioner strengths*, CDF, 2001 and *Changing neighbourhoods*, Policy Press, 2007, which she co-authored with Marilyn Taylor), and is a longstanding member of the *Community Development Journal* editorial board.

PART 1

Contested concepts of class, past and present

ONE

Class, inequality and community development: editorial introduction

Mae Shaw and Marjorie Mayo

Introduction

Inequality has become a matter of increasing concern worldwide and across a range of interests and actors. Even the powerful World Economic Forum in Davos in 2015 warned of the 'inherent dangers of neglecting inequality', including '[weakening] social cohesion and security' (World Economic Forum, 2015). This broad consensus on the evils of inequality has occurred just as community development has re-emerged in global public policy debates. Such convergence is hardly coincidental or, indeed, unexpected. In contexts across the world, community development is being rediscovered as a supposedly cost-effective intervention for dealing with the social consequences of global economic restructuring that has gradually taken place over the last half century.

Of course, community development has a plurality of meanings and usages, which can generate considerable confusion and contestation (Meade et al, 2015). Historically, it has been deployed to both address inequality and to mask its causes. We have therefore decided to approach the term in as open and inclusive a way as possible. As the book's contributions from different parts of the globe attest, there is a variety of pressures, processes and practices that are involved when people act together to influence change in their communities, whether those communities are centred on place, shared interest or identity. This book asks what might be missing in assessments of the likely contribution of community development in the contemporary context in the absence of the explanatory, albeit contested, concept of class. It argues that a critical understanding of class is central to an analysis of inequality and the ways in which it is framed by community development strategies, both within and between countries. Without such a critical understanding, community development risks obscuring the underlying structural causes of inequality or even reinforcing potential divisions between different groups in the competition for dwindling public resources brought about by global processes of neoliberalisation.

Some of these concerns are not new; in 1978, for example, a group of academics and practitioners in the UK produced a book entitled *Community or class struggle?* (Cowley, 1978), which directly addressed these same questions. That book sought to convey a number of things: that 'the community solution' was potentially a masking ideology for concealing the unequal class relations that created the very conditions that community development was deployed to address; that the construction in policy of 'disadvantage' or 'deprivation' as ways of explaining inequality could actually be what might now be called 'misrecognitions' of class (Mooney, 2010); that the social reproduction of power necessary for the continuing operation of capital was conducted through a range of social formations and practices that included the construction of such deficit categories; and that community development could itself be complicit in creating, or at least reinforcing, unequal relations of power by perpetuating such discourses and practices. What contributors to that book were particularly concerned with was whether it was possible, within the conditions of late capitalism, to reconfigure community development's wider educational role in such a way as to take account of this, essentially structuralist, analysis.

Over time, the possibilities and limitations of this model have been the focus of sustained critique from several sources (for example, Cooke and Kothari, 2001; Bryson and Mowbray, 2005; De Fillipis et al, 2010; Harvey, 2012; Jha, 2015) including feminist concerns about reductionist definitions of class (for example, Campbell, 1993; Green, 1992). What interests us here is the extent to which those arguments still have relevance for addressing the changes and continuities in policy and practice. For, whilst the binary choice posed by the 1978 publication may be regarded as too simplistic to take account of contemporary complexities, it nonetheless poses a set of challenges which remain relevant. Not least, it underscores community development as an intrinsically contested political practice within the wider politics of the state. A central theme of this book relates therefore to what might be gained by renewing class analysis in light of subsequent developments in social theory and the shifting realities of current political and ideological contexts. The local consequences of neoliberal globalisation, in particular, stalk the pages of this book.

Clearly, neoliberalism cannot be considered a monolithic process in any simple sense. In reality it is fluid, multidimensional, hybridised and extraordinarily versatile in working with the social, cultural and institutional grain of diverse contexts in order to enact and reproduce itself (Peck and Tickell, 2002). Nevertheless, it can also be understood as an ideological project, 'born of struggle and collaboration in three worlds: intellectual, bureaucratic and political' (Mudge, 2008, p.703), which has been extraordinarily pervasive across the globe. It is important to consider, therefore, the extent to which the multiscalar reach and penetration of neoliberal strategies and processes that have sustained massive global inequality may also have created an unexpected sense of common cause and solidarity, as 'neoliberal political economy becomes exposed and questioned' (De Fillipis et al, 2010, p.7). An important preliminary task is to recognise this 'context of contexts' and to reassert the significance of prevailing economic and material conditions for understanding the politics of community development, and the role of the market in particular (Peck and Tickell, 2002).

In his discussion of what he characterises as the global development crisis brought about by neoliberalisation, Selwyn (2014, p.3) points out that 'economic thought that understands markets as non-political arenas of exchange logically precludes political economy analysis, as "politics" are externalised from market activities'. By extension, we would argue that analyses of community development that preclude economic analysis externalise and thereby depoliticise the market as a key (f)actor in determining people's material conditions and the choices available to them. In addition, sundering the economic from the political has a decisive impact on the parameters of democratic participation. As Ruth Levitas (2000, p.190) warns:

> When the economic dimension is missing, ignored or denied, the demand for community tends to become ideological in the strict sense of the word. That is, it masks the real economic relationships and conflicts that exist – or itself becomes the subject of conflict.

Of particular significance for an adequate understanding of the politics of contemporary community development, is the way in which democratic debate about values and purposes has been largely 'reduced to problem-solving and teambuilding' and 'human selves are reduced to human capital' (Brown, in Lears, 2015, p29). This charge has particular resonance for those practitioners who find themselves the instruments of such stealth tactics, 'delivering democracy' through managerial regimes which actually undermine democracy as a social and political process of contest and negotiation (Shaw, 2011). It also raises perennial questions about the legitimacy of 'the community' as determined by policy, on the one hand, and those community organisations which potentially challenge state policy, on the other. In this context 'unauthorised' community groups and activists may come under intense scrutiny, their validity questioned or denied. The politics of solidarity – which collectivities are or are not regarded as legitimate and on whose terms – inevitably play a central role in addressing the choices and dilemmas of community development practice in its various guises, as evidenced by a number of chapters in this book.

We will return to the potentially divisive dimensions of community in due course, but turn now to a consideration of the contested concept of social class itself. What might be the implications of differing theoretical perspectives for those concerned with community development? And how might these contribute to practitioners' understandings of the ways in which the composition of social classes and class identity has been changing over time?

Class, identity and difference

While the concept of 'class' has become somewhat marginalised in theoretical debates over the past decades, there is some indication of renewed interest in more recent times, with increasing concern about widening inequalities more generally. Certainly, a range of internationally influential texts has reasserted the continuing salience of class and economic-based inequality (for example, Wilkinson and Pickett, 2009; Dorling, 2010, 2014; Savage, 2010; Piketty, 2014; Marmot, 2015). Nonetheless, until quite recently there was a tendency for the very notion of social class to be dismissed as an anachronistic irrelevance – 'we are all middle class now' – while the term 'working class' has all too often been used pejoratively to refer to a 'moral underclass' that resides below or beyond society in a state of 'advanced marginalisation' (Wacquant et al, 2014, p.1270). As Savage (2010, p.235) argues, the educated middle classes have been constructed as 'the quintessential autonomous and reflexive individuals of contemporary capitalism', a construct that has served to mask continuing relationships of privilege and power. With increasing awareness of the global and local growth of social inequality, however, the idea that class has become irrelevant becomes ever less convincing.

But how are social classes to be conceptualised in the 21st century? In everyday terminology, social classes tend to be defined in terms of people's occupations, along with their educational qualifications (or lack of such qualifications), social status and power: usages that are broadly compatible with the sociologist Max Weber's writings on social stratification (Weber, 1964). Such meanings have normative value as well as providing the basis for empirical quantification, including the compilation of official statistics and the commissioning of market research. However, whilst this way of conceptualizing class may facilitate those interventions, including community development, designed to ameliorate the *effects* of inequality, Weberian approaches lack sufficient explanatory scope to address the wider relations of exploitation, domination and unequal divisions of power (Wright, 2009).

This brings us to the important and necessary distinction between class as gradation in the Weberian sense, and class as relation in the Marxist sense. Marxist perspectives start from an analysis of capitalism as a socio-economic system; in particular the dialectical relation between those who own the means of production, and those who sell their labour power. This directs attention towards the underlying *causes* of social inequalities. As the super-wealthy become even wealthier and the poor become even poorer – 'In developed and developing countries alike, the poorest half of the population often controls less than 10% of its wealth' (World Economic Forum, 2015) – this analysis has particular relevance for those concerned to reverse the dynamics of inequality.

Whilst Marxist perspectives emphasise the underlying structures of social division, there is also a recognition that people's own perceptions of their class position may be quite different. Clearly, class as a subjective cultural identity differs from class as an objective economic position, although there are critical connections to be made between economic and cultural dimensions (Moran, 2015). As subsequent chapters illustrate, people can and often do seek to differentiate themselves from those with objectively similar interests. Skilled workers have often defined themselves against unskilled or unemployed workers, just as members of the 'respectable' working class may define themselves against the 'undeserving' poor, and 'hard-working families' may internalise prevalent images of themselves as superior to 'benefit fraudsters' – or, indeed, 'migrants'. These kinds of divisions have increasingly international dimensions too, as workers are forced to compete with each other for production jobs in the global economy. It is also important to acknowledge that instances of symbolic (and sometimes real) 'horizontal violence' are constructed in language, culture and behaviour as much as in social institutions or political processes (Bourdieu, 1985).

Such divisions within social classes reflect long-running strands in social and political history. But the forms that they have taken have varied, just as occupational structures themselves have varied, over time. For instance, recent research on the ways in which precarious employment is becoming the new normality in globalised labour markets raises new questions for and about class analysis. There have been debates as to whether those engaged in informal, insecure forms of employment (from 'zero-hours contracts' in shopping malls to 'volunteering' as unpaid interns) are beginning to constitute a new class: 'the precariat' (Standing, 2011). At the same time, writers like Hardt and Negri (2000) have critiqued what they see as the reductionism of the traditional Marxist focus on the industrial working class to the exclusion of peasants, women and *sans papiers* (the multitude), who begin to constitute a new global proletariat. And their approach has been contested in its turn.

Meanwhile, feminists and other social movement activists have raised questions of their own, challenging theoretical perspectives that fail to explore the interconnections between social class and other forms of discrimination and oppression including gender, sexuality, race, ethnicity and disability (Oliver, 1990; Anthias, 2001, Dominelli, 2006; Craig, 2012). As second-wave feminists pointed out, official statistics (largely based upon Weberian notions) have focussed upon women's social class in relation to their fathers' and/or husbands' occupations, reflecting assumptions that 'husband and wife are always social equals', self-evidently not always the case (Davis, in Garnsey, 1982, p.426). Women were – and are – subjected to oppression and discrimination within the home as well as within the workplace and the community. Garnsey (1982, p.443) concludes that 'the division of labour between men and women and the inequalities associated with it provide an insight into some of the basic causes of change in occupational and class structure'.

In other words, social class and changes in class structure can only be understood by taking account of women's exploitation and oppression: challenges that feminists continue to raise. As Dominelli (2006, p.31) points out, 'Feminists now accept that women's experiences of gender oppression are differentiated by a range of social divisions such as ethnicity, class, disability and sexual orientation'. These differentiations have represented challenges not only to Weberian notions of social class: as Marxist feminists also recognise, they constitute 'vital areas of social reality which Marxists (including Marx) have simply not addressed' (Davis, 1998, p.75). Black feminists have further challenged the ways in which white women fail to take account of the oppression and discrimination that they, as Black women, experience. In particular, they focus upon white feminists' emphasis on the roots of women's oppression within the patriarchal family, rather 'seeing the family as a site of safety for black men and women living in white racist societies' (Dominelli, 2016, pp.30-1). Racial discrimination has been a longstanding challenge for feminist politics as well as for class-based politics more generally (hooks, 1990; James, 2012).

The development of the concept of intersectionality has been critically important in addressing the multidimensional nature not only of inequality but also of injustice more generally (for example, Anthias and Yuval-Davis, 1992; Skeggs, 2004; Emejulu and Bronstein, 2011). According to Dhaliwal and Yuval-Davis (2014, p.35) intersectional politics start from the assumption that 'people's concrete social locations are constructed along multiple (and both shifting and contingent) axes of difference, stage in the life cycle, sexuality, ability and so on', which are also constitutive of each other. In other words, 'Class ... cannot be experienced or lived outside of "race", "gender" or "sexuality" and the same is true of other categories'. These intersections and interconnections form a continuing theme, running through subsequent chapters in this book.

Changes in class formations and class-consciousness

Previous approaches to the study of class have also needed to take account of the changes that have been taking place in class formations and class consciousness over the last 50 years, with the predominance of neoliberalism on a global scale (De Fillipis et al, 2010). In the shift from industry to finance in many western economies that has characterised the current phase of capitalist development, 'we have seen the return of sweatshops and rise of contingent labour – the latter day version of Marx's "reserve army of the unemployed"' on a global scale (Lears, 2015, p.29). At the same time, processes of 'financialisation' – the vastly expanded role of financial motives, financial markets, financial actors and financial institutions in the operation of domestic and international economies – have contributed to a new neoliberal common sense which has infected all areas of human life, including public institutions and private behaviour (Therborn, 2012; Hall and O'Shea, 2015).

Furthermore, as production has become disaggregated – removed ever further from consumption, and turning increasing numbers of employees into self-employed contractors – those solidarity-bearing institutions and bonds that traditionally nurtured and sustained the counterweight of organised labour have themselves become increasingly fragmented. This has created the challenges for traditional trades union organising described in several chapters in this book. At the same time, the distinction between worker and non-worker has necessarily become more porous, allowing for the possibility of constructive alliances and raising new and potentially enlivening challenges for intersectional politics.

As suggested, there are significant questions to be explored about class identities and class consciousness in the face of the diminution of those traditional organisations whose primary focus has been to promote class solidarity and struggle. Whilst nostalgic images of the heroic solidarity of communities in struggle may endure in folk memory, of course the reality has often been more prosaic. Solidarity has never been entirely unproblematic, with longstanding divisions between the skilled and the unskilled, men and women, and between those regarding themselves as the 'respectable' as distinct from the 'unrespectable' in their communities. Hoggett (2001, p.37) urges us not to ignore the physical and emotional 'injuries of class' whereby skilled workers in the past, as now, have too often maintained their advantageous bargaining position at the expense of their less powerful peers at home and abroad. In more recent times, such 'injuries' have been exacerbated by increasing poverty, precariousness, indebtedness and dispossession, posing particular challenges for those concerned with promoting solidarity and collective action in the contemporary context. This has particularly serious implications for those parts of the world in which repression of union activities, sometimes violent, has become commonplace: Zimbabwe, Hong Kong and China, among others, according to the International Trade Union Confederation (www.ituc-csi.org/repression).

In addition, the demonisation, objectification and stigmatisation of 'problem' communities by political elites and some sections of the media has been intense across the world, including the virtual 'cleansing' of public space as the poor find themselves excluded from streets, parks and beaches (Therborn, 2012). Imogen Tyler (2013, p.27) compellingly argues that such stigmatisation – what she calls 'the politics of social disgust' – 'operates as a form of governance which legitimises the reproduction and entrenchment of inequalities and injustices'. Deficit models of community are certainly not new in community development, but increasing global immiseration and dispossession exhort us to be extra vigilant about framing communities as active subjects in politics, as distinct from passive objects of public policy.

In could be instructive to consider the strengths and limitations of different approaches to social and political action in order to address the contemporary challenges of building renewed solidarity; for example the distinction made by Graeber (2013) and others between 'horizontal' activity, demonstrated by Occupy and other social movements concerned about democratic process, and more traditional or 'vertical' forms of organisation which seek primarily to engage with and influence political structures. An assessment of conducive 'political opportunity structures', as highlighted by several chapters, is crucial to this task.

Community, solidarity and class

As inequality has become an issue of increasing international and local concern, community development has re-emerged as a means of offering ways forward in the face of growing social polarisation and the challenges it poses for social solidarity (Gaventa and Tandon, 2010). In this context, community development workers find themselves struggling to address the pressing problems associated with increasing poverty and social deprivation, while aiming to contribute to longer-term strategies for equalities and human rights. This book explores some of the ways in which community development workers can contribute to social justice agendas, developing strategic approaches which take account of social class, as well as the ways in which class intersects with other axes of social difference and division.

This is in no way to suggest that community development programmes could, by themselves, resolve the challenges posed by neoliberal globalisation if only they were based upon more rigorous theoretical understandings. Rather, the point is that community development workers seek to maximise their contributions to broader strategies for promoting social solidarity and social justice. As Shaw and Martin (2008, p.305) argue, the community development role can be decisive in enabling people in communities to pursue their interests democratically, 'exposing awkward political problems rather than obscuring them ... [as] critical allies and creative actors in the building of a new and inclusive kind of democracy'. This is both more necessary and potentially more problematic than ever.

As debates among social scientists as well as those more directly concerned with the history of community development have shown, the concept of 'community' is inherently ambivalent and problematic (Stacey, 1969; Williams, 1976; Shaw, 2007; Mayo, 2008). Community has so often been used as a warmly persuasive term with resonances of nostalgia and belonging (Savage, 2010). Indeed, focusing upon community has tended to emphasise shared interests and concerns, potentially obscuring social divisions within and between communities, including divisions of gender, age and access to resources such as land and power (Guijit and Shah, 1998; Jha, 2015). This has major implications for community development theory and practice. Issues are too often framed in ways that direct attention away from underlying structural inequalities, simply focusing on addressing the local effects. Focusing upon the concerns of the poorest and most disadvantaged has also been problematic in both rural and urban contexts, potentially diverting attention from the concerns of the marginally less disadvantaged. For example, concentrating community development interventions on meeting the needs of those struggling to make a living in the informal economy can pose the risk of sidelining the concerns of those more organised in the formal economy and exacerbating potential divisions. As a result, opportunities for exploring more inclusive approaches may be missed.

Problems in addressing issues of social class within as well as between communities have international dimensions and challenges. For instance, dependency theorists have focused attention upon the structures of unequal relationships between countries in the wealthy Global North and their dependants in the Global South (Gunder Frank, 1973). By implication, and not without contention, such international social divisions can be conceptualised as taking primacy over structural divisions *within* the Global South, obscuring the nature of class divisions within development contexts themselves. The general point is that national elites do not necessarily identify with the concerns of their less advantaged compatriots. On the contrary, they may identify far more closely with their elite counterparts elsewhere. For example, since 2000 the number of individuals in Africa with assets worth US$1 million or more has grown by 145% (163,000 across the continent) according to data by the research firm New World Wealth. This millionaire class boasts a combined wealth of US$670 billion: more than the GDP of Nigeria and Kenya, two of Africa's biggest economies, combined, and within the next decade, the figure is expected to grow by 45%. Some of the implications of these trends are addressed in subsequent chapters, with significant consequences for attempts to build social justice coalitions transnationally as well as locally.

Similarly, local environmental priorities can be erroneously posed against economic priorities, reflecting anxieties about jobs and economic growth more broadly. Rather than seeing these in terms of an 'either/or' dichotomy, sustainable development can instead be posed in terms of an alternative to the treadmill of production controlled by national and transnational economic actors; that is, transnational capital (Gould et al, 1996). As several contributors to this book demonstrate, there are common interests to be brought together, advocating for development that will provide safe working conditions *and* sustainable environments for surrounding communities and beyond.

Crompton et al (2000, p.7) usefully remind us of the necessity 'to take on board the extensive changes that have been taking place in the spheres of production, distribution and consumption in class societies and to recognize the interdependence of class, gender, ethnicity, and age'. Debates that focus attention primarily on personal identity and difference can easily divert attention away from the need to explore active and purposeful intersections between class and other forms of social division (Phillips, 2004). In any case, and as Nancy Fraser (2014) argues, the economic conditions for capitalist accumulation can only be fully achieved by relying on *un*economic conditions: in particular the social role of women and the family in reproduction, the earth's ecology and political power:

> To understand capitalism, therefore, we need to relate its front-story to these three back-stories. We must connect the Marxian perspective to feminist, ecological and political-theoretical perspectives—state-theoretical, colonial/ postcolonial and transnational. (Fraser, 2014, p.66)

Adopting a cultural materialist framework in *Identity and capitalism*, Marie Moran (2015, p.68) further probes the social logic of capitalism, which seeks to integrate personal and economic rationalities so that 'individuals or collectivities act in a way that manifests, embodies, rationalises or normalises the principle of capital accumulation'. These concerted socialisation processes have important implications for claims making in terms of both recognition and redistribution, and point to the necessity of systematic development work that attempts to reveal – and, where possible, to challenge or disrupt – such logic in particular settings.

Class, inequality and community development: remaking the connections

Without a concept of social class that addresses the kind of challenges highlighted above, those concerned with community development risk reinforcing existing or potential divisions within and between communities, pitting one form of discrimination and oppression against another. This has been a longstanding danger. In the words of a Canadian community development worker and local activist writing back in the 1960s, without a clear class analysis community workers can end up simply 'organizing the poor against the working class' (Repo, 1977), with predictably divisive consequences.

In any case, practitioners could be missing significant opportunities for increasing their effectiveness. For example, without an adequate understanding of social class and related social divisions, the challenges of building alliances between different sections within and between communities are even greater. This applies to potential alliances between the urban and the rural poor around community campaigns for land rights just as it applies to the challenges of building alliances in the face of multinational agribusinesses, or between public service users and providers faced with public expenditure cuts, in an era of austerity. These issues are explored in several chapters here, in local, national and international contexts.

Organisation of the book

Part 1: 'Contested concepts of class, past and present' explores the underlying concepts, examining the varying ways in which they have been understood and applied in community development settings in the past, while taking into account contemporary theoretical challenges. Following this editorial introduction, chapter Two by Frances Fox Piven and Lorraine C. Minnite explores differing approaches to the concept of social class in 'Competing concepts of class: implications and applications for community development'. While focusing particularly upon the Marxian tradition, with its emphasis on exploitation and domination, they also take into account a range of groups that have emerged under neoliberalism in order to assess the implications of these and other changes for community development.

Chapter Three, 'Community development in the UK: whatever happened to class? A historical analysis' by Gary Craig then traces ways in which the issue of class has (or more often has not) been addressed within community development theory and practice over time, drawing on key texts and experiences from across the world. This sets the framework for considering the extent to which the mainstream practice of community development, as it has developed, has been able to locate itself solidly within, and build alliances with, more explicitly class-based forms of political struggle.

These three chapters set the context for Part 2: 'Class, inequality and community development in context', which focuses upon current interpretations and issues in different countries. This section includes experiences from the Global South as well as the Global North. In chapter Four, 'Working class communities and ecology:

reframing environmental justice around the Ilva steel plant in Taranto (Apulia, Italy)', Stefania Barca and Emanuele Leonardi explore the relevance of the concept of working-class ecology in understanding environmental issues and struggles. Through the case study of a working-class community in southern Italy, where the closure of a steelmaking complex threatened people's subsistence and identity, they raise questions about how a sustainable way forward can be envisioned, incorporating both community and labour interests.

Chapter Five by Sekou Franklin, 'Race, class and green jobs in low-income communities in the US: challenges for community development', examines ways in which activists have married concerns about the environment and economic justice with a broader 'green jobs' agenda, targeting low-income residents – especially Blacks living in chronically distressed communities – following the disaster of Hurricane Katrina in New Orleans, USA. This work involved mediating tensions between the skilled trades (labour unions and trade associations) and groups working primarily with low-skilled workers who had severe barriers to employment. As he shows, the green jobs movement thus reflected an attempt to bridge divisions between two disadvantaged groups: labour and skilled workers who experienced extreme job loss in the Great Recession of 2008–09, and the working poor who suffered from chronic unemployment and underemployment. This chapter provides particular insights into the ways in which political opportunity structures can either strengthen or impede progress on these issues.

Chapter Six by Mohd. Shahid and Manish K. Jha, 'Class, caste and community development: the Balmiki community in Uttar Pradesh', moves continents to explore the subtle interrelationships between social class and caste and their implications for community development practice in the Indian context. Using the concept of intersectionality, the chapter highlights how social class and caste interconnect to perpetuate the subordination and oppression of marginalised communities. Based on experiences of working with the Balmiki community, the chapter explores the dynamics of the relationship between social class, caste and common sense, arguing for a Gramscian counter-hegemonic community development practice.

Chapter Seven by Janine Hicks and Sithembiso Myeni, 'The impact of gender, race and class on women's political participation in post-apartheid South Africa: challenges for community development', also explores the intersections of class, race and gender, focusing on the dynamics of power and politics in relation to women's participation and engagement. This chapter draws upon a recent study, implemented by the Commission for Gender Equality (CGE), to investigate institutional and structural barriers to women's full political participation and representation, which impacts both on experiences of women in political parties and on ordinary women's shaping of development priorities and decision making at the local level. Here, too, there are challenges for community participation and development – including particular challenges for equalities – when social movements move into government.

The interrelationships between political structures and community development are also taken up in chapter Eight by Mike Geddes 'What happens when community organisers move into government? Recent experience in Bolivia'. Since 2005, the Bolivian government has been in the hands of the MAS (*Movimiento al Socialismo*), a party that defines itself as the 'political instrument' of the strong social movements in Bolivia that brought Evo Morales and the MAS to power. With a majority indigenous population and strong and radical trade unions, issues of class and race – '*marxismo y indianismo*' – are intimately entwined in Bolivian radical politics. The chapter explores how traditional/European concepts of class have been adapted to the Bolivian context and how issues of class and race are reflected and refracted in MAS policies. Exploring the tensions that are beginning to emerge, the chapter helps to illuminate both the potential and the pitfalls of attempting to embed radical conceptions of class and race in the state, and to foreground community organising and community development principles in government policy.

In chapter Nine, 'Community development: (un)fulfilled hopes for social equality in Poland', Anna Bilon, Ewa Kurantowicz and Monika Noworolnik-Mastalska, explore that country's post-socialist experiences in building communities, moving away from centralised state planning to fostering participatory citizenship and advancing community development. Rapid liberalisation of the Polish economy, characterised by a lack of attempts to foster social cohesion, has led to the 'collapse' of some local communities and exacerbated the sociocultural consequences of economic inequality. Drawing on historical and empirical data, the authors examine community development's limitations in contemporary Poland in the context of these profound social and economic transformations.

Chapter Ten – the final one in this section – 'Rural–urban alliances for community development through land reform from below', by María Elena Martínez-Torres and Frederico Daia Firmiano, focuses upon alliances for land rights between urban and rural workers in the area of Ribeirão Preto, Brazil. Although the local community has been under constant pressure from the agribusiness complex and developers, the residents have continually engaged in struggles to create and recreate community life by producing healthy food and protecting the environment. They provide an example of how alliances between urban and rural people can help to achieve community development based on 'land reform from below'.

Part 3: 'Reconnecting class and inequality through community development' addresses ways of inflecting community development with critical understandings of class and inequality for the future. This section includes discussions of the implications for the education and training of practitioners in a range of settings, with a particular emphasis upon building alliances for social solidarity and social justice.

The importance of a critical understanding of social class is explored in chapter Eleven by Kate Newman, 'Reconciling participation and power in international development: a case study', which focuses on the implications for building local/national/global alliances. In recent years, international NGOs (INGOs) have become increasingly important players in international development: whether through involvement in large service delivery contracts or as representatives of poor and excluded people, bringing their perspectives into national and global policy debates. This chapter draws on the experience of ActionAid, one of the largest INGOs, originally headquartered in the UK and now an international federation of national NGOs. The organisation transformed its form and structure in order to be more deeply rooted in national civil society and better able to involve the voices and perspectives of those living in poverty in debates that affected them. The chapter shows that a lack of attention to class analysis posed challenges for ActionAid's theory of change, demonstrating how inequality, community development and class interacted in this complex INGO.

Next in this section, chapter Twelve by Anindita Adhikari and Peter Taylor, 'Transformative education and community development: sharing learning to challenge inequality', explores some practical examples of how popular education approaches have helped to create possibilities for collective learning among groups who are discriminated against because of their class and/or identity. By drawing on an Indian case study, it presents examples of specific participatory educational approaches and methodologies that have helped communities to co-construct diverse forms of knowledge and led to practical, positive change in their lives, taking account of the challenges posed by the internalisation of divisions by caste as well as class. There are important implications here for the education and training of community development workers, their employers and those with whom they work.

Chapter Thirteen 'Community development and class in the context of an East Asian productivist welfare regime' by Kwok-kin Fung, also addresses implications for the education and training of community development workers, highlighting the underdevelopment of class analysis in the community development training field in Hong Kong. As a consequence of this, collective practices have been largely restricted to issue-based protests or mutual self-help initiatives. With the exception of a few organisations that have integrated labour and community struggles, there have been insufficient attempts to foster action for long-term policy or structural changes. The chapter concludes by arguing the case for developing class analysis in community development education and training. This could enable those engaged in community development to explore how capital, in its different forms, exploits already disadvantaged communities and how divisions of social class intersect with other social divisions.

In chapter Fourteen, 'Community organising for social change: the scope for class politics', Marilyn Taylor and Mandy Wilson examine the narratives behind community organising in the UK, exploring the extent to which community organising has generated the scope and space for transformational social change. Using the UK government-sponsored Community Organisers programme as a case study and drawing from other approaches to community organising such as Citizens UK, the authors assess the potential for tackling the structural causes of social inequality and ask how community organising might look if approached more consciously through the lens of class.

The final chapter by Marjorie Mayo and Pilgrim Tucker, with Matt Danaher, 'Community unionism: looking backwards, looking forwards', concludes the volume by reflecting on some implications for community development as these have emerged across the collection. A number of common themes are explored through specific studies of community unionism in the UK. Although alliances between communities and trade unions have featured sporadically in the history of community development, this has taken on a new urgency in the context of the predominance of neoliberal policy agendas in the UK and elsewhere. This chapter examines the opportunities that the shift to community unionism could bring, both for the reinvigoration and potential growth of trade unions themselves and for the strengthening of broader community struggles against the impacts of neoliberalism and accompanying austerity cuts. Despite the challenges involved, beneficial outcomes are already being generated, stimulating growing recognition of the potential value of such alliances. There are significant implications for community development here, both in terms of theory and practice, helping to build short-term alliances *and* longer-term movements for social solidarity and social justice.

This brings the discussion back to our initial questions about community development's potential contribution more generally. How might community development strategies contribute towards exposing and tackling the underlying causes of increasing structural inequalities *as well as* addressing their social effects in the short term? These questions continue to have relevance in the here and now. At the time of writing there have been upsurges of political energy in a number of different national contexts, engaging young people as well as reengaging those who may have felt alienated from politics altogether. As chapters from different contexts illustrate, critical engagements between informal community politics and the formal politics of the state open up fresh opportunities as well as posing significant challenges. Community development strategies rooted in critical understandings of the underlying causes of social inequalities and divisions could make significant contributions here, building sustainable movements for social solidarity and justice.

References

Anthias, F. (2001) 'The material and the symbolic in theorizing social stratification: issues of gender, ethnicity and class', *British Journal of Sociology*, 52(3): 367-90.

Anthias, F. and Yuval-Davis, N. (1992) *Race, ethnicity, colour and class and the anti-racist struggle*, London: Routledge.

Bourdieu, P. (1985) 'The social space and the genesis of groups', *Theory and Society*, 14 (6): 723–44.

Bryson, L. and Mowbray, M. (2005) 'More spray on solution: community, social capital and evidence based policy', *Australian Journal of Social Issues*, 40: 91–106.

Campbell, B. (1993) *Goliath: Britain's dangerous places*, London: Methuen.

Cooke, B. and Kothari, U. (2001) *Participation: The new tyranny?* London: Zed Books.

Cowley, J., Kaye, A., Mayo, M. and Thompson, M. (eds) (1978) *Community or class struggle?*, London: Stage 1.

Crompton, R., Devine, F., Savage, M. and Scott, J. (2000) *Renewing class analysis*, Oxford: Blackwell.

Davis, M. (1998) 'Marxism and oppression' in M. Davis and M. Mayo (eds) *Marxism and struggle*, London: Praxis Press, pp 74–86.

De Fillipis, J., Fisher, R. and Shragge, E. (2010) *Contesting community: The limits and potential of local organizing*, New Jersey, NJ: Rutgers University Press.

Dhaliwal, S. and Yuval-Davis, N. (eds) (2014) *Women against fundamentalism*, London: Lawrence and Wishart.

Dominelli, L. (2006) *Women and community action* (2nd edn), Bristol: Policy Press.

Dorling, D. (2010) *Injustice,* Bristol: Policy Press.

Dorling, D. (2014) *All that is solid: The great housing disaster*, London: Allen Lane.

Emejulu, A. and Bronstein, A. (2011) 'The politics of everyday life: feminisms and contemporary community development', *Community Development Journal*, 46(3): 283–87.

Fraser, N. (2014) 'Behind Marx's hidden abode: for an expanded conception of capitalism', *New Left Review*, 86: 55–72.

Garnsey, E. (1982) 'Women's work and theories of class and stratification' in A. Giddens and D. Held (eds), *Classes, power and conflict*, Oakland, CA: University of California Press, pp 425–45.

Gaventa, J. and Tandon, R. (2010) 'Citizen engagements in a globalizing world' in J. Gaventa and R. Tandon (eds) *Globalizing citizens: New dynamics of inclusion and exclusion*, London: Zed Books, pp 3–30.

Gould, K., Schnaiberg, A. and Weinberg, A. (1996) *Local environmental struggles*, Cambridge: Cambridge University Press.

Graeber, D. (2013) *The democracy project: A history, a crisis, a movement*, London: Sage.

Green, J. (1992) 'The community development project revisited', in P. Carter, T. Jeffs and M.K. Smith (eds) *Changing social work and welfare*, Buckingham: Open University Press.

Guijit, I. and Shah, M. (1998) *The myth of community: Gender issues in development*, London: Intermediate Technology.

Gunder Frank, A. (1973) *On capitalist underdevelopment*, Oxford: Oxford University Press.

Hall, S. and O'Shea, A. (2015) 'Common-sense liberalism' in S. Hall, D. Massey and M. Rustin (eds) *After neoliberalism? The Kilburn manifesto*, London: Lawrence and Wishart.

Hardt, M. and Negri, A. (2000) *Empire*, Cambridge, MA: Harvard University Press.

Harvey, D. (2012) *Rebel cities: From the right to the city to the urban revolution*, London: Verso.

Hoggett, P. (2001) 'Agency, rationality and social policy', *Journal of Social Policy*, 30(1): 37–56.

hooks, B. (1990) *Yearning: Race, gender and cultural politics*, Boston, MA: South End Press.

James, S. (2012) *Sex, race and class*, Oakland, CA: PM Press and Pontypool: Merlin Press.

Jha, M.K. (2015) 'Community organising and political agency: changing community development subjects in India', in R.R. Meade, M. Shaw, and S. Banks (eds) *Politics, power and community development*, Bristol: Policy Press, pp 65–82.

Lears, J. (2015) 'The long con', *London Review of Books*, 37(14): 28–30.

Levitas, R. (2000) 'Community, utopia and New Labour', *Local Economy* 5(3): 188–97.

Marmot, M. (2015) *The health gap: The challenge of an unequal world*, London: Bloomsbury.

Mayo, M. (2008) 'Partnerships for regeneration and community development: some opportunities, challenges and constraints', *Critical Social Policy*, 17(52): 3–26.

Meade, R. R., Shaw, M. and Banks, S. (2015) *Politics, power and community development*, Bristol: Policy Press.

Mooney, G. (2010) 'The disadvantaged working class as 'problem' population: the 'broken society' and class misrecognition', *Concept*, 1(3) n.p. concept.lib.ed.ac.uk/index.php/Concept/article/view/88

Moran, M. (2015) *Identity and capitalism*, Los Angeles/London/New Delhi: Sage.

Mudge, S.L. (2008) 'The state of the art: what is neo-liberalism?', *Socio-Economic Review*, 6: 703–31.

Oliver, M. (1990) *The politics of disablement*, London: Macmillan.

Peck, J. and Tickell, A. (2002) 'Neoliberalizing space', *Antipode*, 34(3): 380-404.

Phillips, A. (2004) 'Identity politics: have we had enough?', in J. Andersen and B. Sim (eds) *The politics of inclusion and empowerment*, Basingstoke: Palgrave, pp 36–48.

Piketty, T. (2014) *Capital in the twenty first century*, Cambridge, MA: Harvard University Press

Repo, M. (1977) 'Organising "the poor" – against the working class' in J. Cowley, A. Kaye, M. Mayo and M. Thompson (eds), *Community or class struggle?* London: Stage One, pp 65–90

Savage, M. (2010) *Identities and social change in Britain since 1940*, Oxford: Oxford University Press.

Selwyn, B. (2014) *The global development crisis*, Cambridge: Polity.

Shaw, M. (2007) 'Community development and the politics of community', *Community Development Journal*, 43(1): 24–36.

Shaw, M. (2011) 'Stuck in the middle? Community development, community engagement and the dangerous business of learning for democracy', *Community Development Journal*, 46(2): 28–46.

Shaw, M. and Martin, I. (2008) 'Community work, citizenship and democracy: remaking the connections' in G. Craig, K. Popple and M. Shaw (eds) *Community development in theory and practice*, Nottingham: Spokesman, pp 296–308.

Skeggs, B. (2004) *Class, self, culture*, London: Routledge.

Stacey, M. (1969) 'The myth of community studies', *British Journal of Sociology*, 20(2): 134–47.

Standing, G. (2011) *The precariat*, London: Bloomsbury.

Therborn, G. (2012) 'Class in the 21st century', *New Left Review*, 78: 5-29.

Tyler, I. (2013) *Revolting subjects: Social abjection and resistance in neoliberal Britain*, London: Zed Books.

Wacquant, L., Slater, T. and Pereira, V.B. (2014) 'Territorial stigmatization in action', *Environment and Planning*, 46: 1270–80.

Weber, M. (1964) *The theory of social and economic organization*, New York, NY: The Free Press.

Wilkinson, R. and Pickett, K. (2009) *The spirit level: Why equality is better for everyone*, London: Penguin Books.

Williams, R. (1976) *Keywords: A vocabulary of culture and society*, Oxford: OUP.

World Economic Forum (2015) *Outlook on the Global Agenda: Top Ten Trends of 2015*, http://reports.weforum.org/outlook-global-agenda-2015/top-10-trends-of-2015/

Wright, E.O. (2009) 'Understanding class', *New Left Review*, 60: 101–16.

TWO

Competing concepts of class: implications and applications for community development

Lorraine C. Minnite and Frances Fox Piven

Introduction: class and community

The growth of social and economic inequality is the hallmark of our era. It is not only evident in the economic gulf between the Global North and the Global South; as has now been endlessly documented, income inequality is also growing within countries. Perhaps most surprisingly, since our theories of the development of the welfare state predicted otherwise, inequality is also growing – and rapidly – within the rich capitalist countries with the most advanced welfare states. The nations that are leading the trend are the United States and the United Kingdom.

Sociologists, social policy experts and economists have been describing social inequalities for a long time, sometimes merely reporting income or wealth disparities, or taking a Weberian approach that groups people according to their various resources, including not only their income and wealth but also their skills, assets, political influence and social status. Members of a class share common 'life chances', which locate them within a social structure of inequality. Markets in capitalist systems distribute life chances according to the resources individuals bring to bear; thus, the varying forms that resources take and the different levels of skills and other assets that individuals possess account for differences in the probability that an individual or group will procure goods, gain position in life and find inner satisfaction (Weber, 1964, p.424). In other words, inequality begets inequality.

The resulting metrics are familiar. Income and wealth inequality data are reported, as are associated measures of inequalities in education and housing and health and happiness, and also inequality in political influence. The evidence is overwhelming: we live in stratified societies, and that stratification is increasing. The slogan of the Occupy movement, 'We are the 99%, they are the 1%!', may not have been precisely accurate; but it was close enough, which is why it resonated as it did.

These measures of class stratification tell us a lot about our societies. It is obviously illuminating to know just how many people are rich or poor or in between, and just how rich or poor they are, and it also serves in the design and evaluation of public policies. But merely to describe the layers of class does not point us to an explanation of why class stratification develops, or how it can be moderated. For that, we need a different lens: one that supplements the descriptive metrics of stratification with an understanding of the social relations that produce and sustain it. Once we begin to consider social relationships we move closer to a Marxian conception of class.

The Marxist tradition sees class as a system of relationships of exploitation and domination based in the economy (Wright, 2005). Classes reflect the location of people in the mode of production, and particularly whether they own the means of production or are forced to sell their labour to those who do. However, merely owning resources or assets or selling labour power are not the distinctive features of the Marxist analysis. More important are the social relations between owners and sellers and the ways in which their resources and assets are deployed in the production process. Thus very broadly, in the Marxian understanding of class, the wealth acquired by some reflects their relationship of domination and exploitation to others. The bourgeoisie prospers at the expense of the proletariat. However, because relations of production have been transformed since the 19th century, so a relational understanding of class has to be adapted to take account of our contemporary economy and the new kinds of exploitative relations on which it is based.

The Marxian analysis of class was developed in the mid-19th century, when industrial capitalism was just beginning to take shape. It drew its insights particularly from England, where manufacturing was most advanced and rapidly growing. Marx and Engels predicted that the growth of capitalist industrialisation would eventually result in the polarisation of society into two great classes: the owners of the means of production (the bourgeoisie) and those who were forced to sell their labour to the bourgeoisie (the proletariat). The revolutionary core of their argument was not only that the proletariat would grow in numbers but also that, by virtue of being critical to production, their power would grow. Moreover, the experience of the factory system would teach workers the lessons of class antagonism and class solidarity, just as periodic crises would teach them about the irrationality of capitalism.

Capitalism, in short, would first create the proletariat and then shape it into a force for the construction of socialism.

Of course, much of this did not happen. But some did. Capitalist industry expanded and the mass production industries nourished the creation of a solidary working class that learned to use the formidable strike power that industrialism also created. Class formation was not only the result of the experience of the factory. Class identity was also shaped by the working-class towns and urban precincts that emerged; by the pubs and churches and bowling alleys and football teams, and by the culture created by the working class itself (Katznelson and Zolberg, 1986). And then there was the inspiring Marxist idea that history, the growth of capitalism, was ultimately on the side of the proletariat and its dreams of a better and socialist society.

In other words, the growth of unions and class-based political parties can reasonably be seen as at least a partial vindication of the Marxian prediction.[1] Together with the formidable strike power of workers in the mass production industries, this partial empowerment of workers forced a kind of class compromise in these societies, through increased wages, security of employment and the protections of the welfare state. This was the heyday of European social democracy, of the British Labour Party – and, in the United States, of the New Deal.[2] The golden era lasted for about 25 years after the Second World War. It was succeeded by an economic regime that we have come to call neoliberalism; the new regime transformed classes and class relations, particularly in rich capitalist societies.

The term neoliberalism is generally used to denote a new phase of capitalist accumulation, characterised by the accelerated cross-border economic transactions in investment, trade and labour that we call globalisation. The globalisation of markets means heightened competition, and heightened competition also leads to domestic economic restructuring, evidenced in the post-Fordist 'lean' production and 'flexible accumulation regimes' that were initiated in the 1970s. Essentially, heightened competition pushed big companies to seek new locations with lower costs – especially lower labour costs, to spin off departments and workers in the effort to reduce costs and to reduce their contractual obligations, especially to workers.

Just as important as changes in the processes of production and trade, however, was the emergence of new patterns of accumulation. New ways of making profit were not as focused on production as they were on redistributing the surpluses earned by production and trade: from workers to capital and from the public sector to the private sector (Harvey, 2005), with increasing financialisation in the process. This came to include the redistribution of shares earned in the past and held in the form of savings, of pensions and homes, and the redistribution of future shares as when the debts accumulated by students mortgage their future earnings.

The new patterns of accumulation were made possible through concerted political efforts by corporate interests to dismantle the institutions that had forced class compromise in the decades immediately following the Second World War. In particular, unions – already tamed by the period of class compromise – were now attacked and rapidly lost ground in both the workplace and in politics. Class-based political parties were also weakened, both by the decline of their union constituents and by the fragmentation of the industrial working class. In the US in particular, these rollbacks were accompanied by the enormous expansion of the so-called criminal justice apparatus targeting especially rebellious Black youth like those who had figured importantly in the various Black freedom protests of the 1960s. As a result, incarceration rates soared. Even voting rights came under attack – again, especially in the United States.

The parallel neoliberal campaign for redistribution often associated with Margaret Thatcher and Ronald Reagan, the political leaders who championed it, focused on reducing taxes on top earners, rolling back financial and business regulation, opening the public sector to private bidders and shrinking welfare state protections.[3] The results were dramatic. Profits rose and wages stagnated or fell, while relatively secure forms of employment were replaced by irregular and contingent work. And whole programs in the public sector – sometimes wishfully called 'the commons' – became a new arena for private profit as public education was replaced by charter schools and physical infrastructure such as rail, bridges and roads, as well as welfare and criminal justice functions, were all auctioned off to for-profit contractors (Meek, 2014). Meanwhile, soaring profits and dizzying CEO earnings encouraged the flow of huge sums of money into electoral politics, in which the influence of big money bent public policies in directions that would further increase profits.

These neoliberal practices created what can usefully be considered new or newly expanded forms of class relations. They are not necessarily relations of production, but like the relations between the bourgeoisie and the proletariat, they are relations that promote accumulation through domination and exploitation. Consider only one example: the relation of debtors to lenders in the financial sector. The temporary solution for squeezed working people trying to maintain their standard of living in a neoliberal economy is to take on debt. Of course, this solution was encouraged by the financial sector, which advertised its wares incessantly, tempting people with various forms of ostensibly easy credit: homes purchased on what were at first easy terms but with obscure escalator clauses, consumer goods bought on credit, even groceries purchased on credit. In the US, with its meagre welfare state, student debt and medical debt, also ballooned. And debt – the servicing of debt, the mysterious fees on debt, debts incurred in the distant past, debts taken on in the future and the packaging and splicing and reselling of debts – all became a huge source of profits for the financial sector in a process that nearly brought the economy to ruin.

The consequences of these changed class relations at the community level were also devastating. Deindustrialisation, economic abandonment and government and market failure conspired in an orgy of physical and human destruction, leaving behind increasingly impoverished neighbourhoods segregated by race and class, and communities with a shrinking capacity to solve their problems on their own. In the US, a number of cities have reached breaking point. Shut out of the bond markets through downgrades, and facing fiscal austerity imposed by right-wing state governments, they have had to lay off teachers, shrink police and fire services, abandon parks and defer maintenance of critical infrastructure.

In 2013, in the largest and most spectacular case of municipal collapse in the history of the US, the City of Detroit, Michigan, which is 85% African-American, declared bankruptcy. Some of the worse-off among the battered citizens of that city had their water cut off, city workers had their pensions reduced and prime public assets were taken over by the state or handed to creditors. Over the previous three decades, the state of Michigan led the nation in the largest number of corporate tax break 'megadeals' of all state and local governments, costing the state more than US$7.1 billion (Mattera and Tarczynska, 2013, p.3). Consequently, in the previous decade alone, the state slashed funding for the city by some US$1.5 billion. A right-wing Republican-dominated state government enacted the governor's tax reforms in 2011, which shifted the tax burden further onto the shoulders of millions of working-class residents of Michigan. In one year (2011–12), individual income tax revenues increased by US$900 million largely from the elimination of tax credits and deductions utilised by working people, while businesses cut their tax bill by US$1.7 billion. Job growth slowed in Michigan each year after the new tax law was adopted (Henderson and Tanner, 2014).

Detroit's fiscal woes were further aggravated by a bad bet made in 2005 by a bad mayor[4] who, with the help of Wall Street banks, crafted a complex borrowing and derivatives scheme to issue US$1.4 billion in municipal debt while bypassing the required voter approval. The borrowed money was to be used to shore up the city's pension fund, which was heavily invested in the dot.com market and began to lose money when the dot.com bubble burst. The problem with the deal was that the city agreed to pay the banks a fixed rate on the loan, while the banks paid a variable interest on the bonds to investors (Preston and Christoff, 2013).

With the collapse of the global financial industry in 2008, Detroit found itself in the position of paying more to the banks than it had received from them. The city's credit rating was downgraded and the banks, under the terms of the 2005 loan deal, demanded immediate payment of US$300 million to US$400 million. With the city's finances in free fall, the state activated an emergency manager law to disband local democracy in Detroit and to vest executive and legislative power in a single emergency Manager appointed by the governor. That manager was a bankruptcy lawyer with a global law firm that represented most of the banks that held most of the city's debt.

The subsequent deal struck in bankruptcy court essentially privatised the Detroit Institute of Art and transferred control over other assets, such as Belle Isle Park and the Detroit Water and Sewerage Department, to state and regional entities. It also handed over the Joe Louis Arena, a tunnel to Canada, parking lots and priceless riverfront land to private creditors. Pensions, which only averaged about US$19,000 a year per worker, were slashed and future cost-of-living adjustments eliminated for tens of thousands of current and retired city employees. Retired police officers and fire fighters – who, under Michigan law, are not eligible for social security – will now pay up to US$1,000 a month for their healthcare.

Meanwhile, according to *The Wall Street Journal*, 'The city remains cash poor but not broke. With its bankruptcy filing, Detroit stopped paying certain debts, including payments to its pension funds, freeing up cash to pay its lawyers and consultants' (US, 2014). Those payments to lawyers and consultants reached $177 million (with $504,000 going to the emergency manager), surpassing the cost of bankruptcy filings for the big auto companies that dominated Detroit's economic fortunes for most of the 20th century (Davey, 2014). Our (much-condensed) story of Detroit's collapse illuminates the importance of a contemporary class analysis of community development in understanding the complex roles that neoliberalism, finance capital and austerity politics have come to play in the lives of poor and working people.

Community against class

It is high time to direct attention to the role of class in contemporary community development. This means analysing not only the role of class in creating the failures of community development, but also the potential for mobilising weak or dormant class interests to give life to more democratic directions in community development.

An understanding of class in the context of community development must cope with the easily confused relationship between the benign ideas associated with community and the reality of class and class conflict. 'Community' often obscures class relations. The elites of any community tend to emphasise commonalities, celebrating the gods and rituals that tie people together, their 'one-ness' under a particular constellation of domination and distribution. Cultural artefacts and tropes help them to do this, and thus help to obscure not only difference but also domination and exclusion. Humans are congregate animals and those congregations or communities are always divided, as people try to use each other in the pursuit of their disparate and competitive goals. Another way of saying this is that class or group divisions and the conflicts that they generate are always there, and even when they are dormant are only temporarily dormant. At the same time, commonalities and cooperative interdependencies are also always there, even when intensifying conflict obscures them. Resistance by the classes and groups disadvantaged by ongoing arrangements has to overcome the celebration of community, of organic oneness, of common interests.

This is not to argue that divided interests – class interests – are 'true' while the common interests denoted by 'community' are false. Rather they coexist, and historical circumstance can bring one or the other to the fore. Historical circumstance includes the deliberate action of men and women pursuing goals. Still, the coexistence of divided and shared interests is also true. At the beginning of the Second World War, for example, many of the militant leaders of the American labour movement rallied around the president and the flag and signed on to no-strike pledges – not in the interest of preserving God and country, but in the interest of preserving Democracy and country.

In capitalist democracies, the invoking of community to deny class divisions has often been facilitated by rapid economic growth. When the boss appeals to his workers on the grounds that what is good for the company is good for workers and bosses alike, or when political leaders urge workers to restrain their demands in the interest of a common fight against an aggressive foreign power or to make the nation attractive to investors, there can be truth in their claims. At least in the past, the prosperity of the company or the community or the nation did tend to be broadly, if not equally, shared.

But not always. Sometimes, the very relationships of cooperation associated with community become the terrain upon which groups with different and opposed interests also do battle. The Marxian conception of class also entailed ideas about difference, about divergent interests and the potential power to act on those divergent interests. Industrial production depends on the contributions of both capital and labour, and both capital and labour share an interest in productivity. They are also pitted against each other in shaping the process of production and in determining the distribution of the fruits of production. Moreover, it is precisely because capital also needs labour that workers have some power in their contests with bosses. Cooperation and conflict are two sides of the same relationship, and the fact of relationship yields workers some power.

Community development theory and practice are rooted in these coexisting and contradictory meanings of locality. More often than not, community development, with its hybrid history in social work, adult education, community organising, housing and what we today call international development (Mayo, 1975; Craig, 1998), is a professional practice involving the mobilisation of community members in identifying and solving common problems and engaging in self-help and mutual aid. It emphasises cooperative strategies and looks inward to build community infrastructure and capacity and to strengthen social solidarities among community members (Kretzmann and McKnight, 1993; Fisher, 1994; Shragge, 1997; Rothman, 2001; Rubin and Rubin, 2008). The inward focus causes community development to limit goals to what can be achieved without aggravating conflict. Along these lines, Lee Staples argues that community development: 'operates within the existing constellation of power relationships and does not attempt to redistribute resources or to reduce power disparities. It is not adversarial or oppositional' (Staples, 2004, p.7).

However, there is also a substantial critical literature on community development that challenges these limitations and argues for a broader and deeper engagement with questions of power, racial equality, social justice and environmental sustainability (see, for example, Craig and Mayo, 1995; Williamson et al, 2003; Sites, Chaskin and Parks, 2007; DeFilippis, Fisher and Shragge, 2010; Joseph, 2010). Mae Shaw usefully poses the problem as one in which community development can either act as a mirror, 'reflecting back an image of "the world as it is"', reinforcing existing social and economic inequalities; or it can function like a lens 'through which existing structures and practices can be critically scrutinised in order to find ways to create a more equal supportive and sustainable alternative – "the world as it could be"' (Shaw, 2007, p.34).

Community development in a neoliberal age

The introduction of a contemporary class analysis that accounts for social groups and economic hierarchies and maps the problems of local communities to centres of power can help to focus Shaw's community development lens on how neoliberalism is impoverishing people and wrecking their communities. Like 'community', neoliberalism obfuscates class and mystifies class relations. It parades as an emancipatory theory of how to achieve human wellbeing by unleashing entrepreneurial spirit through the marketisation of everything, when in fact it is a strategy of the capitalist classes and their allies among the upper echelons of financial and corporate management and the state to curb the power of labour, deregulate the economy, undermine democratic norms and institutions and shrink the welfare state.

Financialisation and technological innovation, particularly in the areas of computer and information technologies, have rapidly increased the speed and complexity by which market decisions and capital accumulation occur. For the ordinary individual, it is increasingly difficult to understand who decided to close the factory in town and move the jobs offshore, or who owns the new high-rise buildings going up in what used to be a park. If class is seen as relational then the important class actors in processes of neoliberal extraction or 'dispossession' are far removed, both spatially and politically, from the local class actors who are being dispossessed. The victims, so to speak, can demonstrate and organise and vote, and they can participate in efforts at community development, but their efforts alone are unlikely to have much of an impact. They are unlikely to become a force in the neoliberal system of production in the absence of broader disruption of that system.

A simple illustration can be drawn from the securitisation boom of the 2000s, when millions of home mortgages were pooled together, transformed into bonds and other exotic financial instruments and sold to investors. When the overleveraged US housing market collapsed, whole communities were upended. Moreover, the frenzy of slicing and dicing individual mortgages and packaging them for resale over and over again had made it difficult, if not impossible, for millions of foreclosed homeowners to determine who held their mortgage note. This is one reason that efforts to organise the dispossessed have floundered.

From our vantage point, the most promising development is the emerging community-based work by offshoots of the Occupy Wall Street movement and their analysis of the hierarchical institutional relationships entangling the '99%' in expanding forms of debt – from varieties of individually-held consumer debt (credit card, housing, medical and student loan debt, with one in seven Americans pursued by debt collectors) to forms of debt that are collective, such as municipal debt and including the predatory practices of the lenders. The movement calls itself 'Strike Debt' and names finance capital 'mafia capitalism' to underline the idea that the finance industry's system of credit and debt is nothing more than a 'shakedown system' (Strike Debt / Occupy Wall Street, n.d., p.1). The argument is that, instead of taxing the wealthy to finance public goods like education and healthcare, governments collude with finance capitalists to borrow the money, as the aforementioned Detroit story illustrates.

The idea is brilliant: 'debt is the tie that binds the 99%', in the words of Strike Debt activist Yates McKee (McKee, 2012). Debtors and creditors are also bound together, and the power of the debtor is in activating that interdependence by resisting payment of the debt. With US$12.12 trillion in household debt (Federal Reserve Bank of New York, 2016, p.1), and roughly 77 million borrowers in collection (Ratcliffe et al, 2014, p.7), there would appear to be tremendous leverage in a campaign that resulted in significant non-payment. A crisis created by massive default would call for a political solution.

Many problems, some of them obvious, remain. For example, if the history of withholding taxes to lodge a protest against war is any guide, we might expect debt resistance to evolve as an individual act of moral courage that is neither powerful nor compelling enough to draw masses of people into a movement. The shame and stigma of being a debtor leads to isolation that must be overcome. The penalties are high; default can cause financial ruination that may be impossible to escape. A debt resisters' movement has to figure out how to reduce the risks.[5]

Those engaged in community development work need to understand the basic workings of the capitalist economy that creates the manifest problems, such as mass home foreclosure and crippling individual, family and community debt, that community development aims to solve. To assert class as an analytical category for community development is to return to radical critiques of 'community' and of 'development' that have ebbed and flowed in the discourse and practice of community development and to update them with even more vigour than before. Such critiques – for example, of the exclusionary tendencies of community, or of equating development with 'growth' – would push community development practice in an explicitly political and anti-capitalist direction. What would this mean?

A reassertion of class within a political economy framework entails a rejection of what professional community development has become in the United States; that is, an instrument of state policy emphasising the physical renovation of declining neighbourhoods and abandoned downtowns so that private capital can be seduced into returning at the expense of working-class neighborhoods, a practice that rests on the bizarre invoking of community to mean local physical infrastructure. This is not to argue that resources are not urgently needed to address decades of disinvestment in poor communities and the lack of affordable housing. Rather, it is to challenge the tendency of professional community development to ignore the larger causes of disinvestment and the need for a political response.

Thus attention to class also means an attention to class politics and class power. In politically quiescent times, the cooperative strategies of asset and capacity building, civic engagement and non-confrontational entrepreneurialism that have marked contemporary community development will continue. Though the strategies themselves may be non-confrontational, community development practitioners can work aggressively to protect communities and fight for larger shares of new projects or other resources for working people.

Moreover, in doing the inward-facing work of developing communities to advocate for themselves, community development practitioners act as agents of change. By pushing for what can be achieved through the normal processes of doing community work, they will confront the limitations of the status quo, thereby identifying what those limits are. This is an educative function of community development that can help to sow the seeds for the kinds of political action required to make lasting change. If the power of community practice 'lies not in its status as a distinct sector of activity but in the extent to which it contributes to social justice' (Sites et al, 2007, p.533, citing Fainstein, 1999, 2005), when it is possible to do more, one goal of community development should be to prepare people to be available for political mobilisation and movement activism.

Useful examples can be located in the political history of the US of how community development in quiescent times has supported the rise of movements that bent 'the arc of the moral universe ... toward justice', in the words of the 19th-century American abolitionist Theodore Parker (later quoted by Martin Luther King, Jr.) The centuries-long Black freedom movement was rooted in and sustained by a deep history of local organising (Morris, 1984; Payne 2007). Segregated Black communities in both the South and the North developed complex local societies and indigenous institutions like the Black church and fraternal and civic organisations, which nurtured and protected ordinary African-Americans as best they could. At times, these organisations played a conservative role in the development of movement politics, following rather than leading protests and sit-ins and exerting their influence to temper demands and the pace of change. But overall, there is little question that day-to-day efforts at grassroots community organising and community-building helped to cement social solidarities and to teach people about the sources of their oppression, thus laying a foundation for the profound and risky work of the broader Civil Rights movement.

In the wake of the riots that later rocked American cities in the 1960s, new locally-based organisations influenced by the Black Power movement formed to carry through on the demands for equal rights of the larger civil rights movement (Theoharis and Woodard, 2005; Jeffries, 2007; Joseph, 2010). For example, in St. Louis, following the murder of Martin Luther King, Jr. in 1968, a new alliance of groups known as the Black United Front presented the mayor with a 15-point list of demands to open up employment in city government to African-Americans, expand the number of public contracts let for Black businessmen, increase the effort in recruiting Black police officers and restructure the federal government's Model Cities anti-poverty program. New groups such as the League for Adequate Welfare organised some two hundred public housing residents in a march on city hall, calling for an increase in the minimum wage, a reduction in public housing rents, reform of the state's means-tested programmes and an investigation into malpractice charges against 76 caseworkers. The march built on protests the year before during which welfare recipients, who were mobilised by community-based organisations, protested against having completed job training in electronics assembly only to face racial discrimination in hiring at more than a dozen of the city's manufacturing plants. Nine welfare recipients and their children staged a 10-day round-the-clock sit-in at the city's human resources office, calling for pest control and better janitorial services in public housing projects and greater tenant representation on the housing authority board (Lang, 2010).

Local organising campaigns to develop the capacities of working-class Black Americans to survive and resist racial oppression and economic discrimination mattered as part of a larger social movement to reform and humanise US institutions. Their participation in these campaigns helped to prepare them to understand the nature of their oppression and to develop strategies for attacking inequality. Community development can have no higher calling.

Notes

[1] Although very general in its outlines, Marx and Engels predict the political development of the proletariat in *The Communist Manifesto*.

[2] The term 'New Deal' is used here partly for convenience, but some historians do indeed think that the era of the New Deal lasted into the 1970s (for example, see Fraser and Gerstle, 1990).

[3] 'The Thatcher era,' writes Eric Hobsbawm, 'was the nearest thing in the twentieth century to a political, social and cultural revolution….[I]t set out to destroy everything in Britain that stood in the way of an unholy combination of unrestricted profit-maximizing private enterprise and national self-assertion, in other words greed and jingoism' (Hobsbawn, 2002, p.273).

[4] A broad federal probe into the mismanagement of the city's pensions funds netted dozens of people, including Mayor Kwame Kilpatrick, who was eventually convicted of public corruption and is serving a 28-year sentence in a federal prison in Oklahoma.

[5] City officials in recession- and foreclosure-ravaged Richmond, California considered a promising approach: a progressive mayor announced plans to use eminent domain to buy mortgages in default and then to forgive homeowners the debt. The idea was put forth by the Alliance of Californians for Community Empowerment (ACCE), formerly the California chapter of the now defunct Association of Community Organisations for Reform Now (ACORN), and efforts to build a movement to support the plan are underway against a considerable onslaught of investor pressure to halt and punish the city if it proceeds (see Dewan, 2014).

References

Craig, G. (1998) 'Community development in a global context', *Community Development Journal*, 33(1): 2–17.

Craig, G. and Mayo, M. (eds) (1995) *Community empowerment: A reader in participation and development*, Atlantic Highlands, NJ: Zed Books.

Davey, M. (2014) 'Detroit bankruptcy nears an end', *New York Times*, 10 December, www.nytimes.com/2014/12/11/us/detroit-bankruptcy-ending.html

DeFilippis, J., Fisher, R. and Shragge, E. (2010) *Contesting community: The limits and potential of local organizing*, New Brunswick, NJ: Rutgers University Press.

Dewan, S. (2014) 'Eminent domain: a long shot against blight', *New York Times*, 11 January, www.nytimes.com/2014/01/12/business/in-richmond-california-a-long-shot-against-blight.html

Dolan, M. (2014) 'Cost of Detroit's historic bankruptcy reaches $126 million', *Wall Street Journal*, 12 September 12, www.wsj.com/articles/cost-of-detroits-historic-bankruptcy-reach-126-million-1410557043

Fainstein, S.S. (1999) 'Can we make the cities we want?', in R.A. Beauregard and S.B. Gendrot (eds), *The urban moment: Cosmopolitan essays on the late-20th century city*, Thousand Oaks, CA: Sage, pp 249-72.

Fainstein, S.S. (2005) 'Planning theory and the city', *Journal of Planning Education and Research*, 25(2): 121–30.

Federal Reserve Bank of New York, Research and Statistics Group, Microeconomic Studies (2016) 'Quarterly report on household debt and credit,' February, www.newyorkfed.org/medialibrary/interactives/householdcredit/data/pdf/HHDC_2015Q4.pdf

Fisher, R. (1994) *Let the people decide: Neighborhood organizing in America*, (updated edn), New York, NY: Macmillan Publishers.

Fraser, S. and Gerstle, G. (eds) (1990) *The rise and fall of the New Deal order, 1930-1980*, Princeton, NJ: Princeton University Press.

Harvey, D. (2005) *The new imperialism*, New York, NY: Oxford University Press.

Henderson, S. and Tanner, K. (2014) 'Michigan taxes: businesses pay less, you pay more', *Detroit Free Press*, 4 October, www.freep.com/story/opinion/contributors/raw-data/2014/10/04/michigan-taxes-snyder/16683967/

Hobsbawm, E. (2002) *Interesting times: A twentieth-century life*, New York, NY: Pantheon Books.

Jeffries, J. (ed) (2007) *Comrades: A local history of the Black Panther Party*, Bloomington, IL: Indiana University Press.

Joseph, P.E. (ed) (2010) *Neighborhood rebels: Black Power at the local level*, New York, NY: Palgrave.

Katznelson, I. and Zolberg, A. (eds) (1986) *Working class formation: Nineteenth Century patterns in Western Europe and the United States*, Princeton, NJ: Princeton University Press.

Kretzmann, J.P. and McKnight, J.L. (1993) *Building communities from the inside out*, Skokie, IL: ACTA Publications.

Lang, C. (2010) 'Black Power on the ground: continuity and rupture in St. Louis', in P.E. Joseph, *Neighborhood rebels: Black Power at the local level*, New York, NY: Palgrave, pp 67-90.

Mattera, P. and Tarczynska, K. (2013) 'Megadeals: the largest economic development subsidy deals ever awarded by state and local governments in the United States', Washington, DC: Good Jobs First (June), www.goodjobsfirst.org/sites/default/files/docs/pdf/megadeals_report.pdf

Mayo, M. (1975) 'Community development: a radical alternative?', in R. Bailey and M. Brake (eds) *Radical social work*, New York, NY: Pantheon Books, pp 129-43.

McKee, Y. (2012) 'With September 17 anniversary on the horizon, debt emerges as connective thread for OWS', *Waging nonviolence*, 13 July, http://wagingnonviolence.org/feature/with-september-17-anniversary-on-the-horizon-debt-emerges-as-connective-thread-for-ows/

Meek, J. (2014) *Private island: Why Britain now belongs to someone else*, New York, NY: Verso.

Morris, A. (1984) *The origins of the civil rights movement: Communities organizing for change*, New York, NY: The Free Press.

Payne, C.M. (2007) *I've got the light of freedom: The organizing tradition and the Mississippi Freedom struggle*, Berkeley, CA: University of California Press.

Preston, D. and Christoff, C. (2013) 'Only Wall Street wins in Detroit crisis reaping $474 million fee', *Bloomberg News*, 13 March, www.bloomberg.com/news/2013-03-14/only-wall-street-wins-in-detroit-crisis-reaping-474-million-fee.html

Ratcliffe, C., McKernan, S., Theodos, B., Kalish, E., Chalekian, J., Guo, P. and Trepel, C. (2014) 'Delinquent debt in America,' Washington, DC: Urban Institute, 30 July, www.urban.org/research/publication/delinquent-debt-america/view/full_report

Rothman, J. (2001) 'Approaches to community intervention', in J. Rothman, J. Erlich, and J.E. Tropman (eds) *Strategies of community intervention* (6th edn), Belmont, CA: Wadsworth/Thomson, pp 27-64.

Rubin, H.J. and Rubin, I.S. (2008) *Community organizing and development* (4th edn), Boston, MA: Allyn and Bacon.

Shaw, M. (2007) 'Community development and the politics of community', *Community Development Journal*, 43(1): 24–36.

Shragge, E. (ed) (1997) *Community economic development: In search of empowerment* (2nd edn), Montreal: Black Rose Books.

Sites, W., Chaskin, R.J. and Parks, V. (2007) 'Reframing community practice for the 21st century: multiple traditions, multiple challenges', *Journal of Urban Affairs*, 29(5): 519-41.

Staples, L. (2004) *Roots to power: A manual for grassroots organizing* (2nd edn), Westport, CT: Praeger.

Strike Debt / Occupy Wall Street (n.d.) *Debt Resisters' Operations Manual*, http://strikedebt.org/The-Debt-Resistors-Operations-Manual.pdf

Theoharis, J. and Woodard, K. (eds) (2005) *Groundwork: Local black freedom movements in America*, New York, NY: New York University Press.

Weber, M. (1964) *The theory of social and economic organization*, New York, NY: The Free Press.

Williamson, T., Imbroscio, D. and Alperovitz, G. (2003) *Making a place for community: Local democracy in a global era*, New York, NY: Routledge.

Wright, E.O. (2005) 'Foundations of a neo-Marxist class analysis', in E.O. Wright (ed), *Approaches to class analysis*, New York, NY: Cambridge University Press, pp. 4–30.

THREE

Community development in the UK: whatever happened to class? A historical analysis

Gary Craig

Introduction: the background

Community development emerged as a professional practice in the UK during the 1950s and 1960s. Early contestation about its identity emerged around the extent to which it could be seen as a form of social work, urban planning or agricultural extension, or whether it had a distinct identity of its own. Prior to the 1950s, three distinct strands of practice could be perceived: in work by colonial extension officers (explicitly as part of an educational paradigm, implicitly within a framework of political control: see Batten, 1957; Colonial Office, 1958), as an extension of trades union activism (often by unemployed workers: see Hannington, 1936) and as 'community-building' with a social focus, usually in post-Second World War social housing areas, including some of the UK's new towns or overspill estates (National Council of Social Service (NCSS), 1962).

What these approaches broadly have in common is a focus on the situation of the poor and attempts to build their capacity to articulate their own needs. Yet, despite this emphasis on poverty and disadvantage, there was little serious attempt to locate community development within a class-based understanding of the unequal distribution of income, wealth and power. So-called 'radical' community organisation such as that espoused by Alinsky (1969) – an influential US-based urban organiser whose writing circulated widely throughout the UK during the 1960s and 1970s – and some of the US War on Poverty projects (and Rein, 1967), tended in fact to be pluralist in their orientation: the poor simply needed to be helped to organise in order to gain their fair share of resources. Moreover, much early US literature emerged from an explicitly social work paradigm or from more generalised social welfare interventions (for example, Biddle and Biddle, 1965; Kramer and Specht, 1969; Cox et al,1970), and this may partly explain why

Alinsky's work appeared at the time to be rather more radical than it actually was. Although some North American literature – which British community workers tended to rely on until the mid-1960s – had begun to theorise community development as a distinct practice, dominant definitions (such as Ross, 1955) 'continued implicitly or explicitly to stress a class-less view of society, the community and, by extension, community work' (Craig, 1989, p.7). According to Corkey and Craig, for Ross, the 'primary objective [of community work] was undoubtedly that of social control – what he called "community integration." Stability and equilibrium were the important things ... [to be] achieved ... through consensus' (Corkey and Craig, 1978, p.37).

Some of the UK community development literature of the 1970s did begin to address the issue of class (Cowley et al,1977; O'Malley, 1977; Hanmer, 1979), but it was the explicitly structural analysis developed by a 'left' caucus within the UK government's Community Development Programme (CDP) – initiated in 1968 and finally closed ten years later – that first generated a widespread, if imperfect, understanding of how class analysis may help to understand the ways in which community development might contribute to wider class-based political struggles for equality. This will be discussed further on, but it is important to emphasise at this point that the state, at both local and central government levels, never again allowed its own community workers such political space explicitly to work within such a paradigm.

This chapter sets out to trace ways in which the issue of class has (or has not) been addressed within community development theory and practice, drawing on key texts and personal experience. It also seeks to describe the extent to which the mainstream practice of community development has been able to locate itself solidly within, and build alliances with, more explicitly class-based forms of political struggle.

The nature of class

Understandings of the meaning of class have changed over the years since Karl Marx first enunciated his classical theories of class and class struggle. In the period prior to Marx's writings, class had begun to be used as a general term to describe the hierarchical ordering of society, with terms such as 'lower class' and 'ruling [or upper] class' being used to denote people's general position in society, linked to wealth and landholdings in particular. Marx's particular contribution, with his collaborator Friedrich Engels (Marx and Engels, 1848; Marx, 1849), was to locate an understanding of class in historical materialist terms. This analysis focused on the relationship between labour (the proletariat or working class, who have nothing to sell but their labour) and the bourgeoisie (the owners of capital) in the context of rapid industrialisation. According to this analysis, the productive process at the centre of capitalist economies required the exploitation of worker by owner (often mediated by the petty bourgeoisie, such as foremen / middle managers) and this was the basis of class conflict. Marx's theories were therefore rooted in an understanding of class divisions as an economic phenomenon, with economic power being exploited for the benefit of a small group of owners. What was so significant, in his view, was the development of class consciousness: an understanding by the proletariat of the common relationship that both groups have to the means of production. Within the UK (and other industrialising countries) this led to the development of industrial organisations, particularly trades unions, to promote the interests of the working class. As Thompson (1963) argued, those who were to form the British proletariat were very much agents in its creation rather than simply the victims of exploitation, and Marx himself argued that the organised working class would eventually displace capitalism with socialism as an economic model, in which need would be the basis of economic reward. The logic of this model would eventually lead to the abolition of private property, and finally to a classless society.

Paradoxically perhaps, while such workers' organisations (including the Labour Party, created to represent workers' interests in Parliament) have achieved significant economic and social gains for the working class, the distinction between working class and bourgeoisie has become somewhat blurred, and the ideological clarity of Marx's analysis undermined in the process. For example, most of the 'workers' organisations' that were formed to defend their interests have, over time, pursued a parliamentary road to reform, and Marxist understandings of class and class struggle have remained on the margins of mainstream political discourse.

It is widely acknowledged that the consolidation of the UK welfare state and the nationalisation of key industries in the 1930s and 1940s were themselves the result of class struggles (Corrigan and Leonard 1978; Gough 1979). This ensured that – in theory, at least – the benefits of good housing, education and health would be available to all, and ownership of the means of production vested much more widely. The privatisation of many of the UK's key industrial activities in the 1980s (steel, coal, transportation, power generation) might therefore have been expected to lead to an increased level of industrial struggle and sharpened class divisions in response. But consecutive Conservative governments offered significant financial inducements, such as discounted house prices and share issues, and these acted progressively to dampen class-based opposition (Craig, 1989).

A contemporary of Marx, Max Weber (1964), also argued against the evils of social stratification; but he suggested that relationship to the means of production was too narrow a conceptual framework, arguing that socioeconomic hierarchies were determined by status and power as well as by class in economic terms. Within a competitive capitalist system, therefore, Weber's route to equality lay in the acquisition of skills and education and equal opportunities for all. This has become a familiar mantra over the past twenty to thirty years in British political discourse, during a period in which social and economic inequalities have been growing rapidly (at present, five people in the UK own more wealth than the bottom 20% of the entire population (Dransfield, 2014)).

Clearly, class has retained its significance over time, albeit at an implicit level, but its salience has been obscured by an emphasis on 'community' in framing policy. The following section considers the implications of this development, explored by Westwood (1992) in a chapter tellingly called: 'When class became community'.

The meaning of community

The emergence of community development as a professional practice has provoked considerable discussion over time about the meaning of 'community' (Shaw, 2008). For example, Hillery (1964) famously examined the literature and identified several hundred meanings, arguing that the only distinctive common characteristic was that of social interaction. Stacey's influential 1969 paper, 'The myth of community studies', even challenged 'community' itself as a useful sociological concept (in Craig, 2011, p.274).

In the early 1980s, some perceived the evident enthusiasm for 'community' within many national governments as a cynical and superficial gloss on policy programmes: a 'spray-on additive' (Bryson and Mowbray, 1981). This practice – and the accompanying cynicism – could be said to remain to this day. Suffice to say that 'community' remains a contested concept that is often exploited, seemingly in the interests of local 'communities' but more often to protect the interests of government (Cooper, 2008).

Notwithstanding this contestation, community development has tended to regard its arena for practice broadly as threefold: communities defined in terms of their *geography* (a village, a housing estate or an inner city slum, in which many residents share the same concerns), in terms of *identity* (a common identity on the basis of 'race' or ethnic origin, sexuality, gender, disability or age) or in terms of an *issue* (common experience of the effects of some, typically national, policy). Issue-based community development may also be based around very local issues, such as the lack of a safe road crossing outside a school. This kind of work may be the most ephemeral, ending as the problem is dealt with; or it may lead onto more enduring community development work.

From this broad perspective, there seems little reason why definitions of community development or approaches to working with communities should not, at least in theory, have been able to encompass the notion of people at a workplace as a 'community' and therefore a legitimate target for community development work. In the Victorian period, indeed, it was often the case that workers not only shared an industrial space – in a textile mill, coalmine or shipbuilding yard – but also a domestic space. Many mines or mills, for example, were surrounded by cottages and terraces housing the workers and their families – housing which, ironically, was often owned by the bourgeoisie and their agents, thus exploiting the workers and their families in spheres of both production and reproduction. The intellectual, political and organisational barriers to working across community and workplace, however, were significant.

In particular, there has been a very strong (albeit contested) acceptance of gendered roles in society at large and labour movement politics in particular (see, for example, Campbell, 1993). The male breadwinner was seen to be responsible for engaging with the 'hard' work of the industrial process and the politics of trades union organising within the workplace, and the female homemaker for executing the 'soft' work of family maintenance within the domestic and community spheres. One consequence has been that, even to the present day, women dominate most community organisations. In this regard, Remfry (1979) observed the highly male-oriented assumptions underpinning contemporary class analysis; assumptions which became less relevant from the 1970s on when women were more visibly as much a part of the labour market as men. Meanwhile, feminists within the 'community movement' developed their own analysis of the need to link home, workplace and community from the 1970s onwards (see, for example, Mayo, 1977), as did Black and anti-racist workers in relation to the intersection of class and 'race' (see, for example, Ohri et al, 1982). Both groups challenged the narrow interpretations of Marxist structural analysis put forward by the CDP, with its emphasis on the largely white and male working class (Green, 1992; Popple, 1995).

Class and other forms of discrimination and oppression

The importance of understanding the links between class and other forms of oppression and discrimination had been emerging in this period as social movements grew. As Wilson argued: 'The growth of community work and the growth of the Women's movement both date in this country [Britain] from the same period, the late sixties with its upsurge of political consciousness' (Wilson, 1977, p.1): 'They have, perhaps not surprisingly, kept apart', she continued, 'yet they have often operated on the same terrain, attempting to grapple with the problems of urban–industrial daily life' (Wilson, 1977, p.1). From a Marxist feminist perspective this was the terrain of social reproduction in which structural inequalities were being reproduced, including those resulting from discrimination against women. The realities of women's oppression in the home and in the community needed to be confronted, then, as well as the realities of their exploitation in the workplace. Community workers needed to understand these processes, learning from the women's movement's sensitivities to the realities of women's daily lives. Furthermore, she concluded, community workers needed to learn to listen to women and recognise women's right to speak for themselves, if they were to avoid reinforcing gender inequalities still further.

Dominelli (2006) has similarly explored the ways in which gendered relations of oppression could be reinforced through community work to impact upon women community workers as well as women in the community more generally. The ideology of caring as 'women's work' provides illustrations here. 'Women community workers are involved in activities that promote personal and community well-being, for example, creating mothers and toddlers groups, forming play schemes for young children, cleaning up neighbourhoods and worrying about quality of life issues' (Dominelli, 2006, p.35). Meanwhile, men were being deemed 'natural leaders', she continued;, managing projects and busy with the 'hard issues' such as developing job opportunities. These were precisely the stereotypes that feminist community workers were setting out to challenge.

Dominelli also explored the interconnections between women's experiences of gender oppression and other forms of social differentiation, including 'race' and ethnicity as well as social class. There were major implications for community work here too, as Manning and Ohri also pointed out: 'It is essential that all in Britain, including community workers, accept the fact that racism is a dynamic force in this society, which unchecked, will continue to exploit and subordinate black people', they argued (Manning and Ohri, 2011, p.147).

Having explored these issues as they were being experienced at the time, Manning and Ohri concluded with some guidelines for white community workers, starting from the recognition that 'racism is a reality in British society' (Manning and Ohri, 2011, n.p.) and that white people must take responsibility for challenging this. As the Association for Community Workers similarly recognised (ACW, 1982), anti-racist white community workers needed to contribute to the struggle for equal opportunities and for the provision of more resources for the Black community, as well as confronting 'racism, sexism and other forms discrimination both within ourselves and within society' (ACW, 1982, quoted in Popple, 2011, p.221). On such a basis and with knowledge and sensitivity to the issues of concern to the Black community, Manning and Ohri themselves concluded that 'there could be collective action and solidarity among white and black groups' (Manning and Ohri, 2011, p.156).

This brings the discussion on to the question of solidarity and alliance building more generally.

Industry–community links

It was relatively rare in the period prior to the 1960s for systematic attempts to be made to bridge the gap between workplace and community through a common analysis of the nature of exploitation, but some examples stand out. One such is the successful attempts by Annie Besant in 1888 to organise the match working women of Bryant and May's factory in East London, many of whom she had met in a community setting near the factory and whose appalling health resulting from unsafe working conditions she had observed (German, 1989). Besant helped not only to form a union to improve wages and working conditions but also to provide social facilities for girls within the community to improve access to health and education. Similarly, in Glasgow during the First World War unscrupulous landlords attempted to impose substantial rent rises on tenants, generally comprising families whose men were away fighting in the war. Given that many of the women were occupying men's roles in the munitions factories, they were able to exert enormous pressure on the government by threatening a general strike as well as preventing bailiffs from evicting individual families (Cooper, 2008). The government finally conceded, freezing rents for the duration of the war.

During the interwar period, at a time of massive unemployment, the National Unemployed Workers' Movement (NUWM) (including unemployed trade unionists) also made public connections between workers and the domestic sphere. As one organiser explained:

> 'If low-wage workers were threatened with evictions we would put into the house a defence committee of ten to twenty members ... When we had barricaded the front door and ground floor windows, back and front, we would fill the street with unemployed workers or sympathetic neighbours so that the bailiffs or police could not penetrate near the house to do the eviction.' (Edwards, 1979, p.32)

Notwithstanding these and other notable examples, however, there is little evidence that a class-based analysis of exploitation continued to inform those occupying 'community spaces' after these actions were carried through (although there were instances, of course, including trade union supported rent strikes).

A more recent example can be seen in the activities of miners' wives support groups during the 1984 national miners' strike. Miners themselves were faced with not only the intransigence of the coal industry but also the full force of the state machinery – including the police, army and judiciary (supported by a hostile media) – and driven by a deeply ideological prime minister, who was determined to break the power of the National Union of Mineworkers (NUM). Police confrontation led to deaths and serious injuries. Many of the miners' wives and partners understood that the future of the industry was at stake and that this implied an attack on what was then characterised as the social wage (decent affordable housing, accessible healthcare, schooling and so on), which years of both political and industrial struggle had achieved. Support groups were established in many areas, campaigning both to save the mining industry and to defend their communities and the wider gains of the working class. As critics argued, however, their support was never fully incorporated into the miners' struggle. Many miners – not least the NUM National President – still tended to regard women's place to be in the home rather than as an integral part of their industrial struggle (Holden, 2005).

Class in community development literature from the 1970s onwards

As noted earlier, from the 1950s onwards, UK community development steadily developed a distinct professional identity – although this was the subject of much debate. For example, it was recognised that there were different models by which community development workers could operate. These were characterised by one significant report (Younghusband, 1968) as a combination of community (field) work, social planning and community organisation. Over time, however, community work not only became distanced from this characterisation, but also developed sophisticated forms of specialised training and education (albeit often in the interstices of the higher education system), inserted its methods and values into other occupational territories (such as community health, community planning and community education) and built links with practice in other countries and cultural contexts. Little of this, however, has been explicitly informed by class-based analysis of poverty, inequality and deprivation – conditions that are widely understood to be the most significant context for community development practice. Class-based analysis is also generally missing from most of the (now very extensive) literature that has emerged across the world. In addition, class tends increasingly to be used in more general socioeconomic terms; for example, to categorise people by their occupation or other forms of stratification (see Dorling, 2014). A few texts are notable exceptions; these are discussed later in the final section. Generally speaking, however, community development texts have tended to either make no reference to social or economic class at all (see, for example, Twelvetrees, 2008) or else raise it in order to dismiss it as marginal to the wider community work literature (as in the case of Thomas, 1983).

From the 1970s onwards, the most significant – indeed, landmark – exception in terms of size, impact and influence on future theory and practice was undoubtedly the output of the 'left caucus' within the national CDP. Consecutive national and local reports challenged dominant government views of the poor (that they were to a large degree the authors of their own misfortune) and argued that the inner city (in which most projects were based) was 'not only the creation of a capitalist system but also functional to it as the inner city provides an area of changing land use and value with a population who can be used as a reserve army of labour' (Hanmer, 1979, p.206). The titles of some of the best-known reports capture the essence of their essentially

Marxist analysis: *Gilding the ghetto; The costs of industrial change; Profits against houses; Cutting the welfare state (who profits)?*

According to this view, neighbourhood-based community action set within a pluralist framework 'would only achieve limited gains (often at the expense of other 'communities') – unless it was linked to the wider organisations of the working class, such as progressive sections of the trades union movement and political organisations' (Craig, 1989, p.11; Loney, 1983). The CDPs, as part of a government response to poverty, were in a good position to observe that such programmes attempted in different ways to marry the conflict between 'responding to the needs of capitalism on the one hand and maintaining the consent of the working class on the other' (CDP, 1976, p.63). Their central argument was that local neighbourhood work was insignificant, or worse, unless set within a wider structural analysis of the causes of the difficulties facing working-class communities. From this perspective, it was essential to build wider class-based links with tenants' and residents' groups elsewhere and with trades unions and other working-class organisations. A good example of this was the Green Ban work of the Australian Building Workers' Federation, which recognised that the development of a financial services-driven property boom in Australia was likely both to generate job losses for workers and the loss of affordable housing for working-class residents (Mundey and Craig, 1978; see also Connolly, 1979 for a UK-based example). Furthermore, without such strategies community work risked reinforcing rather than challenging the basis of social inequalities. Corkey and Craig (1978, pp.41-2) summarise it well:

> the increased interest in community action [work] in the 1960s must be seen as an attempt to contain and direct working class discontent, and that it must be seen in the context of the British reformist tradition whereby Britain has in effect avoided [class-based] revolution for over two centuries by introducing just enough reforms to dispel protest without altering the power relationships which cause discontent (Corkey and Craig 1978, pp.41-2)

Other contemporary writers outside the immediate CDP circle also addressed the relationship between community action, industrial struggle and class politics. Jan O'Malley, for example, reporting on the housing struggles of tenants in Notting Hill – an inner city London area characterised by exploitative landlords and high rents and 'used in a continuous process of capital accumulation' (O'Malley, 1977, p.9) – observed the connection between industrial development and housing issues. At that time, immigration into the area was seen to depress wages and increase competition between workers for the supply of private rented housing, and thus to facilitate significant rent rises. One lesson from her work was that 'ways must be found of building a coordinating structure which does not destroy the political vitality of local or industrial groups but which is geared to improving information … accessible to both kinds of groups' (O'Malley, 1977, p.179).

In this respect, the class-based nature of such local neighbourhoods was often (and deliberately, according to some) concealed under the veneer of 'community'. In fact, Cowley et al (1977) went so far as to question whether such activities amounted to *Community or class struggle*. They further argued that the rise of community organising was, in part at least, a response to the failure of left parties and trades unions to respond politically to community problems. In their view, community issues should be redefined as class issues. This was the only way that strong links across all working–class organisations could be built to challenge the essentially cooptive power of social democratic politics.

The CDP analysis was explicitly underpinned by a view of the state, in Marxist terms, as 'the executive committee of the bourgeoisie', facilitating the expropriation of surplus value (profit) through either the productive process or rents on land and housing. Other commentators also focussed on the role of the state in capitalist society. The London–Edinburgh Weekend Return Group (LEWRG), a collective of state welfare workers, influentially argued that community struggles could play a central role in challenging capital, highlighting the contradictory position of all welfare workers (including community workers) within the politics of the state. In other words, such workers were essential to the state in the field of capitalist reproduction through housing, education and the family (even if, in a typically contradictory position, many were facing job cuts as a result of economic policy). They put it thus: 'The state is not neutral: It does provide services and resources which most of us need … But it does not do so primarily for the good of the working class. It does it to maintain the capitalist system' (LEWRG, 1979, pp. 2–3). Those who worked *for* the state therefore had to find ways to simultaneously work *in* and *against* it at both central and local levels (Cockburn, 1977).

It is notable that some of the most influential writing over subsequent years has come from other thinkers in the Marxian stable, notably Gramsci and Freire, who both understood the nature of class struggle (albeit in differing ways). Gramsci:

discusses the notion that any ruling elite dominates subordinate classes and groups with a combination of force and consent ... force is exercised through the armed forces, the police, the law courts and the prisons while consent is gained through the political, moral and intellectual leadership within civil society' (Popple, 1995, p.44: see, for example, Gramsci 1975)

It is obviously open to community workers as part of civil society, then, as 'strategic players in helping people make connections between their position and the need for change' (Popple, 1995, p.45), to challenge the hegemony of the ruling class's dominant ideas (its ideology) and power.

Freire's contribution to the development of community work theory and practice has been perhaps most strongly advocated by Ledwith (2005). In her view, Freire's insight into the political nature of education has been critical, together with the process of conscientisation. For Freire, 'education can never be neutral: its political function is to liberate or domesticate ... [it can create] critical autonomous thinkers, or it renders people passive and unquestioning' (Ledwith, 2005, p.53). The critical relationship between theory and practice – praxis – is central to this work. As Freire himself contended: 'My activism can never become disassociated from my theoretical work [and] ... my struggle against capitalism is founded on ... its intrinsic perversity, its anti-solidarity nature' (Freire, 1972, p.88).

Whether through the work of consciousness raising by outsiders such as community workers or *animateurs* (as Freire argues, see for example Freire, 1972) or of 'organic intellectuals' (in the Gramscian tradition, see for example Gramsci, 1999), the importance lay in remaining 'culturally rooted in communities, combining knowledge and ideas with direct experience of class oppression' (Gilchrist and Taylor, 2011, p.53). In other words, the task was to reveal the clear nature of class relations, oppression and power to facilitate the growth of an oppositional ideology and power base.

In the contemporary context, Byrne (2006, p.85) reminds us that, 'in post-industrial capitalism, economic restructuring and changes in policy have interacted to produce more unequal and excluding societies', thereby reaffirming divisions within the working class between what the Victorians would have described as the 'deserving' and the 'undeserving' poor. As Adams (2007, p.236) concludes, such divisions undermine the scope for fundamentally challenging social inequalities: 'realising community wellbeing for the many will not happen in a capitalist market system shaped in accordance with the neo-liberal paradigm' (Adams, 2007, p.236). In addition, as Gilchrist and Taylor observe (2011, p.52), the scope for developing alternative approaches rooted in Marxist analyses has been further undermined by the collapse of communism in the 1990s and the global restructuring of capital.

Conclusion

This brief review of the contribution of class-based theory and practice to the emergence of UK community development raises a number of key issues. First, while there is no shortage of class-based theoretical writings that have relevance for community development, there is little evidence that these have informed practice in any systematic way. Furthermore, dominant versions seem to have virtually rejected the need for any theoretical base at all, assuming that solidarity with the poor and the values of social justice are enough to achieve significant political gains.

Related to this has been the increasingly professionalised nature of community work. While its early struggle to distance itself from other professions that were regarded as having been coopted by the state made it distinctive in some significant respects, community work itself has arguably become part of the state apparatus through the processes of developing qualifications and validation procedures. An adherence to class analyses highlights the contradictions in pursuing this trajectory, since the state will always resist strategies that undermine the process of ideological incorporation. The rapid dismantling of the CDP programme in the mid 1970s demonstrates the state's unwillingness to tolerate this kind of dissent – especially when it is funding it! In fact, contemporary neoliberal processes of marketisation may have significantly reduced the scope for developing alternative approaches through community development (Shaw, 2011).

On the other hand, the historical contradictions within community work in terms of its progressive values, its marginal position within structures and organisations and its relative autonomy to organise across different kinds of political space with both industrially- and community-based populations mean that it retains at least some potential to contribute to political struggles based on the values of equality, respect for difference and social justice more widely. This means that its techniques and methods will always have the potential to contribute to wider class-based struggles against injustice, when generated by that consciousness of class.

References

Adams, T. (2007) 'Stuart Hall: the interview', *The Observer Review*, 23 September, pp 89.

Alinsky, S. (1969) *Reveille for radicals*, New York, NY: Vintage Books.

Batten, T.R. (1957) *Communities and their development*, London: Oxford University Press.

Biddle, L. and Biddle, W. (1965) *The community development process: The rediscovery of local initiative*, New York, NY: Holt, Rinehart and Winston.

Bryson, L. and Mowbray, M. (1981) '"Community": the spray-on solution', *Australian Journal of Social Issues*, 16(4): 255-67.

Byrne, D. (2006) *Social exclusion* (2nd edn), Maidenhead: Open University Press.

Campbell, B. (1993) *Goliath: Britain's dangerous places*, London: Methuen.

CDP (Community Development Programme) (1976) *Gilding the ghetto*, London: Community Development Project.

Cockburn, C. (1977) *The local state*, London: Pluto Press.

Colonial Office (1958) *Community development: A handbook*, London: Colonial Office.

Connolly, J. (1979) 'Resisting the run-down of docklands', in G. Craig, M. Mayo and N. Sharman (eds) *Jobs and community action*, London: Routledge and Kegan Paul.

Cooper, C. (2008) *Community, conflict and the state*, Basingstoke: Palgrave.

Corkey, D. and Craig, G. (1978) 'Community work or class politics?' in P. Curno (ed) *Political issues and community work*, London: Routledge and Kegan Paul, pp 36–66.

Corrigan, P. and Leonard, P. (1978) *Social work under capitalism*, London: Macmillan.

Cowley, J., Kaye, A., Mayo, M. and Thompson, M. (eds) (1977) *Community or class struggle?*, London: Stage One.

Cox, F.M., Erlich, J.L., Rothman, J. and Tropman, J.E. (eds) (1970) *Strategies of community organisation*, Itasca, IL: Peacock.

Craig, G. (1989) 'Community work and the state', *Community Development Journal*, 24(1): 1–18.

Craig, G. (2007) 'Community capacity-building: Something old, something new...?' *Critical Social Policy*, August: 335–59.

Dominelli, L. (2006) *Women and community action* (revised 2nd edn), Bristol: Policy Press.

Dorling, D. (2014) *Inequality and the 1%*, London: Verso.

Dransfield, S. (2014) *A tale of two Britains*, Oxford: Oxfam.

Edwards, B. (1979) 'Organising the unemployed in the 1920s', in G. Craig, M. Mayo and N. Sharman (eds), *Jobs and community action*, London: Routledge and Kegan Paul, pp 82–95.

Freire, P. (1972) *Pedagogy of the oppressed*, Harmondsworth: Penguin.

German, L. (1989) *Sex, class and socialism*, London: Bookmarks.

Gilchrist, A. and Taylor, M. (2011) *The short guide to community development*, Bristol: Policy Press.

Gough, I. (1979) *The political economy of the welfare state*, London: Macmillan.

Gramsci, A. (1975) *Letters from prison*, London: Jonathan Cape.

Gramsci, A. (1999) *The prison notebooks*, London: ElecBooks.

Green, J. (1992) 'The community development project revisited', in P. Carter, T. Jeffs and M.K. Smith (eds) *Changing social work and welfare*, Buckingham: Open University Press.

Hanmer, J. (1979) 'Theories and ideologies in British community work', *Community Development Journal*, 14(3): 200–9.

Hannington, W. (1936) *Unemployed struggles*, London: Lawrence and Wishart.

Hillery, G.A. (1964) 'Villages, cities and total institutions', *American Sociological Review*, 28: 32–42.

Holden, T. (2005) *Queen coal: Women of the miners' strike*, Nottingham: Sutton Publishing.

Kramer, R. and Specht, H. (eds) (1969) *Readings in community organisation practice*, Englewood Cliffs, NJ: Prentice Hall.

Ledwith, M. (2005) *Community development: a critical approach*, Bristol: Policy Press.

LEWRG (London–Edinburgh Weekend Return Group) (1979) *In and against the state*, London: Pluto Press.

Loney, M. (1983) *Community against government*, London: Heinemann.

Manning, B. and Ohri, A. (2011) 'Racism: the response of community work', in G. Craig, M. Mayo, K. Popple, M. Shaw and M. Taylor (eds), *The community development reader*, Bristol: Policy Press, pp 147–56.

Marris, P. and Rein, M. (1967) *Dilemmas of social reform*, New York, NY: Atherton Press.

Marx, K. (1849) *Wage labour and capital*, Koln: Neue Rheinische Zeitung (various editions) (also republished in many formats; for example, Wildside Press LLC 2008).

Marx, K. and Engels, F. (1848) *The communist manifesto*, London: Communist League (also republished in many formats; for example, Progress Publishers, Moscow, 1969).

Mayo, M. (1977) *Women in the community: Community work three*, London: Routledge and Kegan Paul.

Mundey, J. and Craig, G. (1978) 'Joint union-resident action', in P. Curno (ed) *Political Issues and Community Work*, London: Routledge and Kegan Paul, pp 199–218.

NCSS (National Council of Social Service) (1962) *Community organisation: an introduction*, London: National Council of Social Service.

Ohri, A., Manning, B. and Curno, P. (eds) (1982) *Community work and racism: Community work seven*, London: Routledge and Kegan Paul in association with the Association of Community Workers.

O' Malley, J. (1977) *The politics of community action*, Nottingham: Spokesman.

Popple, K. (1995) *Analysing community work*, Open University Press: Buckingham.

Popple, K. (2011) 'Models of community work', in G. Craig, M. Mayo, K. Popple, M. Shaw and M. Taylor (eds), *The community development reader*, Bristol: Policy Press, pp 211–21.

Remfry, P. (1979) 'North Tyneside community development project', *Community Development Journal*, 14(3): 186–9.

Ross, M.G. (1955) *Community organisation: Theories, principles and practice*, New York, NY: Harper and Row.

Shaw, M. (2008) 'Community development and the politics of community', *Community Development Journal*, 43(1): 24–36.

Shaw, M. (2011) 'Stuck in the middle? Community development, community engagement and the dangerous business of learning for democracy', *Community Development Journal*, 46(1): 128–46.

Thomas, D. (1983) *The making of community work*, London: George Allen and Unwin.

Thompson, E.P. (1963) *The making of the English working class*, London: Victor Gollancz.

Twelvetrees, A. (2008) *Community work* (4th edn), Basingstoke: Palgrave Macmillan.

Weber, M. (1964) *The theory of social and economic organization*, New York, NY: The Free Press.

Westwood, S. (1992) 'When class became community: radicalism in adult education', in A. Rattansi and D. Reeder (eds) *Rethinking radical education: Essays in honour of Brian Simon*, London: Lawrence and Wishart, pp 150–65.

Wilson, E. (1977) 'Women in the community', in M. Mayo (ed) '*Women in the community*', London: Routledge and Kegan Paul, pp 1–9.

Younghusband, E. (1968) *Community work and social change*, London: Longmans Green.

Class, inequality and community development in context

PART 2

Class, inequality and community development in context

Working-class communities and ecology: reframing environmental justice around the Ilva steel plant in Taranto (Apulia, Italy)

Stefania Barca and Emanuele Leonardi

Introduction: the confiscation

In July 2012, a local preliminary hearing judge ordered the closure of the most polluting furnaces of the Ilva steel plant in Taranto, the largest and one of the oldest such factories in Europe, finding its management guilty of environmental and public health disaster. After decades of an imperturbable – if unequal – balance among social actors, the confiscation[1] set in motion an unprecedented conflict between environmental and community activists on the one hand and the company owners, backed by government support, on the other. The conflict inevitably extended to the Metalworkers' Union Confederation, sparking a profound and irreversible crisis. In this process, its initial manifestations of loyalty and support to the company – in continuation of decades-long attitudes of quiescence because of the threat of large-scale job losses – encountered the unexpected opposition of substantial parts of the rank and file (and the local population at large), causing the union to lose much of its credibility and a significant number of affiliates. Such an explosive situation – which attracted the attention of the New York Times, The Guardian and The Economist – opened up entirely new social dynamics and an ongoing process of cultural and political reframing at the community level.

How can we make sense of this epoch-changing event in the history of the city? To answer that question, some background data need to be taken into account. The Ilva facility is startling in terms of its physical size, economic relevance and record of pollution. With a surface of 1500 hectares (scattered over 200 km of railway, 5 blast furnaces, 10 coke oven batteries and 6 exclusively dedicated docks), Ilva accounts for more than 30% of Italy's steel production and for approximately

75% of Taranto's GDP. Furthermore, it employed 11,980 workers in 2012 (including blue collar, white collar and managerial staff), which rises to over 20,000 if associated services are considered (Comito and Colombo, 2013). And its gigantic scale is perfectly mirrored by the dramatic data concerning polluting emissions: in 2010, Ilva emitted over 11,000 t of nitrogen dioxide, 11,300 t of sulphur dioxide and 1.3 t of benzene, all well beyond the thresholds established by national as well as EU legislation (Vulpio, 2012). As a consequence, evidence about health issues in the area is truly worrisome: the figures for both early mortality (1980–2008) and cancer incidence (2006–07) show epidemiological evidence of disproportionate risk of a number of causes of death, among which lung cancer and cardiovascular / respiratory diseases, both acute and chronic, prominently figure (Piratsu et al, 2013).

These data give an idea of the sheer dimension of the environmental and public health damage brought about by (and through) the Ilva plant in its 50-year operation and make this case of utmost relevance to current European Union (EU) policies, which regulate a variety of phenomena: industrial hazards; public health monitoring; carbon emissions; contamination of life-support systems by Persistent Organic Pollutants (POP) and heavy metals, environmental clean-up and economic transition. All of these phenomena characterise the Taranto area as an industrially contaminated site, with consequent social and legal implications. In the language of environmental justice – an action research approach that emerged in the US in the mid-1980s and which is currently adopted in social science and community activism worldwide (Bullard, 1990; Sandler and Pezzullo, 2007; Schlosberg, 2007) – Taranto is a 'sacrifice zone'[2] of industrial development; its population configures as a discriminated community, whose right to a safe and clean environment has been disregarded and heavily discounted in politico-economic terms.

This chapter will consider the theoretical implications of the Taranto case for a reframing of the environmental justice approach. The principal argument is that such communities typically experience moments of crisis, or the rupture of pre-existing equilibria, due to a mix of exogenous and endogenous factors. In the case of Taranto, this crisis combined industrial restructuring linked to shifts in global markets with a judicial trial resulting from a long series of workers' and citizens' mobilisations. The 2012 judicial sequestration constituted a turning point, allowing for the full emergence of the internal contradictions represented by the job / localisation blackmail and the possibility for openly questioning the cultural premises on which such blackmail rested.

The chapter is structured as follows. First, it will illustrate and discuss the environmental justice approach from a working-class community perspective and propose an innovative framework for integrating the two, which is termed the Working-Class Community Ecology framework (WCCE). Subsequently, a WCCE approach is applied to the Ilva case in order to show how it can account for the environmental injustice played out in a working-class community.

Environmental justice and working-class communities

In its first theorisation, by African–American sociologist Robert Bullard, environmental justice (EJ) is primarily a social struggle arising from the awareness of how the social costs produced by uneven development in the capitalist system have unequally affected different social groups, especially (but not exclusively) along lines of racial discrimination. As Bullard (1990) pointed out in his Dumping in Dixie, work has been a potent mechanism of environmental injustice and racism, considering that the most unhealthy and low-paying jobs in the US are those most likely to be filled by African–Americans and Latinos: 'Requiring people to choose between jobs or the environment is inherently unfair. The solution to this dilemma lies in making workplaces safe for workers. Anything short of this goal places workers at an unfair disadvantage' (Bullard, 1990: 86). Largely credited as the founding text for environmental justice studies and activism, Dumping in Dixie was built on a full recognition of the importance of 'job blackmail': the threat of relevant job loss as a structural cause for the production of environmental injustice. It is significant, however, that labour unions rarely figure in the book, suggesting that environmental justice activism had shifted to citizens' grassroots organisations and community organisers at the neighbourhood level.

This move from union to community activism as the privileged terrain on which grassroots environmental struggles are played out has been interpreted in social science as a shift from the conceptual framework of class to that of subalternity (Pulido, 1996). In the last decade, 'environmental conflict' has become an important way to describe subaltern environmentalism, or so-called 'environmentalism of the poor', generating a new array of social science research (Martinez Alier, 2002). Environmental justice, subaltern environmentalism, environmentalism of the poor and environmental conflict are all ways of conceptualising the various struggles of working-class people over environmental costs and benefits, both in the urban and the rural space. Such struggles, however, often contain an unobserved or under-theorised link between labour and environmental concerns. For example, most social science research on environmental conflicts pays attention to community agency while overlooking the role that workers play in such conflicts and the wider relevance of work in mediating people's understandings of the environmental issues at stake. Paradoxically, work and its complex relationship to environmental concerns is probably the least examined aspect of environmental justice struggles and of environmental conflicts.

And yet work is – and has always been – relevant to these struggles, for the simple reason that 'subaltern' people, racially discriminated people or 'the poor' are typically also working-class people: people who occupy the lower ranks of the labour hierarchy, making a living out of the most dangerous and most unhealthy jobs while also living in the most polluted places. Furthermore, historical research has demonstrated that – despite many contingent, internal stratifications and differentiations – working-class communities do share common experiences and often develop a strong sense of belonging and identity based on some form of control over the work process, its social meaning and its scope. They thus develop a more or less explicit perception of the work / environment tradeoff that shapes their lives and the places in which they work and live. Their own bodies and mental capacities, as well as those of their families, are at stake in the continuous transformation of the local environment. They may even feel partially responsible for such environmental change, viewing it as a bargain that they have to make in exchange for survival. Such bargains are often overly simplified as 'jobs versus the environment', which obscures the nature and diversity of environmental activism that develops from working–class ecological consciousness (Barca, 2014a).

The history of work / environmental coalitions shows how they tend to be heavily influenced by cycles of economic expansion and recession and by political opportunity structures at the national level, which typically condition the extent to which job / localisation blackmails on the part of corporate or state policies are challenged and counteracted. Notable examples are the United Farmworkers Union's boycott campaign against pesticide use in California in the mid 1960s (Montrie, 2008) and the recent One Million Climate Jobs campaign in South Africa, in which a large coalition of unions, community and environmental activist groups fought for a socially just ecological transformation of the national economy (Cock, 2014; Leonardi, 2012). It is at the grassroots and local levels, however, that the convergence between labour struggles for decent work conditions and community struggles for environmental justice face the strongest challenges. In too many cases, labour unions have maintained a detached attitude toward environmental issues or even openly opposed grassroots environmental action at the local level. Nonetheless, this has not completely impeded workers' environmental activism (Gould et al, 2012; Obach, 2004; Barca, 2012a).

The Italian case is significant in this respect. Several important trial cases against large polluting companies, especially in the petrochemical and asbestos sectors, have stemmed from occupational health grievances. Typically, those struggles have been based on 'popular epidemiology' research – collecting evidence about workers, which has then become class action – involving workers' families and larger communities, including local neighborhoods; the urban population affected by air, water, and soil pollution; local fishing, sports, and environmental associations, women's organisations and health professionals. While Italian trades unions strongly supported environmental regulation – especially in the industrial sector – during the 1960s and early 1970s, since the economic recession of the late 1970s they adopted a much more reductive approach to workers' health and environment grievances. In some cases local unions have even aggressively boycotted environmental justice actions and practised various forms of ostracism toward members who supported them. Like the one taking place in Taranto today, those struggles have incorporated all the dilemmas and contradictions typical of the work–environment relationship in industrial societies, which makes them all the more interesting (Allen, 2012; Allen and Kazan-Allen, 2012; Barca, 2012b).

Broadly speaking, environmental injustices involve communities through complex intersections between labour and social conflicts, production and reproduction struggles, in the local space. Consequently, what most weakens and impairs working-class struggles for environmental justice is the division between labour and environmental movements at the grassroots level as well as at national level. With the aim of countering such divisive politics, an original framework for theorising the relationship between working-class communities and environmental justice is offered here.

Working class community ecology

In what terms can we speak of working-class communities as an environmental subject, and how can we understand their ecologies? How does the concept of working-class community help us to advance our understanding of ecological crises and of environmentalism? J.K. Gibson-Graham's (2006) concept of 'community economy' in a post-capitalist perspective is utilised here to answer these questions, and is extended to the ecological dimension in order to develop what a Working-Class Community Ecology (WCCE) framework. In A Post-Capitalist Politics, Gibson-Graham elaborated an extended and revised conception of 'class' as something that can be used to foster self-recognition in terms of interpersonal connection and interdependency (Gibson-Graham, 2006). This idea of class – extended to a human community – is employed to counter the market / capitalist logic of individualisation and competition, which may not eradicate community and interdependence entirely but can nonetheless dismiss them as marginal and irrelevant: 'Making them visible again is a step toward rendering them objects of politics and ethics ... the keystone of our counterhegemonic project of 'differently politicizing' the economy' (Gibson-Graham, 2006, p.84). In other words, 'class' can be an important starting point for negotiating a 'community economy' based on an ethic of solidarity and interconnection.

Our Working-Class Community Ecology framework extends this approach to the working-class community's environment as a crucial dimension in which to find the coordinates of such interconnection. In doing so, it applies a view of ecology as interdependence among humans and non-human nature, advocating for an ethics of partnership; that is, of mutual support and co-evolution (Merchant, 2010 [1990]). In other words, community wellbeing cannot be thought of outside of its interdependencies with the physical and biological environment and the non-human world. The WCCE therefore extends the concept of 'class' to include workers' families and all those who share with them the space that they inhabit (the air that they breathe, the ecosystem in which they reproduce, the living and non-living world with which they share the local space). Sharing Gibson-Graham's understanding of community as 'being-with' or 'being-in-common' (2006, p.81), WCCE looks at the working-class community as a web of interconnections between production and reproduction in place.

In this framework, community is understood as a relationship of solidarity and interdependence centred on the different forms of labour that sustain the local economy and society – whether the work is salaried or unsalaried, productive or reproductive and care-giving, material or immaterial. In this sense, the WCCE pays due attention to what is (re)produced by the community, who (re)produces it, how, and at what social cost – primarily in terms of occupational, environmental and public health. Further, it gives special importance to mapping the alternatives that are available for community livelihood and wellbeing.

The WCCE not only includes ecological interrelations within the community economy sphere, but also includes working-class ecological consciousness and environmental activism. 'Working-class ecological consciousness' refers to the experience of nature, the environment and environmental politics made by working-class communities. Such ecological consciousness is profoundly shaped by positionality; working-class communities typically experience nature from subordinate social positions as those most affected by pollution and other industrial hazard, and by different kinds of 'differential vulnerabilities' (Bullard, 2008). Such positionality tends to produce a self-perception of working-class communities and other marginalised groups as 'the real endangered species' (Peña and Pulido, 1998; Barca, 2014b), threatened in their very survival by a kind of industrial development that is premised on the production of sacrifice zones and disposable bodies. However, the opposite is also true: working-class communities do struggle to reshape the local and national environment through their active involvement in politics by way of grassroots / union organising, for example in campaigning for pollution regulation and prevention measures, public health monitoring and environmental clean-up and prosecution of environmental crimes. This is the essence of environmental justice struggles, whether or not they recognised under this label.

Environmental justice struggles expose the essential weakness of the capitalist productive system by demanding its compatibility with the reproduction of life in the local space. The potentially disruptive character of such a demand should not be underestimated: the full compliance of industrial plants with environmental and public health regulation, and the internalisation of environmental clean-up and reparation activities on the part of polluting entities imply a fundamental rejection of the profit-maximising principle that drives private enterprise, with its inevitable production of social cost. In other words, EJ struggles open the possibility for post-capitalist political economy scenarios of compatibility between the production of surplus and community / ecosystem wellbeing.

Labour and the environment in Taranto

The case of the Ilva steel plant in Taranto can be considered as a paradigmatic example of environmental injustice in its specifically industrial form. Established in 1960, the plant was publicly managed (under the name of Italsider) until 1995, when it was included in the wave of privatisations set in motion by the Italian government and hence sold to the holding company owned by the Riva family (Riva Fire). Originally met with enthusiasm by the local population and institutions alike (Battafarano, 2011), the steel plant did not take long to show the nefarious side of its vast industrial scale. Taranto is today a 'sacrifice zone' created not only by Ilva's facilities but also by other polluting activities variously linked to them: a refinery, waste landfills and illegal dumping sites. In other words, the symbiotic – if contradictory – relationship between Taranto and Ilva accounts for the combined effect of economic relevance and environmental impact (Petrarulo and De Angelis, 2013). In turn, this explains how Ilva has progressively become a paradigmatic example of job blackmail: quite simply, the steel plant can be defined as an industrial machine, producing death in its different shapes: chemical poisoning (Curcio, 2013; 2014), fatal injuries (Campetti, 2013) and socially induced suicides (Ferraro, 2014). As a consequence, the surrounding community suffers constant discrimination as its right to a healthy environment is disregarded and subordinated to politico-economic imperatives.

Environmental injustices such as those perpetrated in Taranto are premised on various forms of symbolic violence; first and foremost, that of silencing critical voices and disregarding social and scientific evidence that would challenge the dominant view that, without Italsider / Ilva, Taranto would face mass unemployment and socioeconomic marginalisation (Barca, 2014b). Even more problematic, however, is a second form of symbolic violence; that is, intentional denial that producing the inexpressibility of environmental injustice implies a widespread internalisation of the official narrative on the part of its very victims. Whereas the former narrative indicates the sedimentation of an institutional arrangement that prevents social change, the second highlights a mental attitude of closure towards the possibility of even imagining economic alternatives to the centrality of the steel plant. In Foucauldian terms, a cognitively dissonant worker was the subjective outcome of the specific form of industrial / environmental governmentality deployed in Taranto. In that sense it could be said that, in bodily experiencing the separation between his[3] social status (the working class) and his spatio-temporal situatedness (the surrounding environment), such a worker was split between occupational euphoria (Ilva guarantees jobs and development) and communitarian fear (Ilva is undermining Taranto's basic livability).

Although directly focused on the Ilva workforce, it could also be argued that such governmental apparatus extends to the Taranto population as a whole. By internalising the job blackmail as an inevitable horizon, communities tacitly accept a situation in which they depend materially and symbolically on the wealth created by the steel plant. This tight identification between local community and company may in fact take the shape of loyalty and thus entail a reduction of social conflicts and – at least potentially – an increase in productivity (Wheatley, 2005). Such a contradictory – and ultimately passivising – position is nicely captured by local journalist Tonio Attino:

> We, the people, had witnessed and participated in the demolition of our coast, our fields and our history. We joyfully cheered that monster which only half a century later we would begin to hate. Hatred spurred from the sudden discovery of something that we were not able to see beforehand, which was hidden under the illusion of wealth. This something is the fact that the monster pollutes and kills and – sadly – it has been polluting and killing for a long time. (Attino, 2013: 165–66)

The 'sudden discovery' to which Attino refers can be easily recognised: it is the awareness, brought about by the 2012 sequestration of Ilva's heat treatment lines, that one's own health and wellbeing have been the bargaining chip in the economy–environment tradeoff. The disruptive effect of the confiscation is perhaps better illustrated in a telling interview collected for the film documentary Pulmões de aço: Resistências locais frente a injustiças globais (Lungs of steel: local resistance against global injustices),[4] in which an Ilva steelworker recounts how he and his workmates were suddenly struck by the discovery that their 'sacrifice' – as breadwinners and workers in a risky job – had been meaningless, because industrial toxins had in any case escaped the factory gates and got into their children's bodies through their mother's milk. In other words, the confiscation tore aside the veil of collective illusion into which the Taranto community had been lured for half a century, making it clear that the damage had extended far beyond what was reputed to be acceptable.

There had been instances of social mobilisation in Taranto prior to 2012; For example, during the 1970s, a vocal minority of Italsider workers openly raised the issue of workplace health and safety. The overall outcomes of their protests were the introduction of small improvements in the organisation of work shifts and the installation of filters, though not in adequate numbers. In the course of the 1980s, the Italian League for the Environment (Legambiente) – a left-wing organisation that was assuming the leadership of the anti-nuclear movement in the area – took a more prominent role in mobilising for anti-pollution regulation. In 1988 and 1989 a few demonstrations called by Legambiente attracted significant participation by workers, raising legitimate hopes for a common front for sustainability inside and outside the factory (Corvace, 2011). Nevertheless, such potentialities for united political action did not materialise and, during the 1990s, the global steel crisis dramatically reduced the workers' space for manoeuvre. Moreover, the 1995 privatisation profoundly modified the workforce structure: older, unionised labourers joined pre-retirement programmes and were replaced by young workers with no experience in confrontational industrial relations. This shift entailed a massive process of employment casualisation, the main implication of which was a further weakening of the unions (Nistri, 2013), leading them to embrace non-confrontational bargaining and surrender to the job blackmail. The 2000s quite simply ratified the divergence between workers and environmentalists: a coalition of community and environmental groups called High Tide (Altamarea) formed in 2008, but it conducted its campaigns in marked isolation from organised labour (Ruscio, 2015). To sum up, the work / environment opposition – as epitomised by job blackmailing – continued to dominate social life, despite the hopeful scenario glimpsed in the late 1980s.

However, a novel element emerged in 2012: the confiscation represented a crucial rupture concerning the internal solidity of the cognitively dissonant worker as the subjective figure (in Foucauldian terms) of job blackmailing. The abrupt realisation that the steel plant was not the eternal, indisputable destiny of Taranto and that the judiciary could actually block production – by appealing to the superior social value of the reproduction of life – entailed a twofold reaction: the first epitomised by employees' protests against the court decision, demanding to keep Ilva in operation, and the second a massive contestation of the job blackmail itself. Crucially, while the first reaction is progressively losing ground due to new legal investigations and a proliferation of alternative imaginaries, the second is gaining consensus and catalysing the impulse of participation, which has been growing in the local community since the confiscation was ordered. One example of this process is the emergence of the grassroots organisation Comitato Cittadini e Lavoratori Liberi e Pensanti (CCLLP) (Committee[5] of Free and Reflective Citizens and Workers) in the context of the disorientation that followed the fractural moment of confiscation, when the job blackmail showed its first cracks. As their manifesto makes clear:

We are FREE because we decided to break the chain of a miserable blackmail which forced us to choose between health and work. Now we choose them both. Now we choose not to be aider and abettor of those who are culpable of environmental disaster and of poisoning Taranto. We are REFLECTIVE because we no longer accept others to think for us, after they have brought us to environmental devastation, financial turmoil and unemployment. We no longer accept to be used as bargaining chips by institutions and corporations which manage a corrupted and disastrous capitalistic system. We want to participate, to re-appropriate our rights without delegating anything to anybody.[6]

The Committee was born in the midst of the social conflict sparked by the confiscation. On 2 August 2012, a national demonstration was organised in Taranto by the trades unions' confederation to protest against the legal judgment. In front of a crowd, at first astonished but progressively attentive, a large and vociferous group of rank and file workers made its way to the stage and interrupted the official talks, manifesting open support for the magistrates' authority in revealing violations of environmental and public health law and openly denouncing the unions' complicity in the tradeoff.

Significantly, CCLLP members referred to themselves as citizens and workers. This explains why, after two years of campaigning, the social composition of the movement was a profoundly mixed one; its original core was made up of Ilva workers who were formerly involved in union activities and had now become self-organising. Around it, a nebulous ensemble of different subjects has been gravitating: non-Ilva – often precarious – workers; the impoverished middle class; the unemployed; inhabitants of particularly affected neighborhoods, students and engaged civil society (such as paediatricians, physicians and academics). In short, the movement seems to mirror that class extension along community and ecological interrelations that defines our understanding of a WCCE.

Another element seems to support the possibility of reading the Committee through the lenses provided by WCCE: its relationship with local communities and environmental advocates has been thoroughly positive, as have been its connections with different struggles for sustainable community development taking place all over Italy, such as the No TAV movement in the Susa Valley (Leonardi, 2013) and the Zero Waste platform in Campania (Armiero and D'Alisa, 2012). This constitutive openness towards similar experiences has allowed the movement to develop a line of thought in which the relationship between labour and the environment transcends capitalistic compatibilities: first and foremost, the primacy of profit-making over social and ecological wellbeing. For example, the Committee's most recent campaign has been advocating state intervention: not immediately to make Ilva's production 'greener' (a goal that may be considered at a subsequent stage) but rather to grant full employment for the current Ilva workforce in the clean-up of the local environment. These activists argue that the costs of restoring decent environmental conditions must not be paid for (again) by the victims of 50 years of industrial growth, but by those who have profited from it, namely the Italian state and the Riva family. It is highly significant that such a strategy of recovering the local environment and economy through the clean-up operations represents the very reversal of job blackmail.

A further important aspect of the 2012 rupture concerns a possible new relationship between the CCLLP and the metalworkers' unions. As the legal judgment marked the end of workers' unconditional trust in the unions' confederation (Leogrande, 2013), this fracture has had a twofold effect: on the one hand it sparked disorientation fuelled by the haunting spectre of unemployment, but on the other it provoked the collapse of unionisation (from over 80% unionisation in 1993 to around 45% – and declining – in 2013). In other words the confiscation opened up a new scenario of political loyalties and social identification, which is still in a very fluid state. In this complex context, the Committee's initial rejection of the unions as interlocutors has been developing into a more nuanced approach, especially since the left-wing section of the Metalworkers' Confederation has started to incorporate several of the Committee's arguments. In fact, after having supported protests against the confiscation in 2012, the union's secretary, Maurizio Landini, eventually acknowledged the fundamental importance of the judicial investigations and stated that designing a sustainable economic policy for the Italian steel sector represents a challenge that both political parties and trades unions organisations should take on (Landini, 2013; Comito and Colombo, 2013). Against this background a new radicalism for the union can be imagined and enacted precisely with regard to the possibility that such a sustainable economic policy be informed by a post-capitalist mindset. For this to happen, however, a profound transformation of union practices is required. Such transformation is being prefigured in Taranto by the CCLLP through the development of what might be termed community unionism. As one activist compellingly put it:

The political division here is not that between workers and environmentalists, but that between capital and labour, which creates the job blackmail and also an extreme individualisation of struggles. But Taranto people want to reclaim their city and their destiny. We want a different economy, not an industrial one. We all need to become unionists. (Ranieri, 2013)

Conclusion

The cultural and political reframing process in Taranto is highly complex and still in progress at the time of writing; as such, the following conclusions should be regarded as strictly provisional. Moreover, further research is certainly needed in order to more explicitly articulate the theoretical hypotheses advanced here. Nonetheless, based on the available evidence, some first inferences can be made about the possibilities opened up by the 2012 confiscation of the Ilva plant.

First, it is the authors' conviction that the CCLLP represents a good example of what the Working-Class Community Ecology framework aims to make visible, namely the specifically ecological dimension of the working-class community, in terms of both ecological consciousness and environmental / social mobilisation. The rupture constituted by the confiscation has allowed at least a section of the Taranto working class to address environmental concerns beyond the straitjacket of the jobs blackmail. Like so many other working-class communities, Ilva workers have been forced to perceive the environmental discourse as something alien to their world. In fact, their democratic options and the exercise of their citizenship rights have been limited by the position that they occupied within the industrial order. In short, they did not seem to have a right to be environmentalists. Yet this social perception – which finds expression in the cognitively dissonant worker – has been thoroughly shaken by the confiscation, allowing for the emergence of a working-class ecological consciousness, as exemplified by the Committee.

Second, the Committee's advocacy opens the possibility for developing a new, post-Ilva social pact for Taranto, working towards a post-capitalist scenario of compatibility between the production of surplus and community / ecosystem wellbeing. Such a pact, however, will not be sealed in aseptic governmental meeting rooms. On the contrary, it needs to be fuelled by new conflict lines from below and by new modalities of social mediation at the institutional level. This is why the emergence of community unionism in the area is so interesting. What can be witnessed at the moment is only an embryo of an expanded notion of class and the first steps of its ecological self-organisation. Nevertheless, this remarkable link between class and ecology at the local level can be related to recent discourses of just transition: a global strategy advocated by the International Trade Unions Confederation (ITUC) and the International Labour Organisation (ILO) and already adopted by a variety of trades unions and grassroots labour movements worldwide. Perhaps the answer to the work / environment dilemma – in Taranto and elsewhere – will require new forms of community unionism, able to reconnect labour and environmental justice struggles in order to negotiate the local particularities of such politics of just transition and to build national and international solidarities around it.

Notes

[1] The term 'confiscation' is used here in the sense of 'seized by authority' as a temporary penalty for environmental wrongdoing. See www.thefreedictionary.com/confiscation

[2] The term is used in environmental justice literature to designate 'a geographic area that has been permanently impaired by environmental damage or economic disinvestment'. These areas are typically inhabited by minority and/or low-income communities. See http://en.wikipedia.org/wiki/Sacrifice_zone

[3] Over 99% of the Ilva workforce is male (De Palma, 2013).

[4] See the Facebook page of the movement: https://www.youtube.com/watch?v=bNK7br4nlYE

[5] To keep the English translation closer to the Italian original, the word 'committee' has been chosen here. It must be noted, however, that in the context of social movements it refers to self-governed grassroots organisations that refuse traditional channels of political representation.

[6] See the Facebook page of the movement: www.facebook.com/CittadiniELavoratoriLiberiEPensanti/info?tab=page_info

Acknowledgement

This research is co-funded by the European Social Fund through the Operational Human Potential and by the National Portuguese Funds through the Foundation for Science and Technology in the context of the Post-Doctoral Grant SFRH/BPD/96008/2013, Centro de Estudos Sociais, Universidade de Coimbra.

References

Allen, B. (2012) 'A tale of two lawsuits: making policy/relevant environmental health knowledge in Italian and U.S. chemical regions', in C. Sellers and J. Melling (eds) *Dangerous trade: Histories of industrial hazards across a globalizing world*, Philadelphia, PA: Temple University Press, pp 154–67.

Allen, D. and Kazan-Allen, L. (2012) *Eternit and the great asbestos trial*, London: IBAS.

Armiero, M. and D'Alisa, G. (2012) 'Rights of resistance: the garbage struggles for environmental justice in Campania, Italy', *Capitalism Nature Socialism*, 23(4): 52–68.

Attino, T. (2013) *Generazione Ilva*, Lecce: Salentobooks.

Barca, S. (2012a) 'On working-class environmentalism: a historical and trans-national overview', *Interface: A Journal for and about Social Movements*, 4(2): 61–80.

Barca, S. (2012b) 'Bread and poison. The story of labor environmentalism in Italy', in C. Sellers and J. Melling (eds) *Dangerous trade: Histories of industrial hazards across a globalizing world*, Philadelphia, PA: Temple University Press, pp 126–39.

Barca, S. (2014a) 'Laboring the earth. Transnational reflections on the environmental history of work', *Environmental History*, 19: 3–27.

Barca, S. (2014b) 'Telling the right story: environmental violence and liberation narratives', *Environment and History*, 20(4): 537–46.

Battafarano, G. (ed) (2011) *Taranto capitale. Economia, lavoro, ambiente, società*, Taranto: Scorpione.

Bullard, R. (1990) *Dumping in Dixie: Race, class and environmental quality*, Boulder, CO: Westview.

Bullard, R. (2008) 'Differential vulnerabilities. Environmental and economic inequality and government response to unnatural disasters', *Social Research*, 75(3): 753–84.

Campetti, L. (2013) *Ilva connection*, Lecce: Manni.

Cock, J. (2014) 'The "green economy": a just and sustainable development path or a "wolf in sheep's clothing"?', *Global Labour Journal*, 5: 23–44.

Comito, V. and Colombo, R. (eds) (2013) *L'Ilva di Taranto e cosa farne*, Roma: Edizioni dell'asino.

Corvace, L. (2011) 'Dalle navi dei veleni all'AIA. La questione ambientale a Taranto', in G. Battafarano (ed) *Taranto capitale: economia, lavoro, ambiente e società*, Taranto: Scorpione Editrice, pp 61–76.

Curcio, R. (ed) (2013) *Mal di lavoro*, Cuneo: Sensibili alle foglie.

Curcio, R. (ed) (2014) *Il pane e la morte*, Cuneo: Sensibili alle foglie.

De Palma, A. (2013) 'Ilva: una storia di fusioni', *Il de Martino*, 22–23: 11–33.

Ferraro, S. (2014) 'Fabbriche del suicidio. Lavoro, patologie e "produzione" di morte', in A. Simone (ed) *Suicidi. Studio sulla condizione umana nella crisi*, Milano: Mimesis, pp 29–50.

Gibson-Graham, J.K. (2006) *A post-capitalist politics*, Minneapolis, MN: University of Minnesota Press.

Gould, K.A., Lewis, T.L. and Timmons Robins R. (2012) 'Blue-green coalitions: constraints and possibilities in the post 9-11 political environment', *Journal of World System Research*, X(1): 91–116.

Landini, M. (2013) 'Prefazione', in V. Comito and R. Colombo (eds) *L'Ilva di Taranto e cosa farne*, Roma: Edizioni dell'asino, pp 5–12.

Leogrande, A. (2013) *Fumo sulla città*, Roma: Fandango.

Leonardi, E. (2012) *Biopolitics of climate change: Carbon commodities, environmental profanations and the lost innocence of use value*, Doctoral Dissertation, University of Western Ontario.

Leonardi, E. (2013) 'Foucault in the Susa Valley: the No TAV movement and processes of subjectification', *Capitalism Nature Society*, 24(2): 27–40.

Martinez Alier, J. (2002) *The environmentalism of the poor: A study in environmental conflicts and valuation*, Cheltenham: Edward Elgar.

Merchant, C. (2010 [1990]) *Ecological revolutions. Nature, gender and science in New England*, Chapel Hill, NC: University of North Carolina Press.

Montrie, C. (2008) *Making a living: Work and environment in the United States*, Chapel Hill, NC: University of North Carolina Press.

Nistri, R. (2013) *La ballata degli affumicati*, Bari: Edizioni Dal Sud.

Obach, B. (2004) *Labor and the environmental movement. The quest for common ground*, Cambridge, MA: MIT Press.

Peña, D. and Pulido, L. (1998) 'Environmentalism and positionality. The early pesticide campaign in the United Farm Workers' Organizing Committee, 1965-71', *Race, Gender and Class*, 6(1): 33–50.

Petrarulo, C. and De Angelis, C. (2013) *Pane e veleno. Il contraddittorio legame tra Taranto e l'Ilva: se ora l'azienda ha il raffreddore, la città ha già da tempo la polmonite*, Avellino: De Angelis.

Pirastu, R., Comba, P., Iavarone, I., Conti, S., Minelli, G., Manno, V., Mincuzzi, A., Minerba, S., Forastiere, F., Mataloni, F. and Biggeri, A. (2013) 'Environment and health in contaminated sites: the case of Taranto, Italy', *Journal of Environmental and Public Health*, http://dx.doi.org/10.1155/2013/753719

Pulido, L. (1996) *Environmentalism and economic justice: Two Chicano struggles in the south*, Tucson, AZ: University of Arizona Press.

Ranieri, C. (2013) 'Essere tutti sindacalisti', *S-connessioni Precarie*, www.connessioniprecarie.org/2012/11/24/essere-tutti-sindacalisti-intervista-a-cataldo-ranieri-comitato-lavoratori-e-cittadini-liberi-e-pensanti-taranto/

Ruscio, B. (2015) *Legami di ferro: dalla miniera alla fabbrica, dal cuore della foresta amazzonica brasiliana al quartiere Tamburi di Taranto*, Ancona: Narcissus.

Sandler, R. and Pezzullo, P. (eds) (2007) *Environmental justice and environmentalism: The social justice challenge to the environmental movement*, Cambridge, MA: MIT Press.

Schlosberg, D. (2007) *Defining environmental injustice: Theories, movements and nature*, New York, NY: Oxford University Press.

Vulpio, C. (2012) *La città delle nuvole*, Milano: Edizioni Ambiente.

Wheatley, M. (2005) *Finding our way: Leadership for an uncertain time*, San Francisco, CA: Berrett Kohler.

FIVE

Race, class and green jobs in low-income communities in the US: challenges for community development

Sekou Franklin

Introduction

On April 14, 2008, over a thousand activists gathered in Memphis, Tennessee to celebrate the life of Dr Martin Luther King, Jr on the fortieth observance of his assassination. Organised by Green For All, an organisation that advocates for green jobs initiatives, the 'Dream Reborn' conference brought together environmental, anti-poverty, criminal justice, labour and faith-based activists. Many conference attendees were attracted to the green jobs movement, sharing larger concerns about climate change after Hurricane Katrina struck the Mississippi Gulf Coast in the late summer of 2005.

For activists working in low-income Black communities, Hurricane Katrina had a similar impact on their political orientations as the Three Mile Island crisis had on America's perceptions of nuclear proliferation. That disaster in central Pennsylvania ignited a wave of protests against the nuclear industry in the late 1970s and early 1980s. The protests ushered in new measures regulating nuclear waste disposal, emergency planning and utility price controls (Joppke, 1992–93). Similarly, the Hurricane Katrina disaster helped to cultivate alliances between municipal officials, environmentalists and activists working on racial and economic justice initiatives. It focused attention on how municipalities could advance sustainable development measures that reduced carbon emissions while also addressing poverty and unemployment.

Green jobs programmes that targeted low-income residents, especially Blacks living in chronically distressed communities, are the focus of this chapter. The people affected by such programmes include individuals with histories in the criminal and juvenile justice systems and other marginalised populations such underemployed youth, people living in transitional housing, and low-skilled workers (Holzer et al, 2003; Holzer, 2007; Jones, 2008). These programmes are situated here within the broader arena of community development activism because they entail grassroots-led planning initiatives that prioritise the concerns of communities facing systemic patterns of racial and class marginalisation. The advocates involved in community development activism (and specifically green jobs advocates in this study) used a variety of strategies such as grassroots lobbying, protest and even forming partnerships with urban planners or municipal officials (Shaw, 2009). Some green jobs advocates were previously active in the environmental justice movement, which since the early 1980s has focused attention on the ecological practices of public agencies and pollution-emitting industries that disproportionately harm communities of colour and poor communities (Bullard, 1994; Shepard and Charles-Guzman, 2009; Zimmerman, 2010; Brown, 2011a). Environmental justice activists actually shaped the direction of the 'Dream Reborn' conference in Memphis.

This chapter argues that green jobs programmes targeting a marginalised workforce were more likely to be adopted in cities in which advocates were able to leverage municipal officials (especially mayors) and collaborate with local economic and racial justice activists on clean energy and other community development projects. At times, varying political cultures influenced municipal adoption, as cities located in states with a strong tradition of anti-union sentiment were the least likely to adopt these programmes. Yet still, in cities that did adopt green jobs initiatives, national and local advocacy groups worked closely with municipal officials and activists to navigate intergovernmental structures and funding streams in order to support workforce development projects for disadvantaged communities. Advocates also repositioned the sustainable development (and green jobs) agenda within the broader framework of community development. The success of this repositioning strategy depended on cultivating cross-sector alliances between environmentalists, labour, economic and racial justice groups and civil rights organisations in support of green jobs programmes.

Community development activists involved in green jobs initiatives were intentional about developing labour–community coalitions that could buttress their initiatives, especially those that could challenge pro-growth urban machines. Yet accomplishing this objective often required building relationships between the skilled trades (labour unions and trade associations) and groups representing people with severe barriers to employment, such as low-skilled workers, formerly incarcerated persons, homeless and transitional housing residents and poor youth. The green jobs movement thus reflected a larger attempt to bridge divisions between two disadvantaged groups: labour and skilled workers who experienced severe job loss in the Great Recession of 2008–9 and working-poor and low-skilled residents suffering from chronic unemployment and underemployment.

The remainder of this chapter examines how green jobs advocates and municipal officials established programmes that targeted low-income communities and communities of colour. The conceptual framework guiding this study draws from linkage theory, which describes how public officials and activists affix environmental or clean energy programmes (or sustainable development programmes) to economic justice and job creation initiatives (Fitzgerald, 2010). Included in this examination is a discussion of why racial equity and social class are central to the green jobs agenda and the broader implementation of community development initiatives.

This study uses both qualitative and quantitative data including event history analysis to examine the adoption of green jobs initiatives in 77 cities from December 2007 to March 2011. The period under study begins with the date that Congress passed the Energy Independence and Security Act (EISA) of 2007, which was the height of the congressional budget fights in March 2011. The EISA encompassed two provisions championed by advocacy and civil rights groups: the Energy Efficiency and Conservation Block Grant (EECBG) and the 'Green Jobs Act' that established the US Department of Labor's 'Pathways out of Poverty' Demonstration Program. Cities were allocated funds if they developed robust sustainability initiatives, or – in the case of the 'Pathways out of Poverty' grant – if awardees developed collaborative partnerships with the skilled trades, labour unions, non-profits and workforce development agencies.

Linkage, green jobs, and community development activism

Municipal officials are routinely criticised for being captives of powerful economic interests and developers whose agendas are particularly injurious to poor residents. Paul Peterson (1981) argues that federalism and a constrained political economy limit the capacity of cities to implement economic justice policies. These realities encourage city leaders to privilege powerful pro-growth interests, municipal privatisation and downsizing policies and other business-friendly measures, usually to the detriment of working poor and historically disadvantaged communities (Reed, 1999; George, 2004).

However, Fitzgerald's (2010) analysis of sustainable community development offers a counterargument to the pro-growth model of municipal governance. She argues that municipal officials, activists and community development institutions can use linkage strategies to extend green jobs initiatives to residents from marginalised communities. Linkage strategies 'connect sustainability or climate change initiatives to economic development goals such as creating workforce development programs to train residents for green jobs' (Fitzgerald, 2010, p.15). These strategies place equity-based agendas such as racial and economic justice at the forefront of sustainable and community development initiatives. Accordingly, they differ from property-led economic development agendas, which are predisposed to marginalise low-income residents.

Green jobs advocates promoted three linkage strategies during the period of this study, the first of which was community workforce or benefits agreements (a policy to which advocates also refer as 'high road agreements'). These are 'legally binding agreements' usually between a city or developer and community stakeholders such as environmental activists, antipoverty groups, civil rights organisations, labour unions and community development or financing institutions (Parks and Warren, 2009, p.89). The agreements solidify support for projects from stakeholders, but only with the promise of 'tangible benefits' such as living wage jobs, collective bargaining rights, environmental protections, affordable housing or other community-based or labour-friendly policies. Community workforce agreements were endorsed by green jobs coalitions in Seattle, Washington, Pittsburgh, Pennsylvania and Nashville, Tennessee (Ho and Rhodes-Conway, 2010; Levin, 2011; Ruprecht, 2011). Portland, Oregon actually created the national model for how to incorporate a workforce agreement into a comprehensive home-weatherisation programme; this model is examined later in the chapter.

The second linkage strategy is green worker programmes targeting low-skilled workers for pre-apprenticeship, clean energy jobs. These may be non-profit programmes, such as the Sustainable South Bronx's BEST programme, Asheville, North Carolina's Green Opportunities (GO) training programme and the Green Collar Job Training programme sponsored by Providence, Rhode Island's Groundwork. They can also be administered by municipalities such as the Oakland Jobs Corps, Boston's Green Youth Corps and Newark New Jersey's Green-Collar Apprenticeship Programme (City of Oakland, 2008; Menino, 2009). They are typically funded by federal or state workforce development grants.

Green worker initiatives offer short 'on-ramp' training that can last several weeks or 12 to 18 months. The most effective programmes provide industry-recognised certification and make concerted attempts to place the trainees in jobs or union apprenticeship programmes. Adrienne Parkmond of The WorkPlace, Inc. in Bridgeport, Connecticut coordinated the city's green worker programme, which trained 500 participants, mostly Blacks and Latinos from high-poverty communities. All participants were required to participate in a four-week training called 'Green Survey 101' (Parkmond, 2011). Case managers then transitioned the participants to a second round of trainings, which – depending on their vocational preference – lasted between eight weeks and 18 months.

Opportunity Maine, a policy advocacy group in Bangor, Maine, coordinated another green jobs programme for rural residents from 2010–12. Six groups assisting with the training provided specialised assistance with vocational skills, wrap-around services, career coaching and environmental education. This 'cross-sector' approach has produced positive outcomes for other workforce training initiatives around the country (Swanstrom and Banks, 2009; Brown, 2011b). Indeed, the 'Pathways Out of Poverty' grant that financed Opportunity Maine's programme mandated that applicants demonstrate a commitment to the cross-sector approach.

In reality, municipalities may not have the resources to finance the two aforementioned linkage strategies (community workforce agreements or green worker programmes), but may be receptive to a third category of green jobs: partnerships with workforce and community development agencies, vocational technical centres or community colleges. Most public–private partnerships are formalised by a city council resolution, a planning department or economic development agency or a Memorandum Of Understanding (MOU) between the city and the participating organisations. The Urban League of Greater Madison, Wisconsin coordinated the city's green jobs programme, which was funded by the Department of Energy's block grant (City of Madison, Wisconsin, 2010). Minneapolis, Minnesota partnered with Renewable Energy Network Empowering Workers (RENEW) to coordinate its green jobs initiative (Minneapolis Department of Community Planning and Economic Development, 2010), and Washington, DC's Green Pathway programme entailed a partnership between the city and Goodwill Industries of Greater Washington.

These three linkage strategies – workforce agreements, worker training and public–private partnerships – accentuate the central themes of linkage theory and the importance of national and grassroots advocacy groups in shaping community development policies. They exemplify how advocates and municipal officials leveraged intergovernmental structures on behalf of clean energy projects for historically disadvantaged residents. Compared to urban planners or economic development administrators, grassroots organisers and advocates are more sensitive to the needs of disadvantaged communities in the design of community development planning projects (Lewis, 2009; Speer and Christens, 2012, p.420). Concern about the growing political influence of business interests, which moderated community and housing development agencies, renewed interest in how grassroots institutions can promote alternative and equitable frameworks for development.

National advocacy groups – such as Emerald Cities Collaborative, Apollo Alliance, PolicyLink and Green For All – assisted with green jobs initiatives. These groups had strong ties with local anti-poverty, civil rights and labour groups. In fact, early in President Barack Obama's first term, his administration promoted several policies to finance sustainable development initiatives in cities. However, because states were plagued by high levels of partisan polarisation (Conlan and Posner, 2011), local advocates and municipal officials had to lean on the expertise of these advocacy groups to design green jobs programmes. By 2010, these groups were working in at least two dozen cities. They sent their policy analysts to various cities to help local activists craft workforce development programmes and authored studies explaining the economic benefits of green jobs and how they could augment civil rights and social justice agendas.

Despite the effectiveness of national and local advocates, each state's political culture affected the adoption of green jobs programmes. Cities located in the US South, a region characterised by racial and political conservatism as well as a pro-business climate that has been averse to robust environmentalism, were resistant to green jobs. For example, non-southern states were more likely to have a Property Assessed Clean Energy (PACE) law. PACE allows cities to extend special assessment statutes, initially designed for street and sewage repairs, to private property-based energy efficient improvements and renewable energy projects (Farrell, 2010). The absence of PACE statutes and related policies in southern states reduced local financing options for green jobs and weatherisation programmes in the South.

In addition, southern states were historically opposed to redistributive and pro-labour measures, as well as policies that placed a high value on racial equity (Dixon, 2010; Levin, 2011; Lewis and Hamilton, 2011;

Swarts and Vasi, 2011). Public policies such as green jobs that were presumed to assist low-income and African–American workers received greater opposition in southern states. This was quite troubling given the region's longstanding history of racial segregation and enduring high rates of poverty and environmental decay.

Racial equity, social class, and the green economy

Although the movement for green jobs promoted policies to mitigate the adverse effects of climate change, it was intent on linking the issue with concrete programmes that could address poverty and other inequities in communities of colour. Civil rights and racial justice groups, especially African–American leaders, were particularly concerned about the marginalisation of these communities in the debate about climate change and the green economy. These concerns were highlighted in the *Green Equity Toolkit* authored by the Applied Research Center, a racial justice incubator located in the San Francisco Bay Area (Liu and Keleher, 2009). In a separate study, Mason (2009) found that Blacks, Latinos and women had difficulty obtaining employment in green sectors targeted by the American Recovery and Reinvestment Act (ARRA).

To address these concerns, advocacy groups made a concerted effort to link climate change mitigation strategies with racial and economic justice initiatives. The National Association for the Advancement of Colored People (NAACP), National Urban League, Wider Opportunities for Women (WOW), National Hispanic Environmental Council and the Climate Equity Alliance all endorsed initiatives promoting green jobs and climate change policies (Cox, 2012). In 2008, the Joint Center for Political and Economic Studies – the nation's foremost African–American think tank – formed the 18-member Commission to Engage African–Americans on Climate Change. Furthermore, African–American leaders and groups were at the forefront of championing racial equity in the green economy and linking this concern to climate change policies.

In addition, the Hip Hop Caucus's Green the Block campaign lobbied the Department of Energy, the Environmental Protection Agency and the Department of Housing and Urban Development to create a National Day of Service on 11 September 2009. The next year, the Hip Hop Caucus convened the 'Green the City Advocacy Summit' in collaboration with the National Conference of Black Mayors (NCBM). The summit was part of the NCBM's 'Green The City' initiative, which helped African–American mayors to develop long-term environmental sustainability initiatives (NCBM National Office, 2010). Black mayors such as Cory Booker of Newark, New Jersey, Ron Dellums of Oakland, California and Adrian Fenty of Washington, DC were among the early sponsors of green jobs programmes for low-skilled workers.

Extending employment opportunities to the most marginalised or low-skilled workers was another concern of green jobs advocates. Influenced by the living wage movement in the 1990s and early 2000s, many advocates agreed with the claim that 'if a job improves the environment, but doesn't provide a family-supporting wage or a career ladder to move low-income workers into higher-skilled occupations, it is not a green-collar job' (Gordon and Hays, 2008, p.3). The labour unions also shared this sentiment, as indicated by green workforce initiatives sponsored by the United Steelworkers, the International Brotherhood of Electrical Workers and the Service Employees International Union. However, the blossoming of the green jobs movement coincided with the Great Recession of 2008–9. In some respects, this created a policy window for advocates to promote the green economy as a pathway out of recession; the US Department of Labor even identified green jobs as a high-growth sector. On the other hand, the recession exacerbated underemployment in the poorest communities and dislocated millions of skilled workers, including union members, from career-track occupations. It then destabilised municipal budgets and forced cities into massive layoffs and cutbacks to services.

Some cities facing budget cuts used green jobs initiatives to retain dislocated workers or channel resources to prime contractors and subcontractors, even though the programmes were intended to assist individuals with the most severe barriers to employment (Barbosa, 2010; Scott, 2010). Elsa Barbosa, Campaign Director for the Los Angeles-based organisation Strategic Concepts in Organizing and Policy Education (SCOPE), coordinated the coalition that won a citywide green jobs ordinance in April 2009. The legislation was a monumental victory for community activists. However, the city's budget deficit undermined the effectiveness of the law (Barbosa, 2010). The initial jobs went to municipal workers who were facing layoffs, instead of the unemployed residents who the legislation initially targeted. Job competition between skilled / union workers and low skilled / chronically underemployed residents dovetailed with contentious debates about race and the green economy. People experiencing barriers to employment were presumed to be disproportionately African–American or Latino, whereas skilled or union workers were deemed as being mostly white or having political connections to workforce investment boards and public officials. Whether these assumptions were correct or not, they produced tensions between the two sectors. Hence the most effective local coalitions attempted to minimise tensions between labour and grassroots, Black and Latino activists.

National advocacy and labour groups such as the Blue–Green Alliance, Apollo Alliance, Green For All and PolicyLink were instrumental in cultivating relationships between the two sectors. They helped green jobs coalitions and municipal officials with policy designs that were union-friendly while also carving out targeted hiring or workforce development policies for severely disadvantaged workers. In some cities, the skilled trades and unions even established pre-apprenticeship programmes for these workers.

Clean Energy Works Portland (CEWP)

Clean Energy Works Portland (CEWP) is a community workforce agreement that exemplifies how advocacy groups can synthesise concerns about climate change with racial equity and economic justice principles. Established in 2009, the programme set a goal of retro-fitting 100,000 older homes for weatherisation and energy efficient upgrades between 2010 and 2030, with the expectation that it would reduce carbon emissions and create 10,000 jobs in the region (Green For All, 2010). It was financed by Department of Energy grants and a homeowner-friendly revolving loan fund. CEWP was designed by environmentalists, labour unions, civil rights and anti-poverty groups, minority contractors and city officials. Green For All and the Apollo Alliance advised the various stakeholders on how to incorporate equity-based principles into the programme design.

Economic justice activists endorsed CEWP because it set aside 30% of the jobs (or 'project hours') for workers from the region's poorest communities. Civil rights and racial justice activists believed that this hiring policy would capture low-income minorities, who were typically excluded from this type of employment opportunity. The agreement also had a living wage provision, guaranteed health coverage or an optional payment for health care costs and had a best-value contracting policy to give minority firms mentorship opportunities and access to weatherisation contracts. The CEWP's collective bargaining language reflected the interests of Oregon's American Federation of Labor-Congress of Industrial Organizations (AFL-CIO), the local affiliates of the United Brotherhood of Carpenters and Joiners of America and Laborers' International Union of North America, which also worked on the agreement.

The early findings of the CEWP offer valuable insight into the success of the agreement. In the pilot phase of project, 55% of the work hours were carried out by women and people of colour, the median wage of all workers was close to $18.50 per hour and more than 80% of the workers hired by prime contractors were eligible for health insurance (Jacob, 2013). Within two years of the launch of the project it expanded across the state; it has since been renamed Clean Energy Works Oregon.

The adoption of municipal-based green jobs initiatives was influenced by advocacy groups, which lobbied municipal officials and partnered with local activists. Simultaneously, the groups championed racial equity and economic agendas within climate change mitigation and clean energy policies. The next section examines which cities adopted green jobs initiatives that targeted historically disadvantaged populations, how long it took for the cities to adopt them and how state and local political cultures influenced municipal adoption.

Tracking changes in adopting green jobs programmes

The remainder of the chapter uses a variation of event history analysis – the Cox regression model – to examine the adoption of green jobs programmes (community workforce agreements, green worker initiatives and public–private partnership) in 77 of the largest US cities (those with populations above 200,000) from December 2007 to March 2011.

Social class is evaluated through indices on unemployment and public sector unionisation. The unemployment variable measures the increase or change in unemployment patterns from 2008 and 2009. All the cities in this study were located in metropolitan regions that experienced an increase in the ranks of the unemployed. Cities with a high percentage of unionised public employees are also expected to be friendly to green jobs policies. The aforementioned variables (right-to-work, region, PACE, unionisation and unemployment) were identified as political culture variables and entered into the Cox regression as a cluster.

The last three variables were each entered in sequentially, thus providing a total of four Cox regression models. These are referred to as the Green For All (GFA) variables because they have been closely associated with racial and economic justice activists involved in green jobs initiatives. Included in this cluster were cities residing in states that approved of a law or related measure supporting green training programmes (such as the Green Jobs/Green Homes New York Act of

2009), a green tax credit incentivising targeted employment or a green training programme in a state workforce investment agency. Cities led by Black mayors were identified, since they have been among the most vocal advocates of green jobs. Finally, the study assesses the role of prominent advocacy groups that worked with local activists and municipal officials, specifically Emerald Cities Collaborative, Apollo Alliance, PolicyLink and Green For All.

Findings and discussion

To simplify the remainder of the discussion and to make it more accessible to the reader, the presentation of the Cox regression table is excluded and only the relevant findings are reported.[1] The overall fit of the regression model is good. The only statistically significant variable for all four models is if a city is in a 'right-to-work state', which prohibits union security agreements or agreements between unions and employers. This adversely affects policy adoption, as cities operating in right-to-work states were the least likely to create green jobs programmes in the 39-month period following the passage of the EISA. This finding was expected, considering the animus towards economic justice movements in right-to-work and southern states. Although the regional variable was not significant, the fact that all but two southern states (Kentucky and West Virginia) have been right-to-work states suggests that region has been closely related to right-to-work laws. The remaining variables (strong union cities, rising unemployment and PACE) did not influence the adoption of green jobs.

The regression findings further indicate that Black mayors were more likely to implement green jobs programmes. This occurred despite the adverse effect of right-to-work laws. The potential for adopting green jobs also increased when Black mayors and national advocates worked together. Interestingly, too, the combined influence of Black mayors and advocacy groups partially mitigated the influence of right-to-work laws. Thus, Black mayors emerged as being more likely to implement jobs programmes when pressured by reputable advocacy groups.

To further investigate the importance of Black mayors and advocacy groups, time variations to policy adoption (measured in months from the passage of the 2007 energy bill to March 2011) were examined. Region and right-to-work laws were the two variables that harmed the implementation of green jobs programmes. On the other hand, Black mayors and green advocacy groups working in pro-labour states (states that did not have right-to-work laws) and states that had a state-wide green jobs initiative were quick to adopt a policy. Overall, cities working with national advocacy groups that created green jobs initiatives had an average adoption time of 20 months. Black mayoralties adopted them within 23 months. Accordingly, it appears that advocacy groups were slightly more successful in convincing cities to implement green jobs programmes at a faster rate than cities led by Black mayors.

Conclusion

The green jobs movement advocates for pollution reduction policies and emerging opportunities in the clean energy economy. Simultaneously, the movement anchors these initiatives in a racially and economically inclusive framework, which gives specific attention to historically disadvantaged communities. By examining municipal-based green jobs programmes, this chapter places the green jobs movement under the umbrella of community development activism. Community workforce agreements or citywide jobs programmes, green worker initiatives targeting historically disadvantaged residents and public–private collaborations are three linkage strategies advanced by green jobs activists. Variations in the adoption of these programmes were shaped by the organising activities of green jobs advocates, their ability to work with innovative municipal officials and local and state political cultures. The findings indicate that cities in right-to-work states had the greatest difficulty adopting green jobs. Yet cities with Black mayors and those working closely with national advocacy groups were able to minimise the influence of right-to-work laws and adopt green jobs programmes. National advocacy groups (Emerald Cities Collaborative, Apollo Alliance, PolicyLink and Green For All) had close ties to local activists, and together they helped municipalities to navigate the complex intergovernmental structures and funding streams that supported green jobs initiatives.

The push for green jobs exemplifies a community development model that synthesises concerns about the environment, equity and the economy. As such, this model provides important lessons for municipal officials and grassroots activists about the potential impact of green jobs initiatives in ameliorating poverty and other inequities.

Notes

[1] For a visual presentation of the Cox regression model, contact Sekou.Franklin@mtsu.edu.

References

Allison, P.D. (2014) *Event history and survival analysis* (2nd edn), Los Angeles, CA: Sage.

Barbosa, E. (2010) Interview, 10 December. Barbosa is the Campaign Director for the Strategic Concepts in Organizing and Policy Education, Los Angeles, CA.

Brown, F. (2011a) Interview, 11 March. Brown is the Associate Director of Program Development for the Kinsley Association, Pittsburgh, Pennsylvania.

Brown, R. (2011b) Interview, 9 March. Brown is the Co-Director of Opportunity Maine in Bangor and Portland, Maine.

Bullard, R.D. (1994) *Dumping in Dixie: Race, class, and environmental quality*, Boulder, CO: Westview Press.

City of Madison, Wisconsin (2010) *City announces energy efficiency grants for small business, green job training*, press release, 29 October. City of Oakland. California (2008) Agenda report, 22 July, Office of the Mayor to Office of the Administrator.

Conlan, T.J. and Posner, P.L. (2011) 'Inflection point? Federalism and the Obama administration', *Publius? The Journal of Federalism*, 41(3): 421–46.

Cox, R. (2012) Environmental communication and the public sphere (3rd edn), New York, NY: Sage Publications.

Dixon, M. (2010) 'Union threat, countermovement organization, and labour policy in the states, 1944–1960', *Social Problems*, 57(2): 157–74.

Farrell, J. (2010) 'PACE financing: Responding to concerns', The New Rules Project, 1 April, https://ilsr.org/wp-content/uploads/files/ILSR response to PACE concerns.pdf

Fitzgerald, J. (2010) *Emerald cities: Urban sustainability and economic development*, New York, NY: Oxford University Press.

George, H., Jr. (2004) 'Community development and the politics of deracialization: the case of Denver, Colorado, 1991–2003', *The ANNALS of the American Academy of Political and Social Science*, 594(1): 143–57.

Gordon, K. and Hays, J. (2008) *Green-collar jobs in America's cities: Building pathways out of poverty and careers in the clean energy economy*, Oakland, CA: Green for All and the Apollo Alliance.

Green For All (2010) *Clean energy works Portland: A national model for energy efficiency retrofits, a report from Green For All*, Oakland, CA: Green For All.

Ho, S. and Rhodes-Conway, S. (2010) *A short guide to setting up a city-scale retrofit program*, Oakland, CA: Green for All and the Center on Wisconsin Strategy.

Holzer, H.J. (2007) 'Collateral costs: the effects of incarceration on the employment and earnings of young workers', Discussion paper no. 3118, October, Bonn, Germany: Institute for the Study of Labour.

Holzer, H., Raphael, J.S. and Stoll, M.A. (2003) 'Employment dimensions of reentry: understanding the bexus between prisoner reentry and work', Urban Institute Reentry Roundtable, 19–20 May, New York University Law School.

Jacob, A. (2013) *Clean energy works Portland final technical report*, Portland, OR: Bureau of Planning and Sustainability.

Jones, V. (2008) *The green-collar economy: How one solution can fix our two biggest problems*, New York, NY: HarperOne.

Joppke, C. (1992–93) 'Decentralization of control in U.S. nuclear energy policy', *Political Science Quarterly*, 107(4): 709–25.

Levin, N. (2011) Interview, 7 March. Levin is the Executive Director of the Tennessee Alliance for Progress and the Coordinator of the Nashville-Davidson County Green-Collar Jobs Taskforce.

Lewis, H. (2009) 'Rebuilding communities: a twelve-step recovery program', in S.E. Keefe (ed) *Participatory development in Appalachia*, Knoxville, TN: University of Tennessee Press, pp 67–88.

Lewis, J.H. and Hamilton, D.K. (2011) 'Race and regionalism: the structure of local government and racial disparity', *Urban Affairs Review*, 47(3): 349–84.

Liu, Y.Y. and Keleher, T. (2009) *Green equity toolkit: Standards and strategies for advancing race, gender and economic equity in the green economy*, Oakland, CA: Applied Research Center.

Mason, C.N. (2009) *Race, gender and the recession*, New York, NY: NYU Wagner.

Menino, T.M. (2009) *Going green: Mayor Menino announces $300,000 in empowerment zone funding to create green-collar jobs*, press release, 25 June.

Minneapolis Department of Community Planning and Economic Development (2010), Request for city council committee action from the department of community planning and economic development to council member Lisa Goodman, community development committee, 23 March, Minneapolis, MN: City of Minneapolis.

National Conference of Black Mayors (NCBM) National Office (2010) *NCBM special report: Sustainably green*, Atlanta, GA: National Conference of Black Mayors.

Parkmond, A. (2011) Interview, 9 March. Parkmond is Executive Vice-President of The Workplace, Inc. in Bridgeport, Connecticut.

Parks, V. and Warren, D. (2009) 'The politics and practice of economic justice: community benefits agreements as tactic of new accountable development movement', *Journal of Community Practice*, 17: 88–106.

Peterson, P. (1981) *City limits*, Chicago, IL: University of Chicago Press.

Reed, A. (1999) 'Sources of demobilization in the new black political regime: Incorporation, ideological capitulation, and radical failure in the post-segregation', in A. Reed (ed) *Stirrings in the jug: Black politics in the post-segregation era*, Minneapolis, MN: University of Minnesota Press, pp 117–62.

Ruprecht, L. (2011) Interview, 9 March. Ruprecht is the Sustainable Community Development Coordinator of ACTION-Housing, inc. in Pittsburgh, Pennsylvania.

Scott, M.E. (2010) Interview, 10 December. Scott is the Research Coordinator for the Strategic Concepts in Organizing and Policy Education, Los Angeles, CA.

Shaw, T.C. (2009) *Now is the time!: Detroit Black politics and grassroots activism*, Durham, NC: Duke University Press.

Shepard, P. and Charles-Guzman, K. (2009) 'The roots of environmental justice', in M.P. Pavel (ed) *Breakthrough communities: Sustainability and justice in the next American metropolis*, Cambridge, MA: MIT Press, pp 35–47.

Speer, P.W. and Christens, B.D. (2012) 'Local community organizing and change: altering policy in the housing and community development system in Kansas City', *Journal of Community and Applied Social Psychology*, 22(5): 414–27.

Swanstrom, T. and Banks, B. (2009) 'Going regional: community-based regionalism, transportation, and local hiring agreements', *Journal of Planning Education and Research*, 28: 355–67.

Swarts, H. and Vasi, I.B. (2011) 'Which US cities adopt living wage ordinances? Predictors of adoption of a New Labour tactic, 1994–2006', *Urban Affairs Review*, 47(6): 743-74.

Zimmerman, K. (2010) *Dare to change: Environmental justice leadership for climate justice, sustainable communities and a deep green economy*, Oakland, CA: Movement Strategy Center.

SIX

Community development practice in India: Interrogating caste and common sense

Mohd. Shahid and Manish K. Jha

Introduction

A textbook much referred to by social work educators and community development practitioners in India contains the following passage, which reflects on the process of community building in a village near New Delhi, the capital of India:

> A meeting of all the villagers was called with the help of the student worker. All the male members, especially the adults, were personally requested to attend the meeting. The meeting was attended by all the leaders. *There was no preferential order of sitting except for the fact that the lower caste people belonging to Jhimer, Chamar and Bhangi did not sit on the carpet.* (Gangrade, 1971, p.59; emphasis added)

Thus, what is stated as a matter of fact – that 'there was no preferential order of sitting' – makes manifest a blatant case of untouchability and indignity for some of the most marginalised caste groups in India. While the usage of derogatory 'call names' like Chamar and Bhangi for these marginalised caste groups now constitutes a criminal offence punishable by law in India, the institution of caste nonetheless continues to provide a common cultural idiom to Indians: 'wherever one may be in India one is in a universe of caste' (Mandelbaum, 2005, p. 228). As Srinivas (2010, p.3) puts it:

> Caste is undoubtedly an all India phenomena in the sense that there are everywhere hereditary, endogamous groups which form a hierarchy and that each of these groups has a traditional association with one or two occupations. ...

> Relations between castes are invariably expressed in terms of pollution and purity.

It is these notions of 'pollution and purity' that govern the nature and extent of social interaction between different caste groups. Thus caste is more than an occupational category or an income-based class; rather, it represents a system of rigid social stratification.[1] This is why Ambedkar called caste a 'closed class' (cited in Rodrigues, 2002, p.257). In other words, caste-related subdivisions of society are not based upon the comparatively open character of the class system but rather have become self-enclosed units: beyond class in any traditional sense.

Historically, castes at the lower end of the caste hierarchy have experienced the worst forms of exploitation. Nevertheless, the normative social order in India – more specifically, in rural India – continues to relegate the marginalised caste groups to physical and symbolic segregation. The location of segregated caste clusters in Indian villages speaks volumes about the inbuilt caste hegemony that exists within the social topography. The connotation of the specific caste groups sitting 'on the carpet' and 'off the carpet' may seem to imply a thin line of physical distance between such groups, but in reality these are the explicit markers of the subtle but powerful forms of untouchability.

It is regrettable that, in India, human service professions such as social work and community development have never effectively come to grips with measures to prevent social disorganisation through changes in the social system. Historically, the inspiration for community development has its roots in the Community Development Programme (CDP) launched by the Indian government in the 1950s. In this programme, the hierarchical caste structure was not given sufficient attention. Rather, under the label of 'voluntary labour', the oppressed caste groups were actually compelled to undergo forced labour (begār) (Desai, 2006). As a result, the term 'community development' has been regarded, in many cases, with an element of contempt. And as has been argued, community development has continued to work largely in support of the prevailing social, economic and political system (Nanavatty, 1985, p.316). While nuances of the social structure and caste system are undoubtedly taught in social work education and its community development counterpart, somehow the elitist orientation of much social work education has obfuscated *Dalit* and *Adivasi* perspectives in its pedagogy (Rao and Waghmore, 2007, p.1). Indeed, reflecting on social movements and mass-based organisations fighting against inequality, exploitation and oppression, Andharia (2007, p.101) notes that 'many of the organisations were aligned to the left, politically or ideologically and believed that professional social workers [and, by extension, community development workers] offered band-aid solutions and were counterproductive for ushering a structural change'.

It is further lamented that unlike countries such as Australia, UK and the US, where community development emerged both as a philosophy and as a political strategy, in India the term generally connotes a failed paradigm (Andharia, 2007, p.98). Jha (2009) has added to the contemporary discussion on intercommunity relations in India, asserting that these can never be comprehensive without taking account of certain landmarks seen through momentous ruptures in the forms and nature of dialogue between communities, such as the recurrent incidents of communal riots and caste-based violence.

It is the authors' view that community development must therefore recommit itself to human rights and social justice (Jha, 2009, p.315). In this sense, this chapter supports the view that community development is a professional practice that enjoins practitioners to make sense of oppressive sociocultural realities and to promote anti-hegemonic community development. The pertinent questions therefore are: how should academics, educators and practitioners make sense of these normative but oppressive social frames? And how is the process of the subordination and oppression of marginalised groups – more specifically, the lower caste groups – normalised as a natural social reality? It is here that this chapter endeavours to throw light on the interplay between macro structural values and micro oppressive realities.

The background of the study

This chapter focuses specifically on the Balmiki community, a substantial majority of whose members are still – at the time of writing – engaged in the inhumane practice of manual scavenging. Positioned lowest even in the untouchable caste group, the community engages with 'impure' and 'polluting' natural wastes as their primary occupation. This chapter draws from an empirical study undertaken during the process of the conversion of the dry toilets[2] and the related rescue and rehabilitation of the Balmiki community, which had hitherto been engaged in manual scavenging in the Budaun district of Uttar Pradesh (India). Studying these processes of change provides valuable insights into the nature of the barriers facing them, together with valuable insights into their experiences of liberation, once these practices and norms had been effectively challenged.

The study was first undertaken in December 2010 and followed up in June 2011. In the first visit two villages were sampled and studied, while in the second visit one previous study village was kept common and one new village was sampled. The field visits entailed interactions and focus group discussions with 'liberated' manual scavengers and their family members, and also with members of other castes / communities whose dry latrines had been converted into flush latrines. The research was based on the personal narratives of 'liberated' women manual scavengers together with those of other caste / community members in relation to their experiences of stigma, exploitation and violence in their engagement with manual scavenging. The aim was also to elicit their perspectives on the 'legitimisation' of manual scavenging. Kakar (1990, p.3) has noted that there is no better way to gain an understanding of a society than through its stock of stories (myth, fable, parable and tale), which constitute its dramatic resources. Every child in India is exposed to stock narratives. The study endeavoured, therefore, to make sense of the ramifications of these popular common-sense narratives on manual scavenging and on those engaged in such scavenging. The Gramscian lens of hegemony and common sense are used to make sense of these narratives.

Hegemony and common sense

Gramsci's work carried forward classical Marxist thinking on the pervasive power of ideology, values and beliefs in reproducing class relations and concealing contradictions through his widely influential notions of *hegemony* and *common sense*. Gramsci exposed hegemony as a process whereby consent was organised through moral and intellectual leadership (Sassoon, 2000, p.45). In this sense, Gramsci's concept of hegemony provides an understanding of the manufacture of consent by the powerful through the institution of cultural values (Peters, 2010). This adds a number of dimensions to the traditional notion of hegemony. Critically, Gramsci located hegemony in the daily operations of power and in the ways in which we interpret the world and create meaning, thereby excavating the ways in which dominance is legitimised by consent rather than coercion. Applying a Gramscian lens to community development, Ledwith (2001, p.110) notes that Gramsci's impact on political consciousness, most particularly through the concept of hegemony, has been profound in its analysis of the insidious nature of power and the role of consent. This is the lens that she uses in articulating community work as critical pedagogy.

Critically for our argument, Gramsci also reflected on how common sense works in the internalisation of the hegemony of the dominant group by subaltern social groups. Unlike English, the Italian notion of common sense (*senso commune*) does not so much mean good, sound, practical sense but rather 'normal or average understanding' (Ives, 2004, p.74). In other words, everyone has a number of 'conceptions of the world', many of which are imposed and absorbed passively from the outside world or from the past, and which are accepted and lived uncritically (Forgacs, 2000, p.421). As Gramsci (2010, p.419) put it: 'Common sense is not a single unique conception, identical in time and space. It is the "folklore" of philosophy, and, like folklore, it takes countless different forms'. For example, many elements in popular common sense contribute to people's subordination by making situations of inequality and oppression appear to be natural and unchangeable. This insight on the seamless link between hegemony and common sense will be helpful in analysing and exploring the oppression inherent in the narratives built around manual scavenging and the people engaged therein.

The Balmiki community in India

Speaking on *The political rights of the depressed classes* in the Indian Round Table Conference (12 November 1930 to 19 January 1931) held in London, Ambedkar observed the following:

> There are communities in India which occupy a lower and subordinate position; but the position assigned to the Depressed Classes is totally different. It is one which is midway between that of the serf and the slave, and which may, for convenience, be called servile – with the difference that the serf and the slave were permitted to have physical contact, from which the Depressed Classes are debarred. (in Das, 2010, p.21)

Even today, the scavenging communities of Balmikis represent the most depressed of all depressed classes across India, although they have different nomenclatures in diverse spatial zones (Kailash, 2002; Beck & Darokar, 2005; Kalyani, 2005; Suzuki, 2010). *The people of India project*, which provides an ethnographic account of caste and communities in India, reported as follows:

The Balmikis consider themselves lowly placed like members of the communities of the same caste-clusters in various parts of the country. They recognize the Varna system and place themselves among the Shudras. The other communities also consider the Balmiki a lowly people ...

Economically, the Balmikis are a poor community. Only few of them own any land. ... They served other communities on the basis of generational contracts (Jajmani system) against payments in cash and kind of various nature as sweepers and scavengers. (Singh, 1992, pp. 156–8)

The trappings of economic misery and the inherently demeaning tradition of sweeping and manual scavenging have resulted in the powerful stereotyping and stigmatisation of the Balmiki community. Consequently, this has led to the development of a low self image among the members themselves and an almost fatalistic acceptance of the all-pervasive context of their lowly existence.

The Balmikis, who are listed as a Scheduled Caste in Uttar Pradesh, are followers of the Hindu religion. However, it may also be noted that even among other religious groups like Muslims there are castes (Biradari) engaged in sweeping and manual scavenging. For example, the community of *Halalkhor*, also known as *Shaikha / Sahani*, is dispersed over a number of the districts of Uttar Pradesh; they practise Islam and are similarly engaged in these menial jobs (Singh, 1992). In Awadh and eastern Uttar Pradesh there is a *Lal Begi* community among both Hindus and Muslims, members of which practise sweeping and manual scavenging. As a mark of distinct identity, *Lal Begi* Muslims have designated themselves as *Hasnati* (Singh, 1992). It is noted that manual scavengers have adopted or experimented with a variety of religions, sects and nomenclatures, or have accepted 'sanitised' names, but their plight has not changed. Bhagwan Das (2007), the celebrated author of *Mein Bhangi Hon* (I am the scavenger), registers deep anguish and disappointment when he writes:

Samajik istar nahin badalta, nirdhanta samapta nahin hoti, chhuaa chhūt nahin mitatī, gulami khatma nahin hoti. Achhūt-achhūt rahega aur bhangi, bhangi. Badlega to kewal nam badlega. (Das, 2007, p.106)

Social status is not going to change, poverty is not ending, untouchability shall not end, and slavery won't end. Untouchable shall remain untouchable and a bhangi,

bhangi. Only the name would change. (Translation by authors)

It is here that field engagement with the communities involved in manual scavenging and their experiences of subordination and oppression helps to make sense of the normative social order, elucidating the subtle ways in which the inhumane practice of manual scavenging becomes legitimised. This approach should reveal the critical understandings that community development practitioners need in order to grasp the interplay of hegemony and common sense in reinforcing oppressive realities.

Class, caste and community development

As already explained, the practice of the manual sweeping of household dry latrines has been forced upon a specific group of people as their ascribed status. Furthermore, a study by Safai Karmachari Andolan (SKA)[3] indicates that 95% of those engaged in manual scavenging are women. Our experience in the Budaun district of Uttar Pradesh – where, from July 2010 to June 2011, a total of 47,000 dry latrines were converted to flush latrines and 2,000 workers were liberated from manual scavenging – reveals that *all* of the workers were women. This demonstrates the extent to which manual scavenging particularly affects women. The concept of intersectionality (Pal, 2001, p.175; Kumar, 2008, p.160) – which postulates that vulnerable groups experience multiple barriers when one discrimination intersects with other forms of discrimination – is therefore illuminating here. Women engaged in manual scavenging exemplify the ways in which gender, caste and class operate to exploit and marginalise these women by mutually reinforcing a set of cultural norms that have been so difficult to contest.

In-depth interactions with individuals and focus group discussions in the three villages of Budaun district have enabled the women 'liberated' from manual scavenging to articulate their experiences. This research has also elicited the response of other community members; in particular, the patrons whose household dry latrines the women used to clean. Such discussions focused on the subject of manual scavenging and the ways in which 'common sense' normalises the subordination and oppression of those engaged in its practice.

Both explicit and subtle forms of subordination and oppression were evident in the accounts of those women who had been 'liberated' from manual scavenging. They shared their sufferings and concerns in focus group discussions, as well as their past experiences of being unable to afford to be sick because each day they had to be at work (*'Bimar bhi nahin ho sakte, kaam par jana hi jana hai'*). Even when needing to visit relatives or for marriages or other such ceremonies in nearby villages, they felt under constant pressure because they thought that their patron families would deal with them badly if they took time off work. There was no question of a weekend – or, for that matter, of any holiday at all. Despite this grim reality, both officials and community 'elites' maintained that families engaged in manual scavenging either could not or would not undertake jobs requiring hard labour and skilled expertise, so long as manual scavenging provided them with 'easy money'. During the field interactions, however, Balmiki women energetically rebuffed these arguments about 'easy' money. In unison, they asked us to calculate what 'easy' and 'big' amounts they actually received from patron families. On average, one Balmiki woman covered 20 to 30 households; some families paid 15 to 20 INR per month (25 p in UK currency), while others merely provided leftover food and some cereals or clothing annually and/or on festive occasions and celebrations. Since there was neither any alternative nor any possibility of imagining one, the women were mostly dependent on these offerings of leftover food (*Joothan*), used clothes (*Utaran*) and the few pennies that came to them from manual scavenging. The irony of their position is captured well in the saying *'Joothan aur Utaran ke payar ne mujhe nikamma bana diya'* ('the love for leftover food and used clothes made me idle') (Das, 2007, p.75).

The women also explained that, in the past, as manual scavengers they had been relegated to the status of 'untouchables' – and as if that was not undignified enough, it was also their responsibility to ensure that they did not touch other community members.[4] In a context in which they were dependent on these very patrons for their livelihood, they had no choice but to comply. Since they had stopped manual scavenging, however, they had been able to move freely about the village. From this new position of ex-scavengers they argued that, if others did not want to be touched by them, then they had better take care of it themselves! They would no longer feel obliged to give way, as they had in earlier times (*'Ham apna chalte hain jise bachna ho to bache'*). This bold response reflects increasing levels of self-confidence and assertiveness among these liberated manual scavengers.

Their accounts also show how far they had come in terms of their experiences and self-perception as a result. In the past, they had been made to experience acute hunger and misery and their occupation had made them vulnerable to infections and diseases, adding further pressure on the family purse (see also Prasad, 2007). As untouchables, their mobility had also been severely restricted, and they had come to consider themselves unworthy and undignified; they had been left to live with a low self-image and socialised into accepting manual scavenging as their destiny. As such, manual scavenging had perpetuated a variety of forms of subordination, oppression, misery, ill health, alienation and exclusion. The notion that manual scavenging was their providence – a notion that was prevalent among both manual scavengers and other community members – served to negate critical consciousness formation and undermine attempts to organise themselves against this undignified practice.

The following account illustrates some of the ways in which these norms and stereotypes had been reproduced in the past. A village elected representative had the following to offer when asked about engaging the former manual scavengers and their family members in Mahatma Gandhi National Rural Employment Guarantee Act (MGNREGA)[5] work:

> They [families engaged in manual scavenging] are not accustomed to do hard work nor can they do it. They have less physical strength. Moreover, women would not do manual work and male members also cannot do physical labour. They have been used to easy and gainful manual scavenging work.

In another village, an elder reflected on the conversion of dry latrines into flush latrines in his house and the village:

> The village has been freed from a stinking environment. At night you could not go out. At the time of child birth and cutting of umbilical cord the Harijan used to ask 500 rupees [£5] and if we were unable to give, then they did not turn up for scavenging. If they did not come for a week then there would be hell. They used to exploit us because of this. They used to get grain/cereals/maize, food in the evening, clothes and cash during marriages and festivals. We got rid of them.

Such comments suggest that manual scavenging was actually beneficial for the scavengers at the expense of other community members and that it was the patron families who were generous enough to put up with, and feed, the manual scavengers. Many similar comments were heard, such as 'they don't have the temperament for hard or skilled work';

'they are habituated to this work and can't do anything else' and 'manual scavenging is for the advantage of Balmiki community'. Furthermore, other castes and communities have used similarly stereotypical cultural constructions to reinforce the belief that there could be no substitute for manual scavenging and that the manual scavengers and their families did not desire change.

Given these stereotypes, it was unsurprising to encounter women arguing that they had taken to manual scavenging with an element of reverence (*'hamne to daliya ko pooja maan liya tha'*). Many admitted that they had initially even been resistant to give it up. On being asked why they were reluctant to consider other occupations, they vehemently responded:

> We do want good food, clean clothes, and good work. But how do we secure them? There was no escape from manual scavenging for us! Who will give us work? How should we venture in starting a new enterprise? Not being in a position to find answers to any of these concerns, we accepted manual scavenging as our destiny.

These expressions reflect an element of frustration but also weary resignation to their roles as manual scavengers. They also reveal how the women in question had been socialised into suppressing any other aspirations. They raised these concerns when the district magistrate and his team visited their village. He assured them that if they wished to quit manual scavenging they would be provided with welfare and social protection (long overdue entitlements, such as old age and widow pensions), as well as training and loans for alternative occupations. It may also be noted that this represented an interesting community development intervention whereby government district functionaries, civil society organisations (such as Balmiki Sena), local bodies and development professionals with social work backgrounds worked collectively to end manual scavenging and induce sustainable change.

Perhaps unsurprisingly, the women responded as if they had long awaited this opportunity. The wicker baskets that they had used for scavenging were burnt (*daliya jalao*)[6] to mark the end of – and their liberation from – manual scavenging in their village. They went on to share with the researchers that they were all now in work or self-employed in tough manual and/or skilled occupations. Some had taken loans and purchased buffaloes, for example, while others had trained in masonry work and become skilled masons. They were convinced that this had only been made possible by the sincere and resolute support efforts of the district administration. As a consequence of these initiatives, *daliya jalao* (liberating manual scavengers) became a joint mission of the district administration, alongside the practical business of converting dry latrines into flush ones. During our last visit in June 2011, as per district officials, the Budaun district was about to achieve the status of a district free from manual scavenging and dry latrines.

This case study illustrates ways in which hegemony has cultural, political and economic aspects. Challenging these had been effective overall for the research participants. However, this had entailed compromises between social groups, as a result of which sectional interests were transformed and a notion of the general interest was promoted (Gramsci, 2010). It is clear that the caste system provided legitimacy for manual scavenging as a caste-based occupation. As such, despite feeling that manual scavenging was menial and inhumane, the manual scavengers had been subtly manoeuvred into accepting it as their destiny: '*Saab Hamne to Daliya ek puja man lee thi*' ('Sir, we took *Daliya* (wicker basket) as worship'). This is how manual scavenging became acceptable; it was therefore no surprise that there was some resistance from the scavengers themselves when faced with attempts to end the practice, as well as very different reactions when former scavengers gained confidence as a result of their liberation.

Conclusion

This chapter has explored the mythical constructions, stereotypes and 'common sense' notions that confined the female manual scavengers of the Balmiki community to a subordinated and inhuman life. Being compelled to undertake manual scavenging as a result of oppressive intersections of class, caste and gender reinforced the plight of the Balmiki community. Their cultural entrapment, economic misery and powerlessness worked in tandem to render their worldview opaque. It is rightly noted that oppression has a domesticating function (Freire, 1996, p.33). It is essential here to understand that a speaker who is a manual scavenger is not simply an individual speaker but rather the 'spokesperson' of the community, culture and normative social order. In other words, the normative social order has hegemonised the world of the marginalised; furthermore, this hegemony has been dynamic, finding a range of ways to control the oppressed and leading them to accept their subservience as normal and 'natural'. Gramsci (2010) provides a way of understanding how this 'common sense' works in the internalisation of hegemony. It is because of this that the Balmiki community had been made to unquestioningly engage in manual scavenging as their traditional hereditary caste-based occupation.

Community development practitioners have to be conscious of the fact that common sense is not necessarily *good* sense, and that the normative social order might in fact be reflective of a hegemonised social reality. They need to make sense of the realities of marginalised groups and depressed classes like the Balmiki community and enable them to envision alternative choices and life chances. This becomes all the more important in a diverse and highly stratified society like India. Our field engagements have demonstrated that the traditions and particularity of hereditary occupational structures can be challenged, and that communities' collective engagement in processes of change could trigger radical transformations in people's beliefs and practices. Community workers need to make sense of existing normative social values and counter these with the professional values of respect for human worth, dignity, diversity and social justice, thus promoting anti-hegemonic community development practice.

Notes

[1] According to B.R. Ambedkar, Indian society is a gradation of castes forming an ascending scale of reverence and a descending scale of contempt (B.R. Ambedkar, in Das, 2010).

[2] Dry latrines are non-pour flush toilets, normally located at the extreme end of the houses where people defecate and the human excreta (commonly referred to as night soil) is cleaned manually and carried to the dumping site by people belonging to a specific caste. Accordingly, dry latrines are the raison d'être for the practice of manual scavenging.

[3] SKA is a civil rights organisation representing mainly the children of those engaged in manual scavenging. The organisation is committed to the cause of liberating and rehabilitating those engaged in manual scavenging through research studies, massive protest marches and written petitions. See http://safaikarmachariandolan.org/

[4] They were made to monitor and maintain the enforced apartheid themselves. This is despite the fact that the Article 17 of the Constitution of India clearly states that 'Untouchability; is abolished and its practice in any form is forbidden' (see Bakshi, 2012). The enforcement of any disability arising out of 'untouchability' is an offence punishable by law in India.

[5] By virtue of this legislation, the Indian government guarantees 100 days of unskilled work in a year to at least one member of each interested rural household; rural local bodies are the implementing agencies.

[6] Similar initiatives were organised in Madhya Pradesh by the community-based organisation *Jan Sahas* (People's Courage for Change) through *Garima Abhiyan* (Campaign for Dignity). See www.jansahasindia.org/programsview.php?id=41

References

Andharia, J. (2007) 'Reconceptualizing community organization in India', *Journal of Community Practice*, 15(1): 91–119.

Bakshi, P.M. (2012) *The Constitution of India*, New Delhi: Universal Law Publishing Co., first published in 1991.

Beck, H. and Darokar, S. (2005) 'Socioeconomic status of scavengers engaged in the practice of manual scavenging in Maharastra', *The Indian Journal of Social Work*, 66(2): 223–36.

Das, B. (2007) *Mein Bhangi Hon* (in Hindi), Delhi: Gautam Book Centre, first published in 1981.

Das, B. (ed) (2010) *Thus spoke Ambedkar (vol. 1: A stake in the nation)*, New Delhi: Navayana.

Desai, A.R. (2006) *Rural sociology in India*, Bombay: Popular Prakashan, originally published 1938.

Forgacs, D. (2000) *The Gramsci reader: Selected writings 1916–1935*, New York, NY: New York University Press, originally published in 1988.

Freire, P. (1996) *Pedagogy of the oppressed* (trans. Myra Bergman Ramos), London: Penguin Books, originally published in 1970.

Gangrade, K.D. (1971) *Community organization in India*, Bombay: Popular Prakasan.

Gramsci, A. (2010) *Selections from the prison notebooks* (translated and edited by Quintin Hoare and Geoffrey Nowell Smith), Hyderabad: Orient Blackswan, originally published in 1971.

Ives, P. (2004) *Language and hegemony in Gramsci*, London: Pluto Press.

Jha, M. (2009) 'Community organization in split societies', *Community Development Journal*, 44(3): 305–19.

Kailash (2002) 'Cleaners are yet to be cleaned: the rehabilitation issue of manual scavengers', *Contemporary Social Work*, 19(2): 71–82

Kakar, S. (1990) *Intimate relations: Exploring Indian sexuality*, New Delhi: Penguin Books, originally published in 1989.

Kalyani, D.D. (2005) *Khamosh Daastan* (In Hindi), New Delhi: Mulniwasi Publication Trust, first published in 2003.

Kumar, S. (2008) 'Dalit women at the intersections: voices from the margins', *Indian Journal of Social Work*, 69(2): 159–78.

Ledwith, M. (2001) 'Community work as critical pedagogy: re-envisioning Freire and Gramsci', *Community Development Journal*, 36(3): 171–82.

Mandelbaum, D.G. (2005) *Society in India* (Indian edition in one volume), Bombay: Popular Prakashan, originally published in 1970.

Nanavatty, M.C. (1985) 'Social work education and professional development', *The Indian Journal of Social Work*, XLVI(3): 315–28, reprinted in 1991.

Pal, G.C. (2001) 'Disability, intersectionality and deprivation: an excluded agenda', *Psychology of Developing Societies*, 23(2): 159–76.

Peters, M.A. (2010) 'Foreword', in P. Mayo (ed) *Gramsci and educational thought*, Chichester: Wiley-Blackwell, pp ix–x.

Prasad, B.D. (2007) 'Scavengers and scavenging in Andhra Pradesh', *Indian Journal of Social Work*, 68(2): 189–203.

Rao, V. and Waghmore, S. (eds) (2007) 'Editorial', *The Indian Journal of Social Work*, 68(1): 1–6.

Rodrigues, V. (eds) (2002) *The essential writings of B.R. Ambedkar*, New Delhi: Oxford University Press.

Sassoon, A.S. (2000) *Gramsci and contemporary politics: Beyond pessimism of intellect*, London and New York: Routledge.

Singh, K.S. (1992) *People of India project: An introduction*, (National Series Vol. 1), Calcutta: Anthropological Survey of India.

Srinivas, M.N. (2010) *Social change in modern India*, Hyderabad: Orient BlackSwan, originally published in 1966.

Suzuki, M. (2010) 'Indian government strategy against caste inequality: "liberating" untouchables in the context of welfare schemes', *Journal of Political Science and Sociology*, 12: 65–83.

SEVEN

The impact of gender, race and class on women's political participation in post-apartheid South Africa: challenges for community development

Janine Hicks and Sithembiso Myeni

Introduction and overview

The Commission for Gender Equality (CGE) is an independent statutory body established in terms of section 187 of the Constitution of South Africa Act 108 of 1996. The CGE mandate is derived from both the 1996 Constitution and the Commission for Gender Equality Act of 1996, the latter of which outlines the powers and functions of the CGE. The CGE is constitutionally charged with a broad mandate: the promotion of respect for, and the protection, development and attainment of, gender equality. As part of this mandate, the CGE has the power to monitor and evaluate the policies and practices of state and private sector entities, including political parties. Accordingly, the CGE, in partnership with the National Democratic Institute (NDI) South Africa, undertook a study to examine political parties' institutional and structural barriers to women's full participation and their ability to influence party policy.

Section 19(3)(a) of the Constitution of 1996 provides that 'every adult citizen has the right to stand for public office, and if elected, to hold office', effectively providing a legal framework for the political presence of women. Noting that political parties are the primary and most direct vehicle through which women can access elected office and political leadership, CGE study findings reveal that the structures, policies, practices and values of political parties have a profound impact on the level of women's participation in the political life of their country.

In addition, through their policies and programmes, political parties have an opportunity to respond to service delivery issues specific to women and to begin to address barriers to women's political participation and representation within their political party platforms and structures. These are vital to ensure country implementation of and compliance with the provisions of a range of global, continental and regional instruments, as well as national legislation, aimed at advancing women's rights to equality. This study therefore sought to assess political parties' efforts to promote women's full and equal political participation in party decision-making structures and processes and to respond to developmental needs of women within communities through their manifestos. For the study, the CGE collected data from three political parties: the African National Congress (ANC); the Congress for the People (COPE); and the United Democratic Movement (UDM), which were among the five major political parties represented in the National Assembly between May 2009 and May 2014 (the others being the Democratic Alliance (DA) and the Inkatha Freedom Party (IFP)). This chapter also includes critical reflections from fieldwork in five provinces of South Africa – Western Cape, KwaZulu-Natal, North West, Free State and Eastern Cape – in the form of 12 focus groups with participants between June and September 2013.

This chapter explores the CGE study findings through the lens of the impact of gender, race and class on women's political representation in post-apartheid South Africa. The aim of the chapter is to share an analysis of the policies and practices of political parties and to assess the progress made in promoting gender equality in the new political spaces that have been opened up for women, as well as the challenges for community development. The chapter finally draws some conclusions by considering possible policy solutions to address these structural inequalities more effectively and to enable women to participate more fully as active citizens in post-apartheid South Africa.

Intersectionality, politics and development

An understanding of the impact of the intersections between gender, class and race is essential to understanding the nuances within the experiences of women in political mobilisation and activism, particularly among marginalised groups of women. Such awareness is important to enable policy makers within political parties to redress past and current oppression equitably. There are numerous challenges facing community development in South Africa. First, the post-apartheid reorganising of the state resulted in women's underrepresentation in strategic positions due to political parties' vested interests in winning geographical territory. Analysis reveals that only elite and powerful women are able to assume party leadership positions, resulting in their representation in legislative bodies. The underrepresentation of women in top leadership positions affects their participation and representation – particularly in municipal legislative committees, which are key decision-making sites in relation to community development projects and policy making.

Second, women's low levels of education, barriers to accessing information and subordinate status in society relative to men prevent poor, working-class women from possessing the requisite profile to be nominated as candidates for elections and to hold strategic posts within political parties. This in turn prevents many women from effectively participating in planning and decision making in relation to community development projects, denying them both the experience and the profile necessary to progress to positions of power within political parties. This has significant implications for women's ability to influence development policy and implementation at the community level, and to ensure this responds to their particular vulnerabilities and opportunities. According to the Combat Poverty Agency (2000), community development is a process whereby those who are marginalised and excluded are enabled to gain self confidence, to join with others, to participate in actions to change their situation and to tackle the problems that face their community. For some, community development is seen as a process of offering ordinary citizens the opportunity to share in making important decisions about their living conditions (Anyanwu, 1992). In the context of this chapter, community development is viewed through the lens of women's participation in decision making and collective action leading to an agenda of social change regarding equality, social inclusion and amelioration of poverty.

Challenges and constraints to women's political representation

Dynamics of power and participation

Before assessing women's political participation and influence in community development decision making, it is critical to examine the unequal power relationships at play in these spaces – which are influenced by issues of class, race and gender – both within political parties themselves and between political representatives and ordinary women in communities. These unequal power relationships play out in the policy arena, resulting in some issues not making it onto the agenda, the exclusion of some stakeholders, the rendering invisible of others and the exclusion of many from that critical juncture at which decisions are made.

It is also important to disaggregate the voices of political representatives and to question whether or not these have included the stated needs of women, elderly people, young people and disabled people. There is a danger of homogenising the voices of community representatives; this can deepen the exclusion of and perpetuate inequitable relations between these various actors (Cornwall, 2003) and 'draw a veil over repressive structures (of gender, class, caste and ethnicity) operating at the micro-scale' (Williams, 2004, p.93). In addition, the tendency to disregard differences between and within groups and to emphasise consensus may result in the replication of 'dominant discourses' rather than present a challenge to them (Gaventa and Cornwall, 2001, p.75). An analysis of participatory processes at community level reflects that these tend to be dominated by men, revealing the importance of questioning which stakeholders are present at these processes and whom they represent. With men tending to set the agenda and to dominate discussions and processes, women's participation is further marginalised and undermined. Beall and Todes (2004, p.304) have noted that, in local development processes, 'participation by women is variable and even where women dominate in numbers, they are not necessarily able to achieve "voice" due to power relations within institutions'.

However the issue of representation is just one important element of the broader component of women's *participation* in policy and governance processes. It must be acknowledged that ensuring the advancement of gender-sensitive and responsive policy options requires more than the numbers approach offered by a quota system. In addition, design of decision-making and consultative mechanisms is a critical consideration. In understanding the participation of women – and other marginalised groups – in policy processes, it is also critical to bear in mind that no political space is 'neutral'. When participatory spaces are created, they are 'infused with existing relations of power', which 'reproduce rather than challenge hierarchies and inequalities' (Cornwall, 2004, p.81). This means that established patterns of behaviour, perceptions and stereotypes that exist between groups and classes of people will 'follow' these people into a participatory space and subtly influence the decision-making process underway. These spaces need to be transformed by introducing new rules, techniques and processes to avoid reproducing the status quo. This can be done through, for example, language-use choices, seating arrangements, rules for engagement and decision making and building on existing spaces in which people are already engaging (Cornwall, 2004). Further considerations are the times at which such spaces are convened (to ensure that women are able to manage domestic or working responsibilities, enabling them to participate) as well as transport arrangements to ensure women's safety when travelling home in the evening (Beall and Todes, 2004).

In engaging with political party stakeholders and community members, the CGE's study sought to elicit an understanding of systemic challenges to women's political representation and participation. While the apparent progress in women's statistical representation in elected government (albeit remaining nowhere near the 50% target) and the formal equality attained through constitutional and legislative gains are indicative of great strides in attaining equality, worrying indicators of persistent constraints to women's full participation and substantive equality are present. The study sought to gauge and analyse these factors. Findings reveal significant challenges to ordinary working-class women's ability to influence political party policy choices, election manifestos and concomitant service delivery through local authority structures, as well as significant challenges to the ability of women *within* political parties to assume leadership positions and roles and to influence decision making. These challenges may be clustered into the following five themes: the nature of the electoral system; internal party-political constraints; sociocultural and economic constraints, lack of confidence and the depoliticising of the feminist movement in South Africa.

The nature of the electoral system

In the post-apartheid context of reorganising the state there was a monopolisation of the political space by dominant political parties due to their vested interest in the system of decentralisation as a means to secure more voter support. This challenged women's political agency in terms of influencing party agendas at the national level and mobilising around issues such as women's representation or gender equality issues. This resulted in women being expected to operate within a male-dominated and hostile political environment to advance their own political careers and statuses. Evidence gathered from political parties in the CGE study indicates that the concomitant overreliance of women on party leadership and internal party policy for their positions has resulted in limitations to their agency and impact.

In the 1990s, political parties started to restructure along the lines of the decentralised, territorial structure of the state. Some parties, such as the ANC, did not have operating quota systems at the local branch level to ensure women's representation and inclusion until as late as December 2007. This was partly due to the fact that women activists within the party focussed on candidate quotas rather than branch-level quotas during the initial phases of negotiation and consolidation of democracy, which left local party structures dominated by men. In short, the spatial strategy of institutional design provided strategic opportunities for party-political manoeuvring, such that local party branches – and, as a result, provincial party structures – became sites for capture by male political elites. In addition, political parties have delegated some of their powers and authority to local branches, which serve as the embodiment of male interests. These structures remain resistant to the notion of a gender quota, which requires ongoing navigation and negotiation by party leadership. This is evident in the appointment of provincial premiers by the ANC and the appointment of seven males to one female in the eight provinces under ANC majority rule, deviating from its 50/50 principle.

Internal party-political constraints

Two major political constraints to women's political participation can be identified. The first is related to the structure and agendas of political parties. The political parties studied do not readily promote women in their echelons, let alone facilitate women's occupation of important positions. Male domination is reflected in political party structures and decision-making leadership positions, in which women are underrepresented. As such, women continue to occupy lower positions compared to their male counterparts and men continue to dominate the entire political arena.

Party leaders largely determine who can be nominated to run for political office, and the spatial strategy of institutional design has provided strategic opportunities for party-political manoeuvring such that local party branches have become sites for capture by male political elites, such as teachers, schools principals and local businessmen. The small number of women granted a measure of control or influence at branch level appears to have used this influence as a conduit for advancing their own personal interests and access to state resources – by positioning themselves as local councillors, for example – but has had little power to, nor seeming interest in, representing the needs of women within their party or poor women in their constituency areas (Myeni, 2012). In attempting to understand this phenomenon, research reveals that while such women fulfil an important role in mobilising and campaigning for their parties they rarely occupy the decision-making positions that would enable them to influence the local party agenda. In addition, the lack of financial resources available to branches for their effective functioning results in a situation in which minimal activities exist to promote gender equality. During focus group discussions, there were endless accounts of the weakness of branches and institutional channels for the representation of women's interests and the common failure of women's wings to provide political leadership in order to ensure that a women's agenda is taken seriously.

The second political constraint is related to the design of the electoral system. Available evidence suggests that the nature of the electoral system plays an important role in determining women's representation. As noted, the proportional representation (PR) system is recognised as being the most conducive to women's legislative presence; it creates a greater incentive for political parties to draw up diversified lists of candidates, including women, in order to appeal to a wider base of voters. Where such a system is coupled with a quota system – such as within the ANC – significant women's representation is effectively guaranteed, as reflected in women's current representation in South Africa. However, the CGE study revealed that in the formal political arena, such as in local council meetings, there are very few spaces for women to collaborate and to push a gender agenda. It is apparent that their reliance on male party leadership – and ultimately, their political survival – depends on their allegiance being overwhelmingly to their political parties rather than to a constituency base of ordinary women.

As a result, the PR system is highly detrimental to the effective representation of voters – and, in this instance, ordinary working-class women's interests – since it weakens the relationship between representatives and their designated constituencies because, from the outset, voters choose parties rather than candidates. As a result, notions of accountability – and importantly, constituency support for representatives – are undermined, along with the necessary elements for mobilising women's support for female representatives, feeding women's interests and issues into government deliberations and influencing the political and policy agenda. Thus although women participate in political spaces and gain new opportunities for leadership and learning, these positions and opportunities do not automatically translate into the representation of women's interests. Rather, they are systemically structured to advance the agenda of political party leadership and perpetuate the dominance of male elites.

As a site of both opportunity for women to enter the political domain and ongoing replication of power imbalances and inequity, the institutional design of local government requires further examination.

The 'mixed electoral system' introduced into local governance provides for a combination of constituency and proportional representation. The findings of the study, largely informed by interview data from councillors themselves, indicate that ward councillors elected in single member wards are legitimate actors and instrumental in the advancement of local development interventions. However, as a result of fundamentally patriarchal perceptions and prejudice in relation to women's leadership potential the majority of ward representatives are men, with women only entering into local representation through the PR system, party lists and party quota interventions.

In practice, it is ward councillors who are accorded resources and responsibility to drive community development activities. As a result, when women are effectively excluded from this terrain, their influence over local development priorities and their ability to ensure that resources are allocated to address local women's needs and interests are severely reduced. Accordingly, this direct form of representation does not offer opportunities for women's effective political participation or representation, but rather further perpetuates patriarchal perceptions of women's political leadership. Ultimately, this component of the CGE study indicates that women as electoral representatives face twin challenges – inadequate institutional transformation to ensure local government's responsiveness to women's interests and issues, and inadequate links between themselves as elected representatives and potential constituencies of women – to enable them to effectively challenge bias and discrimination in existing patterns of policy determination and resource allocation.

Sociocultural and economic constraints

Regarding gender and politics, two dominant sociocultural and economic constraints to ordinary working-class women's political representation became apparent through the CGE study. First, such women are constrained by their lack of education and access to information. In most instances candidate nomination procedures require a minimum level of literacy, and this prevents poor, working-class women from registering as candidates for elections. Kameri-Mbote (2001, p.1) argues further that illiteracy is one of the major challenges to women in that they are not able to benefit from the dissemination of knowledge about the universal principles of human rights. This further serves to divide the educated, professional and urban South African women from the less educated and working-class majority in rural areas, who continue to vote in ways that disadvantage women's presence in the political arena. In addition to basic education, many women lack the political training and experience necessary to participate effectively in the political arena. It is therefore important that women are given access to work experience that is conducive to political leadership from an early age – for example, in community-based organisations – as well as empowerment and leadership opportunities.

The second socioeconomic constraint is poverty, which disproportionately affects women. Respondents from focus group discussions were in agreement that it is difficult for women to participate in political life when their major concern is survival and they have no choice but to spend much of their time in trying to meet the basic needs of their families. This means that working-class women have inadequate access to the time and financial resources required to participate effectively in the political process, even in local community-based organisations or development interventions, which could afford them a necessary platform from which to advance their political activism. As a result of resource constraints, women do not have access to the campaign finances necessary to seeking electoral office, such as initiatives to build their individual profiles and gain name recognition. In this way, their economically disempowered position renders working-class women unable to participate effectively in electoral politics – unlike their male counterparts, who enjoy greater representation as well as formal economic participation. At party branch level there are neither adequate financial resources – nor any party policy allocating such resources – to supplement women's campaign finances, and as a result there are minimal activities promoting women's political participation.

Across the board, women are affected by domestic and child care responsibilities, which within a patriarchal society, are typically accorded to women. Without proactive measures put in place, such as affordable and easily accessible child care facilities made available at party meetings and congresses, women's capacity to travel to political party events and processes, or to attend late-evening meetings, is undermined, impacting on their ability to participate in these. The prevalence of women-headed households in South Africa, particularly within rural areas, and reliance upon women to manage household chores, further exacerbates the challenges faced predominantly by working class women, who cannot afford domestic help, to participate actively in political life.

Lack of confidence

Most participants identified lack of confidence as one of the main reasons for women's underrepresentation in formal institutions such as parliament, municipal chambers and political parties. They argued that women with determination and confidence can reach the highest levels in the political process and that women should be encouraged to believe in themselves and to reject the widespread perception that men have to be their leaders. Participants noted that women are equal to and have the same potential as men, but nonetheless put their trust in men to take up the fight for women's rights. Many acknowledged that, while women are very good party mobilisers, campaigners and organisers, fear sometimes prevents them from contesting elections and from standing for leadership positions. In essence it is apparent that, within a patriarchal society, women are fundamentally affected by the economy of power that grants men superior social position and standing and subordinates women to male dominance. It is clear that these deeply embedded notions of worth, confidence and self-esteem need to be addressed in order for working-class women to challenge and assume positions of leadership within the political life of the country and within party politics.

Depoliticising of the feminist movement in South Africa

Many authors have argued that the organic feminism that characterised the period before 1994 has been lost and that the focus has shifted to institutional politics, law reform and a discourse around gender equality (Hassim, 2006; Myeni, 2012). This has resulted in the bureaucratising of feminism and has shifted the focus to liberal individual rights and law reform, changing the discourse of women's equality and justice to focus on gender relations. There is a strong sense that any discourse of gender that reduces equality to a numbers game has already depoliticised feminist activism. Merely appointing more women to positions of power is not a feminist solution, and formal equality does not equal substantive equality. In addition, the technocratic use of gender mainstreaming (such as tickboxes and events) has robbed gender mainstreaming of its radical potential to change institutional cultures and to include women's concerns in policy and legislation.

The momentum of feminist activism has not disappeared completely in South Africa. Women's organisations have regrouped around specific policy areas of community development, participated in the new inclusive processes of policy formulation and sometimes held government accountable to its broad commitments to gender equality and poverty reduction. This means that there has been a resurgence of activism around specific issues for community development, such as violence against women, poverty reduction and HIV/AIDS. However, some of these issues are not given policy priority, due to the lack of a strong women's voice at the national level to raise fundamental questions about the processes of macroeconomic decision making. The new generation of 'femocrats' finds it very difficult to formulate and implement policies that could rectify gender disparities and resistance to gender transformation inside deeply patriarchal institutions.

Reflections for the future

Women's representation mechanisms

The study reveals that there is poor representation of women in leadership positions of political parties. South African political structures are still dominated by men, despite constitutional guarantees to gender equality and state commitment to the Southern African Development Community's Gender and Development Protocol of 2008 (Myeni, 2012). It is clear from the increase in women's representation following South Africa's 1994 general elections that the voluntary quota system adopted by the ANC has had a radical impact on women's political representation. The study revealed that, while some political parties have undertaken progressive strategies to improve women's political participation, these institutional mechanisms are undermined by failures in implementation of policy and quotas, inadequate resourcing of these measures, structural impediments to women's full participation and representation and the prioritising of partisan interests over women's interests.

That mechanisms such as the quota system are not legal requirements embedded in electoral legislation but rather left to internal party policy, with no accountability or enforcement mechanisms in place, poses a further risk to women's political participation. The study found that the government has a significant role to play in ensuring gender transformation within political parties and structures, since it possesses the legitimate authority to enact a 50/50 quota through electoral legislative reform. Political parties should create candidate recruitment committees to ensure diversity in such recruitment and compliance with rules regarding inclusion of women candidates. In addition, opening up the process of candidate recruitment and selection so that it is transparent and participatory can combat the tendency for leaders in some parties to handpick their candidates according to undefined criteria.

Electoral system amendments

The study calls for an examination of the current electoral system so that different types of constituency can be built to strengthen women's political agency. This should respond to the convergence of the electoral systems that operate at local government level, namely the ward and PR systems. The electoral system that was adopted in South Africa in the 1990s did not have a gender lens through which to consider the impact of embedded patriarchal ideology and attitudes towards the adoption of political spaces by women and men. Ideally, interventions are required to secure seats or representation for women in *both* systems of representation rather than only enabling access to proportional representation through the quota system. This study, for example, proposes the introduction of a mixed system of both PR quotas *and* the reservation of seats at ward councillor level. This would ensure women's representation in this sphere of government and thereby their influence in local development interventions to build their own sphere of influence as well as a constituency base.

Political party interventions

Within the context of a patriarchal and male-dominated societal structure it is evident that there are barriers to women entering the political process, indicating the need to transform formal institutions so that women may be promoted not only as party list candidates but also as leaders and office bearers. All respondents and participants were in agreement that the greatest challenge remains the legacy of patriarchy in overcoming entrenched attitudes and perceptions relating to women's leadership. This prevents parties from putting forward women's candidates, prevents women from standing for nomination and prevents men and women from voting for women candidates. This is despite the fact that the inclusion of women's perspectives and women's participation in politics are prerequisites for democratic development, good governance and community development that is responsive to women's needs.

Political parties must ensure that their policies and priorities respond to the needs of women and men – not only in terms of gender-specific policy reforms but also in terms of ensuring that gender is mainstreamed into all party policies. International best practice indicates that political parties should also be encouraged to include motivated and qualified women in leadership positions and to sensitise party members to the importance of opening a supportive space for women among their members, leadership and internal structures.

During election campaign periods, political parties and civil society organisations should mentor women candidates and strengthen their campaigning skills by providing training on fundraising; message development; working with the media; building voter contact and outreach programmes, writing campaign plans and designing targeted methods of voter communication. Political parties should also establish party funding mechanisms for fundraising to support women candidates during their campaigning. Manifestos and campaign messages should be targeted to women voters, articulating parties' positions on gender equality and women's empowerment.

Furthermore, political parties must adopt clear rules for the participation of women delegates at national party conferences, considering that, in these conferences national organisational leaders are elected, resolutions and major party decisions are made and policies are adopted that guide the direction of the party. Parties should consider establishing targets to ensure that a proportion of the delegates attending are women.

Women's political structures such as the African National Congress Women's League (ANCWL) should continue to advocate for measures to promote women's electoral candidacies and to lobby party leaders to ensure that women candidates are given high positions on the lists and assigned to winnable seats. In addition, women's structures could conduct civic education and voter outreach and seek funding for training interventions for women candidates.

Conclusion

This chapter has outlined the reality that multiple marginalisations based on gender, race and class at both individual and institutional levels creates social and political stratification, requiring policy solutions that are attuned to the intersections of these categories. The chapter sought to capture how the intersections of gender, race and class collectively shape the experiences of women with regard to the notion of women's participation and representation within formal political structures and processes. The data presented provides a platform for a more interpretative discussion of the institutional and structural barriers to women's full participation, which is necessary to understand the overlapping and conflicting dynamics of gender, race and class. The data provides further evidence about the state of women's participation and representation, as well as an overview of the critical challenges that still beset women at the intersections of community development, planning and activism and the adoption of these issues by political parties within primarily municipal government structures. The recommendations offered by the study and synthesised in this chapter, will be deliberated by the CGE and political stakeholders in South Africa with a view to strengthen women's political participation and representation through strategies that are cognisant of the persistent barriers experienced by women on the basis of their gender, race and class.

References

Anyanwu, C. (1992) *Community development: The Nigerian perspective*, Ibadan: Gabesther Educational Publishers.

Beall, J. and Todes, A. (2004) 'Gender and integrated area development projects: lessons from Cato Manor, Durban', *Cities*, 21(4): 301–10.

Combat Poverty Agency (2000) *The role of community development in tackling poverty*, Dublin: Combat Poverty Agency.

Cornwall, A. (2003) 'Whose voices? Whose choices? Reflections on gender and participatory development', *World Development*, 31(8): 1325–42.

Cornwall, A. (2004) 'Spaces for transformation? Reflections on issues of power and difference in participation and development', in S. Hickey and G. Mohan (eds), *Participation: From tyranny to transformation*, London: Zed Books, pp 75–91.

Gaventa, J. and Cornwall, A. (2001) 'Power and knowledge', in P. Reason and H. Bradbury (eds), *Handbook of action research: Participative inquiry and practice*, London: Sage Publications, pp 108–25.

Hassim, S. (2006) *Women's organizations and democracy in South Africa: contesting authority*, Scottsville: University of KwaZulu Natal Press.

Kameri-Mbote, P. (2001) 'Gender consideration in constitution-making: engendering women's rights in the legal process', *University of Nairobi Law Journal,* 12 July, pp 156–94.

Myeni, S. (2012) *History matters: Exploring women's political representation in post-apartheid KwaZulu-Natal, South Africa*, PhD dissertation, University of Manchester.

Williams, G. (2004) 'Towards a repoliticisation of participatory development: political capabilities and spaces of empowerment', In S. Hickey and G. Mohan (eds), *Participation: From tyranny to transformation*, London: Zed Books, pp 92–107.

EIGHT

What happens when community organisers move into government? Recent experience in Bolivia

Mike Geddes

Introduction

A country of about ten million people, Bolivia has long been among the poorest states in the world, with high levels of inequality resulting from centuries of colonial and neocolonial exploitation and elite rule. However, since 2005, the Bolivian government has been in the hands of the MAS (*Movimiento al Socialismo*): a party defining itself as the 'political instrument' of Bolivia's strong social movements, which brought Evo Morales and the MAS to power. Morales himself, and many people who came into government with him, came from community organising backgrounds in these social movements.

With a majority indigenous population and strong, radical trades unions, issues of class and race – '*marxismo y indianismo*' - are intimately entwined in Bolivian radical politics. This chapter will explore how such issues are reflected and refracted in MAS policies. It will then examine the Bolivian experience of a 'government of the social movements', in which many leading figures have a background in community organising and social movements. How, and to what extent, have both the policies and the processes of governance of the MAS reflected this? Key policies, such as the introduction of a new Constitution drawn up by a popular constituent assembly, formally entrench indigenous community culture and practices within the state. A growing state role in the economy has provided resources for redistributive welfare policies and increasing living standards. However, as the MAS nears its first decade in power, tensions are beginning to show. While it retains very strong popular support, some accuse the government of an increasingly authoritarian statism and of abandoning its community roots. The entry of social movement leaders into government is said to have weakened the movements themselves, while ex–community organisers now in senior government positions are accused of incompetence. Divisions are emerging between community organisations that were previously united behind the MAS.

In exploring these tensions, the chapter will help to illuminate both the potential and the pitfalls of an attempt to embed radical conceptions of class and race in the state, and an attempt to foreground community organising and community development principles in government policy. In this context, it should be noted that there are both parallels and differences with experiences in other countries – both in Latin America and elsewhere – some of which are discussed elsewhere in this book. The MAS government is sometimes seen as part of a group (also including Venezuela and Ecuador) at the leftward end of a broader continuum of 'pink tide', left-leaning Latin American regimes, in contrast to others such as Brazil, Argentina and Chile. Comparisons can also be drawn between the overthrow of the racist regime in Bolivia and the assumption of power by the African National Congress (ANC) in South Africa.

Class, race and community in Bolivia

For 500 years – since the Spanish conquest of Latin America – Bolivia has been on the periphery of the global capitalist economy, with the surplus from its rich natural resources siphoned off through the continent's 'open veins' to the Global North. A Spanish/*mestizo* elite governed the country and systematically excluded the indigenous majority; entrenched inequalities of class and race both within Bolivia and in the colonial relationship with Spain and the wider 'advanced' world reinforced each other. However, the limited reach of the state meant that in much of the country, outside the main centres, traditional indigenous culture and forms of social and community organisation remained strongly rooted; for example, the main indigenous cultures of the Aymara and Quechua prioritised the communal rather than the individual in relation to land ownership.

During much of the 20th century, Bolivia had a strong and radical labour movement centred in working-class mining communities and influenced by socialist, communist and anarchist ideologies. Following the institution of nationalist–populist regimes from the 1950s on, however, the union movement became more corporatist and state-oriented; with the advent of neoliberal regimes in the mid-1980s – and especially the consequent closure of major parts of the mining industry – the unions' influence declined drastically. Many miners moved from the Andean areas to the lowlands in the east, taking trades union ideas with them into a different context of semi-peasant agriculture. At the same time, major shifts in economic and employment patterns towards precarious and informal work changed the class structure in fundamental ways. A subaltern class structure, including both an industrial proletariat and a peasantry, saw the increasing interpenetration of their characteristic – trade union and indigenous community – forms of organisation in a working class now characterised as plebeian rather than proletarian. But while these changes threatened traditional trades unions, they opened up spaces for the emergence of new, independent grassroots organisations and a shift in the locus of class struggle from the factory floor to neighbourhoods and communities (Spronk, 2013, pp.79 trade union and indigenous community 82).

It was these 'new' forms of organisation that were instrumental in paving the way for the electoral victory of the MAS in 2005. The peripheral nature of the insertion of Bolivia into global neoliberalism in the 1980s and 1990s meant that – even more than is the case with neoliberalism more generally) – market-led policies failed to benefit more than a small elite, provoking growing popular discontent and resistance. The so-called 'water and gas wars' saw mass protests against the privatisation of water supplies – most notably in Cochabamba, where a city-wide movement successfully reversed privatisation – and against the export of natural gas on terms dictated by transnational capital and the Bolivian *comprador* class. The city of El Alto, close to the capital La Paz, saw massive population growth as a result of migration from mining and rural areas, and the mixing of trades union and indigenous organisational forms in neighbourhood and community organisations was coordinated at a citywide level by the Federation of Neighbourhood Committees of El Alto (FEJUVE).

At the same time, in the coca-growing areas in the east, indigenous migrants from the Andes created a similar organisation of the *'cocaleros'* (coca growers). As a result, in Bolivia today, there is very often no clear separation between 'union' and 'community organisation' and between union organisers and community organisers (Kohl and Farthing, 2006).

It was the social movement of the *cocaleros* that formed the basis for the emergence of MAS in 2003. Significantly, MAS describes itself not as a political party but as the 'political instrument' of the social movements. While still rooted in the *cocaleros*, it was successful in bringing together a broad alliance of urban and rural, trades union, community and social movement oppositional forces, which provided the political strength to overthrow the neoliberal government in 2005 and – for the first time – to elect an indigenous president and his party.

The MAS government has been in power continuously since 2005 and was re-elected by a landslide in October 2014. From Morales himself down, the composition of the government – and of its appointments in the state bureaucracy – has reflected its social roots, bringing community and Left activists into many key positions. In responding to the primary concerns of the social movements with US imperialism and domestic neoliberalism, the government has prioritised issues of race and decolonisation. Most notably, a convention dominated by the social movements produced a new Constitution, which makes Bolivia a 'plurinational' state and reflects the majority status of the indigenous 'nations' in the country (Artaraz, 2012, esp Ch 3 pp.55–77). Concepts such as *'vivir bien'* ('living well'), which draw on rural indigenous notions of harmony with nature and question capitalist 'growth', have become important (if often ambiguous). At the same time the MAS programme envisages a transition away from neoliberalism towards socialism, although the extent to which this has been reflected in action remains a major issue.

Ironically, though, at the very moment when rural-based indigenous ideologies have become dominant in a 'government of the social movements', patterns of demographic and social change are undermining the class and social forces behind it. From a predominantly rural society, Bolivia is becoming much more urbanised, with a growing middle class, while capitalist relations of production are superseding small-scale peasant producers (Stefanoni, 2012). Thus, while concepts of collective ownership and *vivir bien* are influencing policies promoted by community activists in government, they are under threat in the wider society. At the same time, the MAS government – like any other – finds itself in a globalised capitalist environment. It is in this environment that activists-turned-ministers and civil servants have had to try to implement policies ranging from land redistribution to retention of surpluses from hydrocarbons and mining, deal with multinational agribusiness interests (which constitute an important export sector) in the east of the country and make a major contribution to food supply. Simultaneously, indigenous concepts such as *vivir bien* have to be reconciled with the economic growth necessary to raise living standards in a very poor country.

It is in this context that this chapter explores what happened when MAS community, social movement, trades union and leftist activists and organisers participated in government for the last decade. In this discussion, reflecting the Bolivian reality, a broad view will be taken of 'community development'. There are important instances in Bolivia of forms of community development professional practice, often funded by foreign NGOs, which would be easily recognisable in the UK context. For example, the Integrated Community Development

Fund – a US$45 million, 7-year USAID-funded programme operating between 2005 and 2012 – supported hundreds of community development projects across Bolivia, creating infrastructure and promoting local economic development. The ICDF employed both professional community development workers and volunteers, as well as training people from local communities (ACDI/VOCA, n.d.). But such instances are only part of the wider practice of community organising, which (as noted earlier) is inseparable from the trades union and social movement engagement of many activists, and which is often explicitly political rather than (formally at least) apolitical as in the 'professional' model (although, of course, a formally apolitical stance may be questionable; the Bolivian government expelled USAID, the funder of the ICDF programme, in 2013 on the grounds that its operations were undermining the government). The role of radical academics engaged in (or closely aligned to) community organising is also a feature of Bolivian experience, and has been important in promoting a close dialogue between 'practice' and 'theory'.

Social movements, community organisers and the MAS government

Evo Morales himself is, of course, the leading example of a community organiser who has moved successfully into government. From an initial position as local activist and then leader of the *cocaleros*, Morales was a crucial figure in the formation of MAS and subsequently *the* dominant figure – the President – in the MAS government.

Morales's approach to politics has been formed by his experiences as a *cocalero*. The organisation of the coca growers in the Chapare in eastern Bolivia has been heavily influenced by the fact that many of the *cocaleros* are ex-miners from the Andean highlands who brought with them radical trade unionism. In the Chapare, however, the *cocalero sindicatos* (unions) developed as a mixture of trades unions and community organisations, both defending the economic interests of the coca growers (albeit in the changed conditions of small scale agricultural production rather than industrialised coalmining) and providing community organisation and facilities. Local *sindicatos*, which have around fifty members, are combined into *centrales* of around ten local groups; several of these then combine into six provincial *federaciones,* themselves forming a central coordinating committee, which in turn is a member of the Central Obrera Boliviana (COB): the national workers union. Involvement in these different levels means that between 3,000 and 4,000 people are involved in leadership roles at any one time. As leadership roles rotate, it is rare to find an adult male in the coca-growing area who has never been in a leadership position. In the absence of an effective state presence, and with the state perceived as an enemy (due to both its neoliberal policies and its commitment to coca eradication), the *sindicatos* have often functioned as the effective local government, dispensing justice, distributing land, developing infrastructure and building schools. In this context, the clear distinction between the state and social movements that exists elsewhere did not exist: the *cocaleros* were both.

Drawing partly on traditional highland forms of communal organisation, the *sindicatos* aspire to highly participatory and deliberative forms of democracy 'from below'. Leadership in MAS means responsibility to the community – far more than is the case in other political parties in Bolivia (and indeed in other countries); this entails listening to and obeying 'the base'. As a result, once positions (in the *cocalero* organisation and in MAS) are agreed through participatory processes, they are difficult to challenge. This stability has helped MAS to prosper but has simultaneously enabled leaders to exercise sometimes-harsh discipline against dissenters, claiming that they are opposing decisions reached by consensus (Harten, 2011).

This is the background of 'community leadership' that Morales – as a leading *cocalero* activist and community organiser – along with others brought to the MAS. Morales continues to combine his role as President with an active presence in the *cocalero* movement.

Other individuals illustrate similar trajectories. For example, David Choquehuanca – Foreign Minister and a member of the core group within the MAS government since its inception – rose like Morales from the grassroots. Choquehuanca comes from an NGO background in which he led programmes for the organisational training of indigenous *campesino* women and worked to sustain and develop indigenous communitarian knowledge. Another example is Nilda Copa, Justice Minister between 2010 and 2012. Copa came from a background of community organising (within the departmental Federation of Campesino and Indigenous Women in Tarija province) and MAS activism (including participation in the Constituent Assembly, which drew up the new Constitution). Other MAS activists, while supportive of the government, have remained outside it, such as Leonita Zurilda: another *cocalera* who is now a MAS leader in Cochabamba.

However, the transition from grassroots to government has not always been so straightforward; other activists have had a more turbulent relationship with the government. For example, Alejandro Almaraz was a leading activist in MAS since the 1990s and became Vice-Minister of Land with responsibility for the transfer of land to poor and landless *campesinos* and indigenous peasants. However, he resigned from MAS in 2003 and from the government in 2010 and has become a leading critic and opponent. Filemon Escobar – miner, trade unionist and an early mentor of Morales in the MAS – was expelled after disagreeing publicly several times with Morales. He still intends to vote for MAS, but warns against a new 'oligarchy of miners and *cocaleros*' (Unitel, 2013, 2014) (similarly, other activists from the powerful mining sector, such as Domitila Barros de Chiungara and Felix Muruchi, criticise the government and MAS for its lack of clear vision and strategy). Felix Patzi, Aymara activist and educationalist, was made Education Minister in 2006 but dismissed when his radical proposals for the promotion of indigenous languages met with opposition from the Spanish-speaking middle class. Roxana Liendo, from a background of grassroots activism in mining and with Aymara *campesinos*, rose to become Vice-Minister for Rural Development but left the government over the Territorio Indígena Parque Nacional Isiboro-Sécure – *Isiboro-Sécure Indigenous Territory and National Park* (TIPNIS) issue (discussed later), and now criticises both the ineffectiveness of government and what she sees as its commitment to extractivism. Finally, Casimira Rodriguez – a founding member of the Bolivian domestic workers union and Morales's first Minister of Justice – was removed from the post after a year amid accusations that she was not a lawyer, merely an organiser of women workers. She argues that she was able to bring ideas of traditional indigenous 'community justice' into the government, although she is now critical of the slow pace of change.[1]

These contrasting trajectories demonstrate the tensions that arise when activists and community organisers move into government. These tensions reflect wider debates, within and outside Bolivia, about the extent to which the MAS government has put into practice the radical ideas (in relation to both the content of government policies and inclusive participatory processes of governance) of the grassroots activism that overthrew the neoliberal regime.

On the one hand, the government and its allies claim that much has been achieved. Thus, Alvaro Garcia Linera – the Vice-President and himself a political activist who was imprisoned in the neoliberal period Linera – argues that this is indeed a government of and for the grassroots. He argues that, previously, 'indigenous people were condemned to be peasants, toilers, informal artisans, porters or waiters, now they are ministers (both men and women), deputies, senators, directors of public companies, constitution writers, supreme court magistrates, governors, and president' (Garcia Linera 2012, pp.1–2).

In contrast, he claims that today 'the subjects of politics and the real institutions of power are now found in the indigenous, plebeian arena' (Garcia Linera 2012, pp.1–2). The state power circuits pass through the debates and decisions of indigenous, worker and neighbourhood assemblies (Garcia Linera 2012, pp.1–2). Important changes have been made to the institutional structure of the state, from the creation of new ministries reflecting MAS policy priorities to the incorporation of traditional indigenous practices of governance at the local level. Bolivia has played a leading role in the Alianza Bolivariana para los Pueblos de Nuestra América – *Bolivarian Alliance for the Peoples of Our America* (ALBA), the supranational organisation of left-leaning Latin American states designed to provide a counterweight to neoliberal institutions such as the World Bank. Above all, Garcia Linera (2012) emphasises the fundamental achievement of the government in politically empowering the indigenous majority and bringing indigenous concepts of community and community organisation into the heart of the government's programme.

In relation to gender, sexism remains widespread, including in the MAS leadership. Domestic violence is rampant and is often regarded as a man's right. Legal abortion is strictly circumscribed, although some progress is being made. However, women – including indigenous women – are well represented in the government and, building on the requirement in the new Constitution that 50% of party electoral candidates must be women, it seems likely that almost half of the new legislative assembly of 2014 will be women: a greater proportion than almost anywhere else in the world.

At the same time as this process of empowerment, supporters of the government argue that there have been impressive material achievements: the new Constitution; a significant redistribution of land; a major reduction in poverty and inequality, compared with the reverse in the neoliberal world; education reform; literacy improvements, expansion of medical services and new welfare payments for the elderly, school children and pregnant mothers. There have also been significant steps towards industrialising and diversifying the economy, reducing external dependency, increasing value-added production and supporting initial moves towards a post-capitalist economy through small-scale communitarian ventures (Fidler, 2014). In key sectors such as mining the MAS government has navigated a complex web of conflicting interests – including those of the state-owned mining sector (a powerful 'cooperative' sector which in practice is a private sector) and transnational companies – through a law that enhances state control over mineral resources while stopping well short of the full-scale expropriation of the multinationals, let alone of capitalist relations, that some would like to have seen (Fuentes, 2014).

Perspectives such as these suggest that a government claiming to be of and for the social movements, while failing to achieve more radical change, has nonetheless done a great deal, and that to expect much more is to ignore the formidable constraints on a small state in a globalised neoliberal economy.

However, this positive assessment has been increasingly challenged by a growing Left and environmentalist opposition (reflected in the trajectories discussed earlier), which has accused the MAS of selling out the 'revolutionary horizons' (Hylton and Thomson, 2007) of the mass activism of the 2003–5 period, of doing far too little to challenge transnational capital and entrenched neoliberalism, of failing to maintain an early momentum of land reform under pressure from big agribusiness and of a 'neo-extractivism' that is in direct contrast to the government's rhetoric of environmental sustainability and *vivir bien*.

Even those who credit the achievements of the MAS government recognise a number of shortcomings. The process of government has sometimes been chaotic, and increasing tensions have arisen within the social movement activist base of the MAS (Farthing and Kohl, 2014). These problems can be ascribed to the combination of a number of factors (Zuazo, 2014):

- First, many of the social movement militants lack experience of government (although many like those from the *cocaleros* will indeed have had leadership experience within the movements), and moving from opposition to proposition has perhaps been particularly difficult. This lack of experience has been exacerbated by the weakness of the Bolivian state apparatus, especially after neoliberal governments hollowed it out.
- Second, the very fact that MAS – and the government – is an alliance of distinct movements with a bottom–up principle of operation and a lack of clear structures means that decision making is often complex and inefficient. As a result, in direct contrast to ideals of participatory democracy, the role of Morales himself as a *caudillo* figure who controls and manages tensions from his dominant position has become increasingly crucial.
- Third, problems have been associated with the opening up of MAS to new (often middle-class) members beyond the social movements in order to widen its social base for electoral reasons and contribute to policy making. As a result, leading voices in and around the government include not only social movement and community

activists and leftist urban intellectuals (a dualism symbolised by Morales as President and Garcia Linera as Vice-President) but also professionals chosen for their policy and management skills, not necessarily their ideological commitment.

- Fourth, with the movement of many of their leaders into the government and the state and the change of focus from opposition to governance, the social movements themselves face major challenges. Moreover, with the effective defeat of the right-wing opposition the need for unity around and in the government is much diminished; in this context, differences between the social movements and the government – and between social movements themselves – have become more prominent.

- Finally, attempts to resolve these problems by institutionalising the party into a more conventional form have created their own difficulties. Reform has involved giving greater power to certain national structures, but this in turn has led to accusations of centralisation and authoritarianism by a small group of top leaders. Participatory principles have become institutionalised and threatened by the exigencies of government, with social movement involvement in government tending to become reduced to formalised processes of engagement with the state and managed via a *Mecanismo Nacional de Participacion y Control Social* overseeing state-organised participatory processes in each government ministry.

The chaotic and problematic nature of government policy making has been highlighted by one issue in particular: the proposal to build a road through the TIPNIS area, a protected zone in the Amazonian lowlands of Bolivia inhabited by small numbers of indigenous people. Despite the protected environmental status of the area, in 2011 the government proposed to build a road through it, citing the need for improved access for local economic development. This led to a march from the TIPNIS lands to the capital, La Paz, organised by a group of the indigenous inhabitants. The march was criticised and physically harassed by government agents but attracted considerable support from some other social movements, while the government's popularity was severely dented. As a result, the government withdrew the proposal. However – and with some encouragement from the government – a counter-march was organised, led by settlers in the surrounding area. These were mostly originally indigenous people from the Andean highlands who had migrated there following the closure of mines under the neoliberal regime, and for whom the road proposal represented better economic opportunities as a result of improved transport links. At the same time, criticisms emerged – and were voiced by the government – of the links between the TIPNIS indigenous group and NGOs backed by foreign states, including the US; meanwhile, the TIPNIS group lost support as a result of their increasing alliance with the right-wing leadership in the eastern provinces. The government then organised a consultation process to try to resolve the issue consensually, but in the context of a lack of trust there has been suspicion that the process was not impartial. Morales eventually promised to eradicate extreme poverty in the TIPNIS area before taking any further steps on building the road. However, criminal charges against TIPNIS leaders and revelations of police infiltration of the protest movement are widely seen as indicative of a resort to coercion by the government (Achtenberg, 2013a, 2013b).

Social movements: in or against the state?

Although TIPNIS has done serious damage to the government, it and other conflicts did not prevent Morales and the MAS government being reelected in October 2014 for a new term (until 2020) with over 60% of the popular vote: a majority that politicians in most other countries would regard as miraculous. For the majority of the population, the criticisms of Left community activists do not outweigh the positive economic and social changes that the government can claim. This emphatic victory offers the government a mandate for extending the process of change.

In this context, Alfredo Rada, the Deputy Minister for Social Movements and Civil Society, points to the recent reconstitution of what he terms the 'revolutionary social bloc' (Fidler, 2014, n.p.) (CONALCAM: the National Coordination for Change) – the major trades unions, *campesino* and indigenous organisations as well as neighbourhood councils and other community institutions – which was shattered by the TIPNIS issue. For Rada, the unity of this bloc is vital to increase pressure and encourage action for change – not only through the social movements but also through 'programmatic proposals that point to further strengthening of the state' in the economy (Fidler, 2014, n.p.).

This poses the question of the state anew for Bolivian community activists. For Rada and others, a close and symbiotic relation between social movements and activists and the state is not only possible but also essential. The occupation of state institutions by radical social movements – and, more broadly, electoralist strategies of political parties that see themselves as the political expression of social movements – are important means of achieving and institutionalising radical grassroots objectives. Vice-President Garcia Linera is clear that the government must have a foot in two camps:

> In Bolivia governance has two platforms. … Politics is carried out in the political–institutional, parliamentary sphere. But politics is also carried out in the *sindicatos*, unions, associations and companies. Governance is guaranteed if one forms parliamentary majorities and coalitions and social majorities and coalitions. The one who does not work on both platforms is lost. (Harten, 2011, p.213)

However, this view is confronted by an influential current – especially strong in Latin America – that rejects the potential of the state as a terrain of social struggle, regarding it instead as a form of domination and electoral strategies as a subordination of grassroots principles to the alienated forms of bourgeois democracy (Holloway, 2005). From this perspective, the embrace of the state is disabling and destructive for the social and community 'sector'. In Bolivia, this current is associated with a critique of the 'electoralism' of the MAS and the 'statism' of the MAS government. According to this view an increasingly authoritarian government is directing change from above, in contradiction to the idea of a government of the grassroots (Gutierrez Aguilar, 2011). Instead of this 'vertical' conception of organisation and action dominated by the state, the concept of 'horizontalism' (Sitrin, 2006) implies non-hierarchical and anti-authoritarian processes and structures and foregrounds action on the ground. In his identification of local 'counter-spaces' as 'territories in resistance', Zibechi contrasts what he calls 'the crisis of the old politics of the factory and the state and (neoliberal) capital's reformulation of old modes of domination' with the rootedness in community-based action of contemporary anti-neoliberal and anti-capitalist movements in Latin America (Zibechi, 2010, p. 14, see also Geddes, 2013, p. 9). Menser (2009) argues that, in direct contrast to MAS's occupation and strengthening of the state, social movements should seek to fracture the state, transferring or reclaiming some parts for civil society. As has been seen, such horizontalist principles inform the practice of the *cocaleros* and are reflected in the principle of 'leading by obeying' to which Morales commits himself. But as the TIPNIS issue demonstrates, some of the actions of his government provide ammunition for the view that the state will always fit principles of community organisation and activism into the logic of power rather than enabling its transformative potential (Dinerstein, 2014).

While the MAS government seeks to strengthen the state, the new Constitution is also intended to 'refound' it, transforming the racist neoliberal state by opening it up to the indigenous majority and the representatives and organisations of the subaltern classes. Certainly much still remains to be done to tackle the old regime, which is entrenched in the state bureaucracy, and its power to hinder progressive change. At the same time, critics argue that – despite a veneer of progressive inclusivity – what is actually emerging is a more fully bourgeois state than the hollowed-out shell bequeathed from the neoliberal period.

Garcia Linera's 'two platforms' analysis embodies an optimism that horizontalism and verticalism – action by the state from above and social movements from below – are both necessary and can support each other (Harten, 2011, p.213). If the MAS government were to demonstrate that such a dialectical relationship is indeed possible, it would have implications well beyond Bolivia – including, for example, for debates around movements such as Occupy and the World Social Forum.

Concluding comments

What conclusions can be drawn about the first decade of a MAS government in which social movement and community activists have been prominent? First, occupation of government and state positions has not (or not yet, at any rate) been translated into a thoroughgoing transformation of the state apparatus, while the principle of governing by obeying the grassroots is at odds with an increasing tendency towards a centralised authoritarianism. So far, the MAS government has achieved more in relation to race than class. The political empowerment of the indigenous population, despite its limits, has been a historic achievement. Major steps have also been taken – from a very low starting point – towards the empowerment of women. In contrast, policies to retain and redistribute economic surpluses have reduced material class inequalities but have not seriously challenged the roots of class in capitalist social relations. As a small state in a globalised world, the MAS government has been more successful in facing down internal right-wing opposition than it has been in facing up to global neoliberal capital. Unsurprisingly, it has found (as has been the case in South Africa, for example) that dominant global interests have been more willing to accommodate a change in the local ethnic character of the government than potential challenges to the capital relation.

Indeed, the impact of government policies has been to stimulate the growth of an indigenous middle class. When combined with rural–urban migration and the associated decline of traditional indigenous agriculture, the result has been to significantly advance the transition to more fully capitalist relations of production: a trend that has not been offset by rather half-hearted government support for community-based forms of enterprise.

The process of change in Bolivia is constantly and fiercely contested, and any attempt to further resolve the issues presented here would be facile. However, what can undoubtedly be said is that the Bolivian experience of the MAS 'government of the social movements' offers much food for thought for community activists elsewhere.

Note

[1] I am indebted to Carlos Revilla and Emily Achtenberg for some of the examples given in this and the preceding paragraph regarding individuals' involvement in MAS and social movements and their trajectories between them. Note that the views attributed to individuals date from the period up to 2014.

References

ACDI/VOCA (n.d.) 'Bolivia: Integrated Community Development Fund (ICDF): improving social and productive infrastructure', ACDI/VOCA, http://acdivoca.org/our-programs/project-profiles/bolivia-integrated-community-development-fund-icdf

Achtenberg, E. (2013a) 'Bolivia: TIPNIS road on hold until extreme poverty eliminated', *Rebel Currents*, 25 April, https://nacla.org/blog/2013/4/25/bolivia-tipnis-road-hold-until-extreme-poverty-eliminated

Achtenberg, E. (2013b) 'Bolivia: Criminal charges against indigenous leaders, revelations of police infiltration reignite TIPNIS conflict', *Rebel Currents*, 27 August, https://nacla.org/blog/2013/8/27/bolivia-criminal-charges-against-indigenous-leaders-revelations-police-infiltration-r

Artaraz, K. (2012) *Bolivia: Refounding the nation*, London: Pluto Press.

Dinerstein, A.C. (2014) *The hidden side of social and solidarity economy*, Geneva: UNRISD, Occasional Paper 9. http://www.unrisd.org/unrisd/website/document.nsf/(httpPublications)/B399D2E1D5EC83DFC1257D3A004512A4?OpenDocument

Farthing, L. and Kohl, B. (2014) *Evo's Bolivia: Continuity and change*, Austin, TX: University of Texas Press.

Fidler, R. (2014) 'Bolivia's Evo Morales re-elected, but important challenges lie ahead', *Boliviarising.blogspot.com*.

Fuentes, F (2014) 'Evo Morales' victory demonstrates how much Bolivia has changed', *Boliviarising.blogspot.com*, http://www.telesurtv.net/english/opinion/Evo-Morales-Victory-Demonstrates-How-Much-Bolivia-Has-Changed-20141020-0074.html

Garcia Linera, A. (2012) 'Moving beyond capitalism is a universal task', Interview by Luis Hernández Navarro, translated by Felipe Stuart Cournoyer. *Boliviarising.blogspot.com*, February 23, http://links.org.au/node/2753

Geddes, M. (2013) 'State space and non-state space in the crisis of neoliberalism: Comparative perspectives', Paper for panel on Austerity, the Local State and Public Services, Political Studies Association Conference, Cardiff, March, https://www.psa.ac.uk/sites/default/files/860_414.pdf

Gutierrez Aguilar, R. (2011) 'Competing political visions and Bolivia's unfinished revolution', *Dialectical Anthropology*, 35: 275–7.

Harten, S. (2011) *The rise of Evo Morales and the MAS*, London and New York: Zed Books.

Holloway, J. (2005) *Change the world without taking power*, London: Pluto Press.

Hylton, F. and Thomson, S. (2007) *Revolutionary horizons: Past and present in Bolivian politics*, London: Verso.

Kohl, B. and Farthing, L. (2006) *Impasse in Bolivia*, London and New York: Zed Books.

Menser, M. (2009) 'Disarticulate the state! Maximising democracy in 'new' autonomous movements in the Americas', in N. Smith, O. Dahbour, H. Gautney and A. Dawson (eds) *Democracy, states and the struggle for global justice*, London: Routledge, pp 251–71.

Sitrin, M. (2006) *Horizontalism: Voices of popular power in Argentina*, Oakland and Edinburgh: AK Press.

Spronk, S. (2013) 'Neoliberal class formation(s): the informal proletariat and "new" workers' organisations in Latin America', in J.R. Webber and B. Carr, *The new Latin American Left: Cracks in the empire*, Plymouth: Rowman and Littlefield Publishers.

Stefanoni, P. (2012) 'Y quien no querria "*vivir bien*"? Encrucijadas del proceso de cambio boliviano', *Critica y Emancipacion*, 7: 9–25.

Unitel, Politicas (2013) 'Filemon Escobar: La COB naciócomo fuerza gravitante de la política bolivian', 17 April, http://www.unitel.tv/noticias/filemon-escobar-dice-que-votar-por-evo-prorrogara-a-las-oligarquias/

Unitel, Politicas (2014) 'Filemón Escobar dice que votar por Evo proroggará a las "oligarquías"', 10 July, http://www.unitel.tv/noticias/filemon-escobar-dice-que-votar-por-evo-prorrogara-a-las-oligarquias/

Zibechi, R. (2010) *Dispersing power: Social movements as anti-state forces*, Oakland, Edinburgh, Baltimore: AK Press.

Zuazo, M. (2014) 'The MAS government in Bolivia: Are the social movements in power?' Translated by R. Fidler, *Boliviarising.blogspot. com*, http://lifeonleft.blogspot.co.uk/2013/07/the-mas-government-in-bolivia-are.html

NINE

Community development: (un) fulfilled hopes for social equality in Poland

*Anna Bilon, Ewa Kurantowicz and
Monika Noworolnik-Mastalska*

Introduction

Economists and researchers of social life in Poland have only recently started to analyse the social consequences of the 1989 political shift in terms of wealth distribution and social divisions in particular. In the immediate aftermath of the 'breakthrough', as it has become known, optimism (generally speaking) rocketed to unprecedented levels and faith in impending favourable social change flourished. In this atmosphere, 'dwelling on the growing diversification of incomes and living standards tended to be construed as an attack on neoliberal market reforms at hand' (Podemski, 2009, p.8). Over the last few years, however, research and – in particular – public opinion in Poland have increasingly gravitated toward addressing social inequalities and attending to transformations in the social structure and the class system.

This chapter seeks to critically examine the role of community development in fostering social cohesion and counteracting social inequalities in Poland. It intends to establish why – despite changing political circumstances and deep political, social and economic transformations – community development in Poland finds itself in an initial, fragmentary and discontinuous stage. The decision to tackle these particular issues is motivated by the fact that community development has occupied a seminal role in the period of political transformation, as formal decentralisation and deregulation policies were launched in many spheres of social life in Poland. Hopes attached to community development concerned first the (re)building of civil society through increasing mutual trust and promoting citizens' cooperation in the (local) public sphere, and second, empowerment of local self-government agencies. Since 1989, community development in Poland has targeted these two goals with the idea that accomplishing them will further social equality and cohesion. To begin, though, the chapter must be situated in the historical context of contemporary Poland.

The years of the Polish People's Republic (1945–89) were characterised as a period of centralised management over local communities. In this model, all programmes had to comply with the principle of 'equal' treatment, which resulted in adopting the same solutions for every community irrespective of specific local problems or needs. Communities were regarded as homogeneous, and differences (ethnic, cultural and social) were ignored. In this context, community development was understood to be the implementation of top–down, standardised political actions. Very few community-led initiatives were officially recognised, some notable exceptions being those based mainly on artistic activities (such as the 1976 *Lucim* Programme) or participatory research (such as the 1985 *Węgrów* Programme) (Theiss, 2001).

Prior to 1989, community development had a different meaning, role and purpose in Poland. Its contemporary meaning, developed in the process of (re)creating civil society after 1989, therefore included ideas such as the formation of communities, participation and emancipation (Mendel, 2007). For the purpose of this chapter, community development is considered to be an educational process that brings about change within communities and is implemented by local means and informed by local interests and values (Cunningham, 1996, p.58).

To understand social stratification and class divisions within local communities fully, it is necessary to explore some of these communities' historical experiences and struggles and to locate them in relation to the global situation. We would argue that, in Poland, social stratification and class divisions are unfolding processes rather than fixed states. This chapter's emphasis on the procedural and 'becoming' nature of contemporary social stratification in Poland is driven by the observation that political transformation in Poland has not (yet) produced social divisions typical of Western Europe, as well as by the insight that local communities have been differentially affected by the changes; this has had particular consequences for the social structure, In fact, economic and political fluctuations in Poland have generated both opportunities and tensions for individuals and local communities.

The history of social stratification processes and community development in Poland

One can hardly comprehend the condition of local communities and social inequalities in Poland without recourse to the past, including not only the times of the People's Republic of Poland (1945–89) but also the previous partition period (1772–1918). Partitioned Poland stood no chance of developing uniformly since the country's territory was divided among the different occupying powers that regarded it as their respective peripheries (Wesołowski, 1966). This resulted in very sparse investment in the development of some areas as well as in enormous differences in economic and cultural development across what used to be the Polish state. Consequently – and crucially – Poland did not undergo the same industrialisation and modernisation processes that swept across Western Europe at that time (Tellenback, 1974), and Polish society was typified by extensive diversification and divisions even before the inception of socialism. The partitioning powers not only thwarted community development but also enforced Russification and Germanisation. This action in turn impeded the identification of local communities with self-government policies and bred a peculiar phenomenon of communal identity being formed exclusively in resistance to the occupiers' power. Poland still copes with the legacy of the period, which is patently manifest, for example, in the oft-cited division into Poland A (western, economically and culturally more advanced areas, once under Prussian rule) and Poland B (eastern, less-developed areas, once incorporated into Russia). The persistence of this trope indicates that neither socialism nor the post-1989 transformation succeeded in bridging the gap between the two regions' developmental levels (see, for example, Maciejewicz, 2012). The split continues to surface in analyses of electoral preferences, axiological positions and attitudes to the Catholic Church in Poland.

The period of socialist rule is identified – and not only in Polish literature – as a time of political centralisation. Accordingly, centrally imposed policies aimed to effect a uniform and even development of local communities. In practice, however, that meant a complete eradication of genuine regional policy (Węcławowicz, 2002), while 'grassroots' responsibility and community development activity atrophied (Sobala-Gwosdz, 2003). In ruling Poland, the Communist Party systematically strove to monopolise the political, social and economic life of local collectives, and simultaneously to fully control the operation of local self-government (Gieorgica, 1991). However, some researchers insist – against the recent mainstream discourse on community development in socialist Poland – that social activism of the time should not be underestimated and that Polish social movements boast a long history and a rich tradition (Szustek, 2008). In fact, civic participation of this kind is alleged to have made a major contribution to the systemic change that occurred in 1989, and the transformation itself is seen by some as a manifestation of the relevance of preexisting civil society (Broda–Wysocki, 2003). Nonetheless, the authors would argue that these manifestations may be more appropriately considered within the category of civil disobedience than that of civic participation. This entailed creating clandestine structures, devising action plans and working towards social and political change through overthrowing the government and/or improving the modus operandi of the state. All of these subversive activities were underpinned by the notion of 'a common enemy', involved a strong identification with like-minded groups and were grounded in a readiness to face persecution for actions against the imposed order. The active engagement of Polish society in this period is dwelled upon here to emphasise an insight – recurring also in the literature – that, in the case of post-socialist societies, what we face may not be so much an absence of typical social structures and social capital that impede social development but rather an inadequacy of 'west European' language to provide an accurate account of these structures and class theories. Even before the onset of socialism, as researchers claim, Polish society did not have the class structure characteristic of west European societies (Tellenback, 1974). Furthermore, socialism, when it came, prioritised both industrialisation on a national scale and the development of the working class and the intelligentsia, the latter of which was severely depleted by the Second World War. Simultaneously, this does not mean that the social stratification in the People's Republic of Poland followed the intended trajectory or complied with the standard model set for socialist societies (Szczepański, 1965; Kurantowicz, 2011).

As already mentioned, the transformation period following 1989 formally initiated the decentralisation and deregulation of most spheres of social life, thereby ascribing to local communities a new role in reforming the social structure and working towards social equality (Kurantowicz, 2011). The notion prevailed that 'it was imperative to constitutionally guarantee the right of local communities to self-government' (Antkowiak, 2011, p.164) and the years following the political transformation were steeped in enormous social optimism and faith that it would inevitably lead to the much-coveted equality. Equality was conceived of as a levelling of the differences in living standards both within Polish society and between Poland and Western

European countries, the latter to be aided by Poland's accession to the European Union. The prevalent discourse of that time emphasised equal opportunities and abundant possibilities, insisting that citizens themselves were responsible for their success in life and that, consequently, Poland was a classless society. Even though inequality became increasingly evident, social inequalities did not stir public debates, because they were presented as a natural effect of the free market and Poland's opening to the global economy. Whatever gaps were acknowledged to exist were expected to be soon bridged.

In the later period, unemployment rates suddenly soared in Poland, finally reaching 20% in the years between 2002 and 2004 (GUS, 2011). The statistics of the time imply that unemployment affected primarily rural as well as small- and mid-sized urban communities, the situation of which was additionally aggravated by latent unemployment (GUS, 2011). In terms of community development, these milieus also began to suffer from the dissolution of neighbourly ties: an apparently significant element of these processes of change in rural and small-town communities. Rather than remaining based on identification with a particular geographical area, the idea of neighbourhood gradually mutated into more of an associative bond, which over time has undercut collective collaboration in small Polish communities and thereby exacerbated increasing social inequalities (Lewenstein, 2006). Consequently, the unequal and uneven development of the country can no longer be ignored in public debates.

Recent critiques of the political transformation foreground its ambivalent social effects. For example, it is pointed out that, although new opportunities and options for development have been offered to both individuals and local communities, the accompanying systemic shift has consistently generated ever-increasing social inequalities and processes of class differentiation (Krajewska, 2011). Some researchers are indeed inclined to identify just two social classes: the 'winners' and the 'losers' (Slomczynski et al, 2007). Although simplifying the actual social structure and situation, this rather crude division helps to demonstrate that the stratification of Polish society has territorial, economic and symbolic dimensions. Substantial differences are observed in regional development, with urban areas overwhelmingly considered to be more advanced. The indices of income concentration and the Gini ratio place Poland among European countries with the greatest social disparities (OECD, 2011; Ortiz and Cummins, 2011; GUS, 2012). Such outcomes have been produced by, among other factors, the prioritising of market development at the expense of social security and the replacement of the 'post-socialist corporatist regime' by limited social protection measures (Whelan and Maître, 2010). While Polish sociology tends to describe the post-breakthrough period in terms of middle-class formation (Domański, 2009), researchers have increasingly exposed the emergence of 'upper classes and far lower classes' (Modzelewski, 2004) or even the rise of 'redundant classes' (Szahaj, 2000). In the authors' view, it can legitimately be claimed that the structure of Polish society had not yet 'managed' to evolve into the fully-fledged structures typical of Western European societies when – propelled by the global economic meltdown and wider processes of globalisation – it started to undergo diversification characteristic of those societies (Bauman, 2011). Hence, as Polish researchers (such as Domański, 2009) insist, Poland knows 'strata' and 'groups' rather than the classically defined social classes.

These tendencies and processes observable in Polish society make identifying, counteracting and levelling social inequalities ever more urgent. As already mentioned, community development has been given a seminal role in relation to these objectives. A range of projects has been launched to boost the process, promote equality and foster an equality-informed new social structure. However, the brief outline of the development of the current social structure in Poland above indicates that social inequalities have been developing within the context of longer-lasting historical processes, which makes the situation of some local communities all the more difficult to alter. The analysis also highlights the historical continuity of these inequalities, which resisted even the concerted efforts of centralised state power. The following section presents an analysis of undertakings aimed at increasing social cohesion and combatting inequalities. Importantly, such undertakings are now viewed as a unique chance for addressing inequalities, while hitherto policies and regional management have fallen short of expectations. The analysis aims to identify frameworks of, barriers to and opportunities for community development offered by such projects in the current context. The analytical material comes from unstructured interviews with project coordinators and from statistical data on employment derived from the project participants after completion of the project.

Community development and work activation projects

This analysis includes two work activation projects, financed by the European Social Fund (ESF), which were introduced at the turn of 2012 and 2013. Each of these projects involved about sixty people in two distinct age groups – the under-25s and the over-50s –ewho are regarded as the most vulnerable to social exclusion caused by joblessness. The participants were residents of the 13 counties with the highest unemployment rates in the region.

The first group (Project A) consisted of the over-50s; that is, those who remembered living and working in the People's Republic of Poland (before 1989). These participants felt inadequately equipped and expendable within the labour market because their qualifications, vocational experience and skills were of no use in the new market economy. This further created a number of barriers that impeded their full immersion in social life. The second group (Project B) was made up of the under-25s, whose experience post-dated the socialist system. They belonged to what has become described as the NEET category (not in employment, education or training). According to the EU-commissioned Eurofound report (2012), young people who are disengaged from the labour market and the education system face the greatest risk of permanent exclusion from the labour market.

Both projects aimed to prepare participants for working in elderly care, thereby introducing them to the labour market and enhancing their prospects for permanent employment. As well as general goals related to work activation the projects also pursued other objectives, such as overcoming perceived psychological barriers caused by long-term or complete disengagement from the labour market, boosting self-esteem and increasing confidence and skills.

Analysis of the project practices identified some problematic areas and issues in relation to the targeted promotion of community development, social cohesion and the prevention of social and economic exclusion. We call these *paradoxes*, because the effects of the projects turned out to be completely different from those envisaged by either the projects or the ESF.

Paradox One: work activation programmes without relevant work opportunities

The statistics produced by follow-up monitoring of the participants who completed training in elderly care show that integration within the labour market – the specific objective of the projects – was only partly successful. For example, only a small number of participants across both groups actually gained employment in elderly care – or any other secure job – while many participants worked without any official contract. In addition, a substantial number of people resumed their former passive lifestyle.

Analysis of the project further revealed a number of significant barriers impeding employment in elderly care.

First, although the general outline of the Human Capital Operational Programme does not specify what vocational skills project participants are required to attain, the institutions that fund particular projects (in this instance the Regional Job Centre) impose their own criteria. In this case, elderly care was one of the sectors that was particularly targeted. With the qualification framework for this vocation already well defined by the Ministry of Labour and Social Policy, a growing number of education facilities in Poland were already providing preparation for work in elderly care. However, even though Poland is undeniably a rapidly aging society, the labour market does not seem to have been accommodating elderly care professionals at a comparable pace. Elderly care tends to be informally provided by kin (children, grandchildren and spouses) rather than by institutions, which is the case in many European countries, and is therefore not recognised as work of high social status. In the context of social inequalities related to employment, it turns out that educating young people for such work, while creating some limited opportunities, may actually perpetuate or even aggravate social exclusion because of low status and low pay. The gendered nature of care also potentially carries an additional risk of increased gender-based exclusion.

There is thus a considerable risk that 'work activation' projects of this type may create expectations that cannot be fulfilled because of factors well beyond the scope of the project or the control of the participants.

Paradox Two: Community development without developing communities

Upon completion of the projects it turned out that, for most of the participants, employment in elderly care was possible only at some distance or abroad, if at all. Although securing employment may be more important than the location of that employment in terms of *individual* development, in terms of *community* development, location is a factor of some significance. When project guidelines are standardised and devised without attention to the demands of the local context, projects are likely to fail to contribute to the local environment. Consequently, the development of the local community, instead of being boosted by its members' involvement in the learning process, was becoming dispersed by migration for work – and, finally, halted.

A further obstacle to the success of such projects lies in the shortcomings of the local institutional infrastructure. Despite acquiring new qualifications, the project beneficiaries were unable to realise their potential because local institutional networks have been lacking and, consequently, self-governance has been weak and local labour markets unsupported. The project experiences show that while the potential and willingness to collaborate were in place, they were hampered by ineffective communication among the local institutions.

Paradox Three: Combating social inequalities without addressing exclusion

Such projects usually include material rewards comprising minimum pay for participation and benefits that enable full involvement, such as reimbursement of travel expenses, accommodation during training, child care allowances and so on. Because of these advantages, some of the participants used the project as a source of easy income – or temporary betterment of their income – without necessarily intending to effect any genuine changes in their lives. Some project coordinators have even suggested that a 'new vocation' seems to have emerged, which could be labelled as 'project participation'. In other words, vocational performance can involve enrolment in successive projects with financial benefits as the primary motivation. As a by-product, a situation can be produced in which projects aimed at fostering participants' vocational involvement can actually enhance their passivity or cynicism, further increasing possibilities for their long-term exclusion.

In addition, such project interventions may not translate into the reduction of social inequalities for reasons unrelated to the participants' attitudes and behaviours. The market economy – premised as it is upon instability, precariousness and illegal job opportunities (coupled with the impossibility of securing legal employment in many cases) – may also preclude people from the processes of challenge and change envisaged in the programme. In such circumstances, the basic objectives of the ESF programme are not achieved – indeed, may not be achievable – while the chances for participants eager to change their situation are limited and squandered in the same measure.

Conclusion

In this complex context, a number of what Poland-specific challenges to community development can be identified. As argued already, these include historically entrenched discrepancies between regions, a precipitate transformation to the free-market economy without due attention to social protection measures and adoption of a neoliberal capitalist economy model more generally (Eyal et al, 1998).

In addition, growing social inequalities and dangerous mechanisms at work are at work in Poland that are also observable in other countries, including the consolidation of social polarization, causing emigration of the young and 'depopulation' of some local communities. Increasing social stratification and precariousness of the labour market frequently prompt decisions to emigrate for work to Western Europe, especially for those from rural areas and small- and mid-sized towns (GUS, 2013). Despite being difficult to measure, foreign migrations undoubtedly have an impact on the potential of local communities for sustained development. Statistics show that the population density in Poland is seriously diminishing due to such emigration (Celioska-Janowicz et al, 2010, p.40). However, the outcomes of emigration are never unequivocal and depend on a range of perspectives: psychological; economic; individual; local, national and global. Sometimes emigration improves the economic situation of individuals or families, but it can also cause negative psychological effects at home (such as the Euro-orphans phenomenon[1] emerging in Poland, especially in the villages). Similarly, while earnings transferred to Poland can improve the economic situation, they can also adversely affect the local labour market. From a national perspective the results of emigration are also complex: on one hand they reduce the unemployment rate, but on the other the depopulation phenomenon is observable, and has wider social consequences.

In relation to the trajectory of community development in Poland, it could be argued that a participatory model of local community, and its associated distinctive pedagogies, are still at an embryonic stage. The tensions between policy-led community initiatives and those that might arise from communities seeking to determine and articulate their own concerns and interests to those in power may be felt, but there is not yet an established practice that starts from a view of 'community as politics' (Shaw and Martin, 2000; Martin and Shaw, 2006). This can be seen in the lack of coherent policies for creating and managing educational initiatives in communities, including bottom-up and regional undertakings as well as EU-sponsored community projects. A common failing of such top-down projects is that they ignore 'community-based, bottom up knowledge which values the learning that comes from experience, including the experience of inequality, marginalisation and oppression' (Johnston, 2003, p.16). In addition, the spurious promotion of civic activity can create a semblance of democratic engagement without addressing those inequalities of power and resources that systematically exclude certain groups and individuals.

It is important to identify the mechanisms that prevent social change and to assess the possibilities for transformative action. The work of John Gaventa (2006) is drawn on here to analyse the relationships between spaces, levels and dimensions of power within the projects described earlier. First, the projects were created, in Gaventa's terms, in a 'closed space' (Gaventa, 2006, p.26). The decisions on the actions undertaken and the premises and aims of the project were taken at European and regional levels, rather than being established with the participants. Simultaneously, the projects represented an attempt to create 'invited spaces' in which participants could engage with the objectives of the project. However, it is difficult to avoid a critical analysis of these attempts. People were expected to prepare themselves for work that turned out to be low-paid and – more critically – not needed in their own local community. As the research presented in this chapter has shown, the participants' new skills and attitudes were used in completely different spaces, if at all. From a community development perspective it is clear that such results do not contribute to sustainable development in Poland, although it is of course possible that those who move abroad may contribute to the development of other communities (including diasporic communities) despite – or because of – the interrelationships of perspectives and experiences in a globalized world.

Analysing the research material, we identified all three forms of power theorised by Gaventa (2006). *Visible power* manifested itself several times, by decision-making agents (such as the EU, Polish government and labour offices) that created the 'invited space' of the projects. This process cannot be assessed unequivocally, for reasons we have identified above. Still, it could be seen as an attempt to prevent social exclusion and to support community development. *Hidden power* can be identified within the local labour market and the wider economic environment, which dictated whether or not the participants found the work for which they were trained. The failure to acknowledge or to address the tensions between visible and hidden power, in this context, can be perceived as one of the reasons that such 'activation' strategies had limited success.

A further reason for failure was created by Gaventa's (2006) third form of power: *invisible power*. Eventually, both the participants' negative experiences and the particularities of the Polish context turned out to be obstacles to the reintegration of participants within local labour markets and local communities. For now, we can say that projects such as those described earlier seem to reproduce social inequalities and enhance the bipolarity of the social structure, even though they may contribute to improving some individuals' lives.

Finally, it could be said that the reason why community development has not fulfilled the hopes for social equality in Poland is at least three-dimensional: a complex issue consisting of particular historical influences, the effects of neoliberal policies and the ambivalent nature of community programmes themselves. In accordance with neoliberal discourse and policy, after the political transformation in Poland local communities were almost left to rely on themselves; this has had wider social and political consequences. Community initiatives continue to be created without considering the tensions between different power dimensions and continue to assume a simple synergy between individual achievement and local development, irrespective of class power dynamics. As the experience outlined here shows, this is a mistake that should be avoided if we are to make more progress in achieving the goals related to community development.

Note

[1] This term refers to the children being left in Poland by one of the parents (or both of them) that emigrated to European countries for economic reasons. It is a form of social orphanhood and has the negative consequences similar to the orphans phenomenon.

References

Antkowiak, P. (2011) 'Decentralizacja wladzy publicznej w Polsce na przykladzie samorzadu terytorialnego' ['Decentralisation of public authority in Poland: example of local territorial self-government'], *Srodkowoeuropejskie Studia Polityczne* [*Central European Political Studies*], (2): 155–74.

Bauman, Z. (2011) *Collateral damage: Social inequalities in a global age*, Cambridge: Polity Press.

Broda-Wysocki, P. (2003) *Rozwój społeczeństwa obywatelskiego w Polsce* [*The development of civil society in Poland*], Warszawa: IPiSS.

Celioska-Janowicz, D., Miszczuk, M., Płoszaj, A. and Smętkowski, M. (2010) *Aktualne problemy demograficzne regionu Polski wschodniej* [*Current demografic problems of Polish East Region*], Warszawa: Raporty i analizy EUROREG 5.

Cunningham, P.M. (1996) 'Community education and community development', in A.C. Tuijnman (ed) *International encyclopedia of adult education and training* (second edition), Oxford: Elsevier Science Ltd, pp 54–60.

Domański, H. (2009) ‚Stratyfikacja a system społeczny w Polsce' ['Stratification and the Social System In Poland'], *Ruch Prawniczy, Ekonomiczny i Socjologiczny* [*Journal of Law, Economics and Sociology*], 2: 381–95.

Eurofound (2012) *NEETs: Young people not in employment, education or training: Characteristics, costs and policy responses in Europe*, Luxembourg: Publications Office of the European Union.

Eyal, G., Szelenyi, I. and Townsley, E. (1998) *Making capitalism without capitalists. Class formation and elite struggles in post-Communist Central Europe*, New York, NY: Verso.

Gaventa, J. (2006) 'Finding the spaces for change: a power analysis', *IDS Bulletin*, 37(6): 23–33.

Gieorgica, J.P. (1991) *Polska lokalna we władzy PZPR* [*Localities in Poland under the leadership of Polish United Workers' Party*], Warszawa: Uniwersytet Warszawski.

GUS (2011) *Obszary wiejskie w Polsce [Rural areas in Poland]*, Warszawa: Zakład Wydawnictw Statystycznych.

GUS (2012) *Europejskie badanie dochodów i warunków życia (EU–SILC) w 2012 r.*, Warszawa: Zakład Wydawnictw Statystycznych.

GUS (2013) *Informacja o rozmiarach i kierunkach emigracji z Polski w latach 2004–2012 [Information on the size and directions of Polish emigration in the years 2004–2012]*, Warszawa: Zakład Wydawnictw Statystycznych.

Johnston, R. (2003) 'Adult learning and citizenship: clearing the ground', in P. Coare and R. Johnston (eds) *Adult learning, citizenship and community voices: Exploring community-based practices*, NIACE, pp 3–21.

Krajewska, A. (2011) ‚Wzrost zróżnicowania dochodów: ujemna strona transformacji polskiej gospodarki' [‚An increase in income inequality: a negative aspect of the Polish economic transformation'], *Zeszyty Naukowe*, 9: 159–78.

Kurantowicz, E. (2011) 'Micro development: among localisation, de-localisation and relocalisation processes in the perspective of Polish social and political transformations', in A. Fragoso, E. Kurantowicz and E. Lucio-Villegas (eds) *Between global and local: Adult learning and development*, Frankfurt am Main, Berlin, Bern, Bruxelles, New York, Oxford, Wien: Peter Lang GmbH, pp 89–103.

Lewenstein, B. (2006) 'Spoleczenstwo rodzin czy obywateli: kapital spoleczny Polakow okresu transformacji' ['A society of families or a society of citizens: Poles' social capital in the transformation period'], *Societas/Communitas*, 1(1): 163–96.

Maciejewicz, P. (2012) 'Bogata Polska ucieka od biednej Polski' ['Wealthy Poland is fleeing from poor one'], *Gazeta Wyborcza* [*Electoral Gazette*], http://wyborcza.pl/1,76842,13101936,Bogata_Polska_ucieka_od_biednej_Polski.html

Martin, I. and Shaw, M. (2006) 'Developing the "community" dimension of learning: three conceptual frameworks', in A. Fragosso, E. Lucio-Villegas and E. Kurantowicz (eds) *Human Development and Adult Learning*, Faro: University of Algavre, pp 11–16.

Mendel, M. (2007) 'Animacja współpracy środowiskowej' ['Animation of the community collaboration'], in M. Mendel (ed) *Animacja współpracy środowiskowej na wsi [Animation of the community collaboration in the countryside]*, Toruń: Wydawnictwo Adam Marszałek, pp 11–32.

Modzelewski, K. (2004) 'Klasa wyższa, klasa niższa' ['Lower and upper class'], *Polityka [Politics]*, 23: 78.

OECD (2011) *An overview of growing income inequalities in OECD countries: Main findings*, DOI 10.1787/9789264119536-3-en.

Ortiz, I. and Cummins, M. (2011) *Global inequality: Beyond the bottom billion. A rapid review of income distribution in 141 countries*, New York, NY: United Nations Children's Fund (UNICEF).

Podemski, K. (2009) ‚Wstęp' ['Introduction'], in K. Podemski (ed) *Spór o społeczne znaczenie społecznych nierówności. [Controversy about the importance of social inequalities]*, Poznań: Wydawnictwo Naukowe UAM, pp 7–9.

Shaw, M. and Martin, I. (2000) 'Community work, citizenship and democracy: remaking the connections', *Community Development Journal*, 35(4): 401–12.

Słomczynski, K.M., Janicka, K., Shabad, G. and Tomescu–Dubrow, I. (2007) 'Changes in class structure in Poland, 1988–2003: crystallization of the winners losers' divide', *Polish Sociological Review*, 157: 45–64.

Sobala-Gwosdz, A. (2003) 'Zróżnicowanie poziomu rozwoju gmin przygranicznych województwa podkarpackiego' ['Diversification in the bordering municipalities development of the Podkarpackie Voivodeship'], in J. Runge (ed) *Granice, Obszary Przygraniczne, Euroregiony [Borders, border areas, Euroregions]*, Katowice: Uniwersytet Śląski. pp 249–62.

Szahaj, A. (2000) 'Solidarność mandarynów' ['Solidarity of mandarinies'], *Polityka [Politics]*, 9: 28–30.

Szczepański, J. (1965) 'Zmiany w strukturze klasowej społeczeństwa polskiego' ['Changes in class structure of Polish society'], in A. Sarapata (ed) *Przemiany społeczne w Polsce Ludowej [Social transformations in Polish people's republic]* Warszawa: Państwowe Wydawnictwo Naukowe.

Szustek, A. (2008) *Polski sektor społeczny* [*Public sector in Poland*], Warszawa: Uniwersytet Warszawski.

Tellenback, S. (1974) 'Patterns of stratification in socialist Poland', *Acta Sociologica*, (1): 23–47.

Theiss, W. (2001) 'Mała ojczyzna: perspektywa edukacyjno–utylitarna' ['The small home country: educational–utilitarian perspective'], in W. Theiss (ed) *Mała ojczyzna: Kultura–edukacja–rozwój lokalny* [*The small home country: Culture–education–community development*], Warszawa: Wydawnictwo Akademickie "Żak".

Węcławowicz, G. (2002) *Przestrzeń i społeczeństwo współczesnej Polski. Studium z geografii społeczno-gospodarczej* [*Space and society of modern Poland*], Warszawa: Wydawnictwo Naukowe PWN.

Wesołowski, W. (1966) *Klasy, warstwa i władza* [*Classes, strata, power*], Warszawa: Państwowe Wydawnictwo Naukowe.

Whelan, C. and Maître, B. (2010) 'Welfare regime and social class variation in poverty and economic vulnerability in Europe: an analysis of EU–SILC', *Journal of European Social Policy*, 20: 316.

TEN

Rural–urban alliances for community development through land reform from below

María Elena Martínez-Torres and Frederico Daia Firmiano

Introduction

When you get to the city of Ribeirão Preto there is a large billboard along the highway that reads: 'Welcome to Ribeirão Preto, Brazilian capital of agribusiness'. Further ahead, a contrasting sign reads: 'Welcome to the Mario Lago Land Reform Settlement. "We don't require a lot. We only need one another" – Carlito Maia'. The contrast in the scenery is also striking: thousands of kilometres of sugar cane contrast sharply with the diverse production that is visible in the Mario Lago Settlement. This chapter explores an example of community development achieved by a group of families who are part of the Landless Workers Movement and who occupied land in Ribeirão Preto, a region in which almost all of the arable land is in the hands of the sugar cane industry.

Historical context

After the 1964 military coup, the Brazilian military–civilian regime brought together two basic strategies for the countryside: one economic, the other military. The economic strategy was to industrialise the entire country and to modernise agriculture, meeting any manifestation of popular dissatisfaction with brute force. In this way, the organised peasantry – such as the *Ligas Camponesas*, or Peasant Leagues, which flourished during the 1950s – were brutally repressed and extinguished by the military (Welch, 2009). During the 1970s, the modernisation of agriculture was based mostly on Green Revolution practices and the expansion of the agricultural frontier, with a policy of providing favourable credits for capital; this created the conditions for the large-scale agroindustrial production of commodities destined for foreign markets. The end result was a rural exodus (Chase, 1999) and an intense cycle of proletarianisation in the countryside.

In the southern region of Brazil, the modernisation of agriculture and the expansion of monocultures such as soy devastated the small-scale production of the majority of farming families, particularly those of European immigrants and their descendants, who were subjected to the same extremely violent methods of expulsion as those in the north. In the southeast – for example, in the state of São Paulo – family-based production was slowly destroyed by the invasion of monoculture, principally sugar cane. The military government created an incentives programme to broaden so-called *Proálcool* production through which, beginning in 1975, the region of Ribeirão Preto became the largest producer of alcohol and sugar in the country. As a consequence of the creation of a sugar–alcohol complex based on monoculture, the high concentration of land and the overexploitation of labour, 2.5 million people were expelled from their farms in São Paulo alone (Silva, 1999). In Brazil overall, more than 50 million people were driven from the countryside between 1960 and 2000 and, 'with the expulsion and impoverishment of small farmers, the objective conditions were created so that a mass movement calling for agrarian reform could be born' (MST, 2009, p.11).

In 1984, displaced farming families, rural wage laborers, small family producers who owned land but lacked formal titles and countless other workers in similar conditions across Brazil founded the movement of Rural Landless Workers (known as the MST: the *Movimento dos Trabalhadores Sem Terra*). Their goal was to achieve political unity among the diverse struggles against different kinds of exploitation, dispossession and subjugation (see Fernandes and Stédile, 2000). With the weakening of the military regime at the end of the 1970s, the working class began to organise politically again, creating strong rural–urban worker alliances, and the regime was finally unable to prevent the return to democratic rule in 1985.

The 1988 new federal Constitution retained the concept of the 'social function of the land' that had been part of the 1964 Statute of Land (McKay et al, 2014, p.227). The concept stipulated – and continues to stipulate to the present day – that land that does not serve a social purpose may be expropriated in order to promote agrarian reform. This stipulation refers principally to unproductive land, but also to properties that violate labour and related laws (Silva, 1997). However, despite the modernisation of Brazilian agriculture, the unproductive *latifundio* (large commercial estates) continued to dominate land use and there was an abundance of idle land in Rio Grande do Sul state, birthplace of the MST (Wright and Wolford, 2003).

The MST grew out of the self-organisation of working families and through the occupation of territory by landless families. Although to this very day there are tensions surrounding the definition of 'unproductive land', the constitutional argument regarding the social function of the land was taken up rapidly by the MST to justify their land occupations, along with the legal strategy of negotiating the expropriation of lands once they had been occupied. It was through this spatial distribution and territorialisation that the MST was able to expand across the country, organising the dispossessed masses of both rural and urban workers and forming a new and important social category: the *Sem Terra* (landless) (Fernandes, 2001).

Building Sem Terra community development

The *Sem Terra* or landless community has primarily been forged through the occupation of land and the creation of encampments. The encampment is a form of geopolitical organisation by landless families who unite and live together in an occupied space or in surrounding areas until the rural settlement is finally established. It is, however, common for such occupations to be evicted by the state (through the police) or the landowner (through hired gunmen). In such cases the families routinely set up a base camp from which to go out and occupy the land in question again. These organised family groups – sometimes 20 families, sometimes 100 – can spend months, or even years, in an encampment before they become formally settled.

In the early years, it was not unusual in such situations that the people involved had never met each other until they came together to occupy a piece of land. Typically, they were people (or descendants of people) who had migrated from the countryside to the city, or they were displaced farmers. But there were others without direct peasant roots who had decided, for a variety of reasons, to adopt the rural way of life. Cooperation between people from different backgrounds and interests could therefore perhaps be described as the first class-based alliance to occur inside the MST. People from different class backgrounds created a sense of community by structuring their living arrangments to cooperate, live and work together to provide for their needs. As one member of the *Gabriela Monteiro* settlement near Brasilia described it: 'It was very difficult; we lived through rain and extreme heat, living in a barrack, but it was worth it because the people worked together for it' (interview conducted by the authors, 17 February 2014). So while it was a period of suffering and struggle, it was also a period in which people strengthened their determination; as such, the camps become spaces for education and training (Starr et al, 2011).

The internal organisation of families that allows community development begins with the formation of family clusters in the camp. Each cluster is made up of between 10 and 30 families. The clusters organise among themselves by affinity groups to participate in different commissions. These are in charge of, and make decisions regarding, all aspects of daily life: from material needs (security; food; camp layout; housing; energy sources; sanitation; transport; communication; production; cooperatives; industrialisation, commercialisation and finance), to human development (education; recreation; training; culture, childcare and sports). Each cluster has a female coordinator and a male coordinator, and these two − along with all the other coordinators from the rest of the commissions − make up the General Coordination of the Camp, which is in charge of organising labour, completing tasks, negotiating with the government and relating to Brazilian society in general. Finally, the General Assembly of the Camp is the highest decision-making body and is made up of every member of the encampment. This is the structural base that will later lead the community development after they have won the legalisation of the land as a settlement[1] by the National Colonization and Agrarian Reform Institute (INCRA).

During its formative years the movement tried to form collective cooperatives in the settlements as an alternative to individual family plots. However, the differences between settlers' interests and commitments, as a result of their previous experiences, made collective working more problematic than had been envisaged. For those coming from *favela* (slum and informal urban settlement) environments, for example, living and working together in collectives fitted well with their culture and their needs. Displaced peasants, however, while open to credit and marketing cooperatives, were not persuaded by the wholesale collectivisation of land and production processes. As the MST became more aware of this internal diversity and the different motivations that people had for being a part of the movement, they began to concentrate on promoting cooperation as a value that can play out in a number of different ways rather than imposing a single model (Scopinho, 2007). This was an important shift that provided the basis for more realistically sustainable communities in the settlements.

Community development is therefore understood to be a practice by which organised families construct or rebuild a peasant community, and with it a sense of belonging. But it also includes the capacity to change policies and practices, through political mobilisations in alliance with urban movements. For example, through continuing campaigning – including repeated occupations of public buildings and blockades of highways – settlers have successfully applied pressure to gain access to credit programmes for housing and agricultural production, as well as gaining services like schools, healthcare and potable water. Another of the movement's important achievements has been the National Law of 2009, which requires that 30% of the food in school lunches provided by public education institutions should be purchased from family farmers. This law benefits many settlements by ensuring the sale of at least part of their production to the government through the Food Aquisition Programme and/or the National School Lunch Programme, which has decentralised purchasing to the local level.

Commenting on changes over time, in his research on the MST, Leandro Vergara-Camus (2009) explains that a key factor in the success of the movement lies in the fact that it creates relatively autonomous, organised communities with independent political structures that facilitate mobilisation. Furthermore, alliance building is fundamental: from the very moment of founding an encampment through to the related land occupation and settlement processes. The material and political support provided by other movements with whom they share class interests has been a key factor.

Rural–urban alliances of the MST in Brazil and the struggle for land in the Ribeirão Preto–São Paulo region

In the process of spreading the struggle for land at the end of the 1990s, the MST organised the region of Ribeirão Preto in the state of São Paulo (Fernandes, 2000). As has been seen, from around the mid-1970s this region had been a primary centre of monoculture for the production of sugarcane. However, beginning in the 1990s, the alcohol–sugar sector began to gain importance at national level as the state opened up the economy and stimulated foreign investment and trade, encouraging multinational companies to increase their investments (Jank et al, 2001, pp.65–7).

Thus, the organisation of families under the MST flag in the Ribeirão Preto region coincided with the transnationalisation of Brazilian agriculture and the gradual capitalisation and incorporation of the *latifundios* into the production of boom products such as soy, sugar cane (to feed ethanol plants for agrofuels), citrus and forest plantations for pulp production (Delgado, 2005; Stédile, 2008). This also coincided with the dismemberment of the workforce, accompanied by a rise in job insecurity, structural unemployment and a major rollback of traditional forms of worker organisation. At the beginning of the 2000s, Ribeirão Preto–SP was a highly urbanised municipality. In 2004, the municipality had a total population of 504,923 inhabitants, and of these only 2,163 people lived in rural areas (Firmiano, 2009, p.73).

In this context the struggle for land took place primarily in the city, through the organisation of workers who had either been expelled from the countryside or who had experienced violent processes of proletarianisation and increased insecurity. In this sense, political alliances with other labour organisations and supporters of the struggle for land reform in the city were an important condition for mobilisation. Organisations like the Brazilian Communist Party (BCP), the United Socialist Workers' Party and progressive sectors of the Catholic Church, along with other labour organisations, created the Land Reform Support Group within the Postal Workers Union. This group backed the first MST militant collective that undertook the grassroots work of organising and mobilising rural landless working families to occupy territories and subsequently establish encampments. This group offered some of the bases necessary so that the collective could organise the workers in what they call grassroots work.

Among the alliances forged by the MST in Ribeirão Preto, the support of the diocese was also fundamental in the consolidation of the movement in the region. In November 2002, a partnership was formed with the archdiocese of Ribeirão Preto, 'through which a space was granted to the MST on the urban outskirts of the municipality in order to realise its activities: the Pau D'Alho site' (Firmiano, 2009, p.96). In this space, the movement consolidated its activities toward a socio-pedagogical project and created the Dom Hélder Câmara Center for Socio-Agricultural Education. Here, the regional secretariat of the MST was also established. With the educational centre built, the regional secretariat consolidated, the support of important sectors of civil society and two settlements set to be built, the movement continued moving forward with its grassroots work, creating new alliances. In this way, the MST broadened its dialogues with civil society organisations and forged urban alliances, including with environmental groups such as the Pau Brazil Ecological Association, with whom they shared similar social, economic and environmental concerns relating to the impacts of sugar cane monoculture.

Discussion of the problems caused by agribusiness and the forging of alliances in the city to spread the agrarian struggle in the region led to the discovery that the Guaraní Aquifer in Ribeirão Preto was at some risk of contamination. This aquifer is one of the largest underground freshwater reserves in the world, and extends 1.2 million square kilometres between Brazil, Argentina, Paraguay and Uruguay. The recharge areas are located where the aquifer is closest to the surface of the earth and where the soil composition allows for the greatest and fastest water penetration. One of the recharge areas was inside a 1,780-hectare estate on the border of the city and the countryside, called the *Fazenda da Barra*, which belonged to an important business group from the city and was dedicated to the intensive and extensive production of sugar cane. According to the Ribeirão Preto Justice Department, from 1994 onward the estate was being investigated by the Prosecutor for the Environment and Land Conflicts for environmental damage, such as deforestation and burning, in addition to investigation for failing to obtain permits for exploration as required by Brazilian legislation. Considering this, the Justice Department called upon the relevant governmental bodies to expropriate the area for land reform purposes (Firmiano, 2009, p.106). However, this only happened after many demonstrations and mobilisations by the MST and its allies.

In 2003, 400 MST member families occupied the estate to reaffirm that due to the low productivity of the area, along with the environmental damage that it had caused, the land should be considered for agrarian reform. The farmers offered to build a settlement that would guarantee work and income for the workers as well as quality food for the population and environmental protection in the area. With this vision they were able to build alliances with more than 100 organisations from different sectors in the region, and with the Justice Department itself. On 2 August 2 2003, 100 landless families occupied the site. As Nogueira (2005, pp.229–300) described it:

> Support groups, some students and other people sympathetic to the movement came from the city. Settlers and campers from other places nearby joined with the local militants and their families to build two barracks and build the camp a structure.

The presence of local allies was very important, both to demonstrate wider support and to avoid violent police action. Named after the Brazilian actor / composer and Communist Party militant, who had passed away the year before, the Mário Lago community was born.

The families were subsequently evicted by force many times, and possession returned to the original owners; but each time, the MST reorganised to occupy the land again. While the confrontation lasted, the MST faced multiple police actions along with a negative media campaign directed against the organisation and the occupying families. But in the meantime, the movement's research teams discovered a piece of relevant information that would turn the whole judicial case around. In 2005, a law had been approved that increased the area of urban expansion. In light of this, the Barra estate had negotiated with other investors to build condominiums on their land. However, the project required that one area inside the Guaraní Aquifer recharge zone be drained. When the MST discovered these plans, they denounced the environmental damage that the estate was inflicting on the aquifer. The workers organised many demonstrations, both in the country and in the city, leading to the reoccupation of the land. It was only in August 2006 that the Justice Department finally authorised the implementation of the settlement project, and by 2007, Mário Lago community was no longer an encampment; it had become a rural settlement. As this account has demonstrated, then, rural settlements such as this were achieved as a result of continuing struggles, fought over considerable periods of time and taking on massive challenges in the process. There were no easy victories, even when the MST had the support of its allies across rural–urban divides.

Community development with land reform from below: the Mário Lago land settlement

An important victory was the concession that the MST won in a Preliminary Conduct Agreement with INCRA that was signed by the local Justice Department on 3 July 2007. This guaranteed the implementation of a rural settlement project based on the ecological, social, political and economic principles espoused by the MST. According to this document, the territory should be granted to (a) areas for collective production composed of agroforestry systems, silvopastoral systems and other agroecological systems; (b) areas for family production, located in *Agrovilas*, or farming villages; and (c) common use areas for the settlers to engage in social, cultural and leisure activities (MP/SP, 2007, p.3). The development of the area would be performed exclusively by the settler families, and the land could not be rented out to anyone else. With regards to the environment, the document foresaw the preservation of 35% of the total settlement area, guaranteeing particularly that the Guaraní Aquifer recharge areas would be protected and that areas deforested by the previous owners would be reforested. It also stipulated the use of environmentally sound agricultural management techniques, prioritising diversification as a means to ensure household food security.

Since then, the MST has put a great deal of effort into building a community in the Mário Lago settlement, honouring all of these agreement, looking to expand the use of agroecological techniques, disseminating agroforestry production systems and sustainable irrigation and water management and strongly rejecting the use of chemical fertilisers, genetically modified seeds, pesticides and the so-called 'Green Revolution' technological package. This emphasis on sustainable approaches relates to two general shifts inside the MST.

The first shift occurred when many farming families using Green Revolution methods went bankrupt and returned to the *favelas,* causing the MST to reflect on the technological matrix employed by their bases. National representatives began a process of debate and analysis, which concluded that the conventional agricultural model – a model that utilises toxic inputs – was damaging to both the settlers and the environment (Correa, 2007). As MST leaders explained to the authors, the movement felt the need to come up with a viable model that would not leave producers dependent on product markets. Through the participation of the MST in *La Vía Campesina* (an international network of movements promoting sustainable family farming), they made contact with indigenous and peasant movements from other regions in Latin America that were already practising agroecology by reviving traditional knowledge (Rosset and Martínez-Torres, 2012; Martínez-Torres and Rosset, 2014). In their Fourth Congress in 2000, the MST adopted agroecology as the national orientation for production in all settlements.

The second shift occurred as a response to structural changes in the Brazilian macroeconomy. Whereas in the past the struggle for land was principally a struggle between landless peasants and semi–feudal landlords, the more recent influx of international finance capital has capitalised agribusiness such that the formerly unproductive large land holdings have become productive agribusiness plantations. As such, the MST has necessarily adapted the nature of their argument and their strategy (Porto-Gonçalvez, 2005; Rosset, 2013). Where they had previously emphasised the inherent unfairness of a situation whereby a small number of landlords had vast amounts of unused land while millions were going landless, they began to shift their arguments in response to these changes. The MST now maintained that it is better for society as a whole for rural areas to be represented by agroecological peasant agriculture, as this both produces healthy food and conserves the rural environment (Fernandes, 2010, Martínez-Torres, 2012, Rosset and Martínez-Torres, 2012). This new recognition in the MST of the importance of peasant agriculture in general, and of ecological peasant agriculture in particular, has had a positive influence in building local community settlements such as Mário Lago.

It should be added that the Mário Lago settlement community has also improved the living conditions of settler families through community development approaches. In these processes, it is important to note the positive alliances that have been made with other organisations and entities in both the country and the city. For example, to implement projects related to production, the community has two particularly important allies. One of these – the *Cooperafloresta* – is a farmers' association located in Barra do Turvo in the state of São Paulo, which helps to implement the Agroforestry Systems (AFS), working alongside the ninety or so families involved in the project. The other, *Estação Luz*, is a non-governmental organisation (NGO) based in the city of Ribeirão Preto that develops social technologies. Among the Mario Lago's current projects in the settlement, there are four that stand out:

- *Rebirth of the Guaraní Aquifer Water*, in partnership with the *Cooperafloresta* and funded by the Secretary of the Environment, aims to protect the aquifer recharge areas through agroforestry production;
- *Project 'Candeia'*, also in partnership with *Cooperafloresta* and funded by the National Biodiversity Fund, works on strengthening agroforestry systems in the settlement.
- *'Agroflorestar'*, in partnership with *Cooperafloresta* and funded by the Petrobrás Foundation, has supported around ninety agroforestry systems in family plots in the community and is currently in its second phase.
- *'Caravana de Luz'* conducts educational workshops on how to implement water collection systems and how to treat different kinds of non-potable water.

To implement these projects, the settlement searches for ways to organise and produce agroecologically in order to create an alternative, collective means of production and to generate income. They exchange labour, working collectively on each other's plots on a rotating basis. So for example, on a given day, from 10 to 20 families get together and work on the agroecological plot of one family, who will in turn contribute to another family the following week. In this way the families help each other to develop a common agroecological production system. The experience of cooperation is a complete change for many of them, and a radical departure from the organisation of the labour process that they previously experienced in the city or in the field. They are, in fact, a part of the 're-peasantization' of the countryside (Rosset and Martínez-Torres, 2012) and peri-urban areas.

For the MST, the settlement is a form of 'agrarian commune': an idea proposed by the movement to create clusters of the peasant economy nearby large urban centres. In the Mário Lago settlement, for example, 264 families live in plots of some 2 hectares. This model allows for both agricultural and non-agricultural activities to be developed and implemented within the settlement, which also 'directly help resolve urban problems ... such as violence, unemployment, low income, a lack of housing and insufficient space to realize social and cultural activities' (CONCRAB, 2004, p.17). In this sense, the MST sees that many of the problems facing city dwellers are also experienced in the rural areas. For example, public transportation is very expensive in Brazil, which recently led to the Free Pass Movement (FPM): a national movement that fights for free, quality public transport. This directly affects the lives of the Mario Lago families, who depend on public transportation to go to the city. In parallel, therefore, the MST in Ribeirão Preto approached the FPM and built an alliance to demand public transportation for the settlement too.

In the same vein, they entered into an alliance with the *Se Vira Ribeirão*, (Ribeirão Turnaround) to create an alternative cultural movement in which the youth of Mario Lago community and other MST settlements in the region develop cultural alternatives to the dominant forms that operate in the city. Politically, the MST – and the Mario Lago community – also builds alliances with political parties and other urban movements around action over health, housing and education in the city. In these ways, the community has been supporting the various struggles that different urban organisations and social movements have been waging, building alliances within the working class to fight together for their collective rights.

However, the community still has a number of serious problems that have an impact upon the implementation of its goals, starting with the lack of infrastructure necessary for its consolidation. For example, ten years after the settlement began, although the state released the funds needed to build houses, the streets and roads inside the settlement still have not been improved. As one settler summed it up: 'This impedes the flow of production, even though we are so close to the city'.

This situation of infrastructural insecurity is not unique to the Mário Lago settlement. According to research conducted by the Institute of Applied Economic Research, in 2001 there were 8,784 million settlement projects being run by the INCRA, home to 920,700 families within an area totaling 85.9 million hectares, most of which were located in the northern regions of the country. The structure established for production by the settlers, both new and old, was the main obstacle to development. More than half of the projects were still in their early stages, about 30% were in the development phase and only 18% were in their final stages of consolidation (IPEA, 2012, p.266).

In spite of the adverse conditions that they face and the gains made, the Brazilian peasant sector still holds only 24.3% of the total agricultural area in Brazil, with just 80.25 million hectares, despite the fact that the sector produces 87% of the nation's yucca; 70% of its beans; 58% of milk; 50% of pigs; 50% of poultry; 46% of corn; 38% of coffee; 30% of cattle; 34% of rice, 21% of wheat and 16% of soy (Martins de Carvalho, 2010, pp.7–8). Nevertheless, for the MST the Brazilian peasant sector remains a key player: both in community and national development through their settlements and through the rural–urban alliances that it has forged in an effort to achieve agrarian reform across the country and to defend food sovereignty.

Conclusion

Ribeirão Preto is a unique place in terms of the starkly contrasting ways of life that characterise surrounding rural areas. On the one hand are the vast sugar cane plantations that make up industrial agriculture in the region and on the other are the diverse agroecological crops of the settlements: yucca, tomato, pineapple, orange and vegetables. The organised peasantry and agribusiness represent very disparate forces that run contrary to one another; they are essentially two opposing and incompatible models.

As this chapter has demonstrated, the Mario Lago settlement community development experience brings together a wide range of urban organisations, in alliance with the rural Landless Workers Movement, in order to campaign on a variety of issues including the distribution of healthy food, transportation, housing and environmental concerns. Although the community is under constant pressure from the agribusiness complex and developers, the residents continuously engage in struggle to create and recreate community life by producing healthy food and protecting the environment. As this chapter has also demonstrated, there have been no easy wins. Their achievements are the result of hard struggles, often fought against the odds, over long periods of time. While they continue to take on the international interests of agribusiness, they simultaneously demonstrate the potential for developing alternative approaches and provide an example of how alliances between urban and rural working people can help to achieve community development based on agrarian reform from below.

Note
[1] The settlement is a Brazilian legal concept that refers to collective rights, in which the land is conceded in usufruct for 99 years, with the possibility of renewal. The permits are inheritable and the settled community has decision-making power over the land. The settlers are owners of their property – houses, animals, machinery and so on – and can sell their property to a new family that arrives as well as transfer the right to use the land, with the permission of the settled community.

References

Chase, J. (1999) 'Exodus revisited: the politics and experience of rural loss in Central Brazil', *Sociologia Ruralis*, 39(2), pp.165–85.

CONCRAB (Cooperative's National Confederation of Brazil) (2004) 'Novas formas de assentamentos de reforma Agrária: a experiência da Comuna da Terra', in *Caderno de Cooperação Agrícola*, 15. Brasília: Distrital Gráfica e Editora.

Correa, C. (2007) *MST (Movimiento de los Trabajadores Rurales sin Tierra) en marcha hacia la agroecología: una aproximación a la construcción histórica de la agroecología en el MST*, Masters thesis on agroecology, International University of Andalucía and University of Cordoba, Spain.

Delgado, G. (2005) 'A questão agrária no Brasil, 1950–2003', in L.O. Ramos Filho and O. Aly Júnior (eds), *Questão Agrária no Brasil: Perspectiva Histórica e Configuração Atual*, São Paulo: Instituto Nacional de Colonização e Reforma Agrária, pp 21–85.

Fernandes, B.M. (2000) 'Formação e territorialização do MST no Pará', *Cultura Vozes*, 94(2), pp 3–18.

Fernandes, B.M. (2001) *A formação do MST no Brasil*, Petrópolis: Editora Vozes.

Fernandes, B.M. (2010) 'El MST, Gobierno Lula y Agronegocio: Territorios en disputa', Conference paper in *Seminario Permanente Internacional sobre Medio Ambiente, Agricultura, Género y Movimientos Sociales*, CIESAS-Sureste, CIDECI-Universidad de La Tierra. San Cristóbal de las Casas, Chiapas, Mexico, 24 June.

Fernandes, B.M. and Stédile, J.P. (2000) *Brava gente: a trajetória do MST e a luta pela terra no Brasil*, Sao Paulo: Perseu Abramo.

Firmiano, F.D. (2009) *A formação cultural dos jovens do MST: a experiência do assentamento Mário Lago, em Ribeirão Preto (SP)*, São Paulo: Cultura Acadêmica.

IPEA (2012) *Políticas sociais: acompanhamento e análise*. 20, Brasilia: IPEA.

Jank, M.S., Maristela Franco P.L. and Andre M.N. (2001) 'Concentration and internationalization of Brazilian agribusiness exporters', in *International Food and Agribusiness Management Review*, 2(3/4), pp.359–74.

Martínez-Torres, M.E. (2012) *Territorios disputados: tierra, agroecologia y recampesinización. Movimientos sociales rurales en Latinoamerica y agronegocio*, paper presented at the 2012 Conference of the Latin American Studies Association, San Francisco, California, 23–26 May.

Martínez-Torres, M.E. and Rosset, P.M. (2014) 'Diálogo de saberes in La Via Campesina: food sovereignty and agroecology', *Journal of Peasant Studies*, 41(6), pp.979–97.

Martins de Carvalho, H. (2010) 'Na sombra da imaginação II: A recamponesação no Brasil' [online], www.mpabrasil.org.br/biblioteca/textos-artigos/na-sombra-da-imaginacao-2-recamponesacao-no-brasil

McKay, B., Alonso-Fradejas, A. Wand, C. and Borras, S.M. Jr (2014) 'Contested land politics and trajectories of agrarian change within an emergent world agro-commodity regime: insights from the BRICS and the periphery', in W.D. Schanbacher (ed) *The global food system. Issues and solutions*, London: Praeger, pp.211–31.

MP/SP (Ministério Público do Estado de São Paulo) (2007) *Termo de Compromisso de Ajustamento de Conduta Preliminar* (Assentamento Mário Lago), Ribeirão Preto [mimeo.].

MST Movimiento de los Trabajadores Rurales Sin Tierra (2009) *Revista Sem Terra*, special edition on Agroecology.

Nogueira, S. (2005) *Movimentos sociais, cultura, comunicação e participação política*. PhD thesis, Centro de Estudos LatinoAmericanos em Comunicação e Cultura, Escola de Comunicação e Artes, Universidade de São Paulo, São Paulo.

Porto-Gonçalves, C.W. (2005) *A Nova Questão Agrária e a Reinvenção do Campesinato: o caso do MST*, En: OSAL: Observatorio Social de América Latina, 16 June, Buenos Aires : CLACSO, http://bibliotecavirtual.clacso.org.ar/ar/libros/osal/osal16/AC16PortoG.pdf

Rosset, P.M. (2013) 'Re-thinking agrarian reform, land and territory in La ViaCampesina', *The Journal of Peasant Studies*, 40(4), pp.721–75.

Rosset, P.M. and Martínez-Torres, M.E. (2012) 'Rural social movements and agroecology: context, theory and process', *Ecology and Society*, 17(3): 17.

Scopinho, R.A. (2007) 'Sobre cooperação e cooperativas em assentamentos rurais', in *Psicologia and Sociedade*, 19, pp.84–94 [online], available from www.scielo.br/pdf/psoc/v19nspe/v19nspea12.pdf

Silva, L.O. (1997) 'As Leis Agrárias e o Latifúndio Improdutivo', *São Paulo em Perspectiva*, 11(2), pp 15–25.

Silva, M.A.M. (1999) *Errantes do fim do século*, Sao Paulo: Editora UNESP.

Starr, A., Martínez-Torres, M.E. and Rosset, P. (2011) 'Participatory democracy in action: practices of the Zapatistas and the Movimento Sem Terra', *Latin American Perspectives*, 38(1), pp 102–19.

Stedile, J.P. (2008) 'La ofensiva de las empresas transnacionales sobre la agricultura', Conference in *V Conferencia Internacional de La Vía Campesina Maputo* [online], Maputo, Mozambique, 19-22 October, available from www.rebelion.org/noticia.php?id=77961

Vergara-Camus, L. (2009) 'The politics of the MST: autonomous rural communities, the state, and electoral politics', *Latin American Perspectives*, 36(4), pp 178–91.

Welch, C. (2009) 'Camponeses: Brazil's peasant movement in historical perspective (1946-2004)', *Latin American Perspectives*, 36(4), pp 126–55.

Wright, A. and Wolford, W. (2003) *To inherit the Earth: The landless movement and the struggle for a new Brazil*, Oakland: Food First Books.

PART 3

Reconnecting class and inequality through community development

ELEVEN

Reconciling participation and power in international development: a case study

Kate Newman

Introduction

Over the past thirty years, international NGOs (INGOs) have become increasingly important actors in the international development sector. They deliver a range of social services to those living in poverty and represent their voices in policy debates nationally and internationally (Thomas, 2008). While the sector as a whole has grown dramatically – Yaziji and Doh (2009, p.16) estimate the annual turnover of the 'NGO sector' to be over US$1 trillion – looking at these organisations at a sectoral level obscures the different choices that each one makes and hides the myriad of different organisational forms, approaches and ways of working with, and on behalf of, people living in poverty.

This chapter focuses specifically on one such international NGO, ActionAid International. ActionAid initially operated in the same way as any other INGO: it was funded by supporters in the Global North and delivered 'community development' in the Global South. But in 2003, it took the brave decision to radically change its organisational structure. This decision was based on its analysis of poverty and the belief that its root causes lie in unequal power relations:

> The structures that reinforce inequity, injustice and poverty are all closely intertwined across geographical and cultural boundaries. Traditionally funded by goodwill from the north, NGO development projects, whilst producing positive outcomes at local levels, are certainly not sufficient to eradicate poverty and often are not sustainable. They have not been able to change the overall pattern of massive and increasing poverty and inequality. The solution lies in a global movement, led by poor and marginalised people, for action against poverty that cuts across national and

> south–north boundaries. The founding of ActionAid International is our participation in, and contribution to, such a movement. (2003 Memorandum of Understanding for the Founding of ActionAid International, quoted in Jayawickrama and Ebrahim, 2013, p.3)

In working to align its organisational form with its analysis of poverty and its causes, ActionAid has spent the last 10 years becoming:

> an international organisation, working with over 15 million people in 45 countries for a world free from poverty and injustice. ... We believe the people whose lives our work affects should decide how we're run. And that's what makes us different. We help people use their own power to fight poverty and injustice. Because that's how real change happens – for families, for communities, for whole societies. (ActionAid, 2016)

This chapter draws on research conducted between 2006 and 2009, which used participant observation, semi-structured interviews and document analysis to explore the challenges and dilemmas that ActionAid experienced in this transition process. The research focused specifically on how the organisation struggled with reconciling a commitment to bottom–up participatory development, focused on building local capacities, with a deeply political analysis of poverty and inequality requiring national and global advocacy. This chapter focuses on one aspect of this transition: the move to strengthen policy engagement, particularly at global and national levels.

It argues that, although an analysis of class and inequality underpinned the argument for organisational form and structure and were considered 'out there' in terms of the relationship between the organisation and the people it existed to benefit, the analysis was not applied 'in here': in terms of who the staff of ActionAid were, their relationships with each other and the people they were working with and on behalf of. This lack of attention to class analysis challenged ActionAid's theory of change and moved the organisation further from the people who it was intending to represent and to whom it intended to move closer. It is suggested here that due to recruitment of a different 'type' of staff – people rooted in policy and activism rather than community development – the class makeup of the organisation shifted, as did the relationships between the organisation and people living in poverty.

Central to the chapter is the need to understand the dynamic nature of power and inequality in this context. It is suggested that it is not enough to pit a rich and powerful Global North against a poor and excluded Global South, but rather that a more complex analysis is needed; one that appreciates how power relations play out differently in different interactions and different spaces. This has implications for how class is conceived, experienced and potentially formed and reformed in different moments through different relationships.

The chapter begins with a brief background on the shifting role and position of NGOs in international development, and locates ActionAid in relation to this. The process that ActionAid underwent to increase its capability in policy and advocacy work is then described followed by an analysis of the consequences of this shift. The chapter concludes by drawing out key conclusions and implications from ActionAid's experience, particularly in relation to how class needs to be understood when working in international development. The chapter utilises quotes and insights from ActionAid staff members throughout, who were active participants in the research that underpins this chapter.

There are two important caveats to mention in relation to this research and chapter. First, the research and ideas discussed are intended to illuminate the complexity of the process that ActionAid undertook. They must be read as such, while recognising that the organisation was brave, radical and committed in its decision-making and vision. In focusing on building alliances globally and locally, the organisation was working tirelessly to address the challenges of inequality and poverty.

Second, the dynamics described here are relevant to a particular point in time. Veneklasen et al (2004, p.20) note that such organisational transitions can take more than ten years; this implies that the research period fell in the middle of the transition. Transitions are not straightforward; they involve messiness and disorder, and are not representative of what has gone before or what is intended to follow. The analysis here refers to a period of time that is now part of ActionAid's history and needs to be understood as such. By the time this chapter is published, power dynamics and culture in ActionAid will have shifted again, as the INGO pursues its social justice agenda informed by reflecting upon its experiences.

Setting the context

In the 1980s NGOs were marginal actors in the development industry, but by the early 2000s they had become increasingly important in international development. Over the same period, diverse development actors coalesced around agreed aims of development shaped by the 'millennium development goals'.[1] These focused on a range of defined targets of social development spanning education, health and gender. Although these targets have been important in bringing human development back onto the agenda, following a period of focus on economic growth there are concerns that this target-based focus has given rise to a technocratic approach to development, suggesting that the challenges of poverty and inequality could be addressed and managed by technical means (see Heyzer, 2005, for example). This context of NGOs' increasing profile and influence, alongside increasing international agreement on the terms of development, has led to two trends that influence the international NGO sector today.

On the one hand there is the growth of relationships between international NGOs and official development bodies. Broad agreement on the focus of development has led to increased direct funding from governments to NGOs. This has meant that, for example, NGOs are increasingly participating in bidding for and delivering large-scale service contracts on behalf of governments in the Global North. These closer relationships with government (and the private sector) have introduced a greater focus on management and professionalisation of the INGO sector.

Eade et al (2000, p.15) comment that while management was often seen as a 'pejorative term' in the 1960s and 1970s – 'at best irrelevant, at worst incompatible with commitment' – by the 1980s and 1990s, 'Corporatism, strategic planning and formal accountability became the order of the day: a way to contain if not to understand the complex environments in which development and humanitarian programmes now had to function'.

The conception of development as a technical rather than a political process, accompanied by a belief that specific inputs will lead to predefined outputs, has meant that staff in many NGOs are now recruited and valued for their technical management abilities more than their personal commitment to social justice.

However, this shift was accompanied by a second trend: NGOs increasingly began focusing attention on the root causes of poverty, which they understood to be embedded in unequal economic, political and social power. Thus although direct poverty alleviation (social service delivery) still figured strongly for most NGOs, many also scaled up their policy and advocacy work at national and international levels, working to challenge or change the relationships and policies underpinning global inequality. This led to a growing presence of NGOs at global meetings as both insiders – building relationships and influencing official delegations – and outsiders – holding parallel meetings, drawing on research and analysis and using a range of media tactics to raise debates on development matters spanning issues as diverse as the environment, women and education rights. It is within this wider context that ActionAid's transition from an international NGO focused on local community development to an international organisation focused on building alliances against poverty and inequality must be understood.

ActionAid's organisational change process

ActionAid was formed in 1972, when it focused on the education and welfare of children in the Global South using child sponsorship as its fundraising model. As the organisation evolved from the 1970s to the 1990s, its analysis of poverty – and therefore its response to it – shifted. Initially it broadened out to work with the wider family, and then it began to focus on community development.

Community was defined on a geographical basis to refer to a village or cluster of villages in a rural area; staff were recruited from the local area and valued for their deep understanding of the local dynamics, their ability to build and sustain relationships locally and their commitment to local poverty alleviation and development. These staff would also bring a specific 'technical expertise' – such as irrigation, health or education – and the practice of community development focused on the integration of these two sets of knowledges. From the early 1990s onwards, ActionAid was also developing its understanding of participation and empowerment processes, leading to an emphasis on responding to local analyses and priorities. This focus on participation, people-centred development and empowerment underpinned the later shifts in organisational practice.

By the late 1990s, ActionAid's approach had evolved to consider the importance of tackling the structural causes of poverty rather than only responding to its symptoms. In 1998, it launched a new strategy, firmly committing the organisation to a 'rights-based approach' to development. This meant that, rather than delivering services such as building health centres or schools, the emphasis was on working with people living in poverty to demand services from their government.

Explaining ActionAid's rights-based approach

In its publication, 'Human rights-based approaches to poverty eradication and development', ActionAid states:

> We believe that people who live in poverty should understand their experiences of want, fear, discrimination and exclusion in terms of human rights abuses, violations and exploitation, and not in terms of natural phenomena, as the consequences of their own failings, or as situations they have brought upon themselves. ....We believe that the rich and powerful, at all levels, structurally deny the rights of the poor and excluded ... [they] capture the state structure and apparatus to deny or violate rights for all, and to maintain the conditions that allow oppression and injustice to continue. (ActionAid, 2008, p.1)

This analysis had major theoretical and practical implications. On a theoretical level, it overtly politicised ActionAid's approach to development: eradicating poverty could not be understood as a technical project, but rather needed to be focused on tackling inequality and transforming society (Johnson et al, 2002). The practical implications of this were widespread, shifting both *how* the organisation understood what needed to be done and *who* needed to be involved. ActionAid's human rights–based approach required staff to work in new ways with people living in poverty: to build their confidence and capacity to hold their duty bearers to account. The focus of community development was no longer about service delivery but about building accountable relationships between local populations and a range of government institutions. The local programme focused on a range of empowerment processes to build the capacity of community members to articulate their demands, access information and secure their human rights. But it was also recognised that people living in poverty could not transform power relations on their own. For community-led development to be successful, an enabling environment needed to be created. Therefore there was also an increased emphasis on policy engagement and advocacy (nationally in the Global South, as well as in the UK and internationally), which focused on changing the policies and structures that kept people in poverty.

Matching development ideology and organisational structure

ActionAid recognised that, if global power relations were to be challenged and transformed, the organisational structure needed to model different relationships and practices. This new structure was therefore intended to enable community development to be designed, driven and managed locally, while also focusing attention on developing analysis and voice as part of national civil society in the countries in which it was working and in global policy spaces.

Central to the organisational design was the belief that it is not enough to engage in policy advocacy *on behalf of* people living in poverty, but rather that their priorities, perspectives and voices needed to be heard *directly*. Work at local, national and international level therefore had to be well connected to ensure that policy positioning linked to grassroots experiences and voices; if these perspectives were to be heard in the international development sector, it was recognised that they also needed to be influential at an organisational level.

Thus, ActionAid International, a global federation of equal members with each member registered and rooted in their nation state and governed by a board of national trustees, was born. An international secretariat was established in Johannesburg, South Africa, and by 2013 the organisational structure was made up of 26 member organisations (15 of which were from the Global South). Its governance structure included an international board and a general assembly, which deliberately sought out members from excluded backgrounds. The strategic decision making of the organisation shifted from a UK board of trustees and UK-based senior management to an international group of directors, primarily from the Global South. Moreover, the international board and general assembly were made of up a range of different types of people, many with a history in activism, social movements and national civil society.

Building capability in policy: recruiting policy experts

Central to ActionAid's solution to global inequalities and poverty was to build a global movement against poverty. This included various strands of work, including a focused effort on partnering with social movements (which could offer political analysis and activism) and expanding and strengthening ActionAid's own policy analysis and advocacy work. This required the recruitment of new and different staff: 'Previously ActionAid staff in Africa had been generalists, or had specific technical development expertise; these were replaced by activists, policy people' (interview, Twinning–Fooks).

New staff members were recruited at every level in the organisation. For example, during the period of this research the Asia regional director had a long history in budget advocacy, supporting campaigning across India, while the head of women's rights was a well-known Zimbabwean feminist activist. Nationally, policy staff members were recruited from a range of backgrounds, including civil society but also civil servants, academics and individuals from donor organisations. Data from a review of education staff in 2008 showed that two thirds of these staff members spent most of their time working at national level; the following quotes (from 2007) are illustrative of the backgrounds of many of the education staff:

> Before I joined ActionAid I was the coordinator for professional development for the Pan African Teacher's centre; and before that I worked with the Ghana Education service, teaching, managing and researching. I have an M Phil in Curriculum development, and a degree in education. (Interview, Konadu)

> I've been at ActionAid for nearly 4 years ... I did lots of things before joining AA, including being a teacher and programme manager, focusing on education, but I wouldn't call myself an educationalist, rather a lobbyist/advocate. (Interview, Nsanjama)

The appointment of activists was coherent with the organisational vision and important in enabling ActionAid to participate in policy debates. However, the recruitment policy also created a challenge. Whereas previously the majority of staff were drawn from community development backgrounds and were valued by the organisation due to their in-depth local knowledge, this had shifted:

> It is the policy–advocacy work which is publicised within ActionAid, seen as 'sexy'. In the early 1990s the iconic people in ActionAid were DA [development area] managers – there were 10 or so with high status, they were 'it', known across the organisation. Now it is all policy people whose names are known ... and they may not know much about what happens in the field. (Interview, Archer)

This impacted on how the organisation connected with the people on whose behalf it was working:

> People come from different backgrounds and they are not really being inducted into what we are about. Policy people are hired straight out of policy, they don't get community work ... We are hiring lots of new people, giving them a

very ambitious agenda and not really grounding them in 'cutting edge work' ... we are trying to do stuff that hasn't been done before and there are no easy models – but we don't necessarily recognise how difficult it is. (Interview, Adams)

The discrepancy between those living in poverty and those working in ActionAid was exacerbated by two other dynamics: the nature of global spaces and the organisational dynamics concerning information flows and decision making.

The nature of global spaces

Batliwala (2002) suggests that the engagement of INGOs in global civil society transformed the nature of civil society at this level, impacting on its democracy and representativeness and disguising differences in power; resources; visibility; access, structure and ideology between movements of directly-affected people and their advocates. Moreover, international NGO's engagement in influencing policy encouraged a close relationship between government officials and NGO policy experts, who used complex technical language in an increasingly exclusive debate (Batliwala and Brown, 2006).

Key to ActionAid's approach to these global spaces (that is, global events such as UN summits) was the idea that the organisation was participating not only as a representative of those living in poverty but also with the aim of fundamentally altering the power relations that characterise those spaces: enabling perspectives and voices from the Global South to be heard directly and powerfully. However, as suggested by Batliwala (2002), to participate in these spaces, you had to be highly educated, familiar with technical language and confident in speaking to policy makers.

ActionAid now had individuals from an 'activist' background or with policy experience on their staff; but given the nature of these spaces, how representative could these individuals be of poor and excluded voices? Was participation in activism and international policy making actually leading to a process of detachment: between a set of staff immersed in policy discourse on the one hand and local development programmes on the other?

Alongside these challenges of who could participate and be heard in such policy spaces was a second challenge relating to the policy development process itself.

Developing policy positions

The increase in policy staff in ActionAid, especially at national level, meant that the process of policy development was fundamentally different from most other international NGOs. In most INGOs, a small group of staff working in the Global North tended to dominate policy and advocacy work (Newman, 2011). For ActionAid, however, policy development was characterised by international negotiation:

> There was a change while I was there … the policy community grew, so there were more people to link with, there were genuine counterparts … There would be an interested Country Director or policy lead then we would work together more … and increasingly you had to sell the idea of working in the UK … there was a different dynamic. (Interview, Watt)

This had an impact on how ActionAid positioned itself, especially in the UK:

> [T]he political lead in ActionAid and the broad priority setting was coming from the South … our reaction to the Gleneagles[2] communiqué was more negative than a lot of the other INGOs and one reason for that was it had to be negotiated between some colleagues in Africa who wanted to slam it, and colleagues in the UK who wanted a more nuanced/carefully couched response. (Interview, Watt)

However, this process was not straightforward, and negotiating a policy position internationally presented challenges:

> Because ActionAid–UK doesn't have autonomy to decide public policy positions this makes the process longer … the process is inefficient, there are either too many people involved in a sign off, or those involved are not taking their role seriously, which is an obstacle to moving forward. (Interview, Calaguas)

International fora run on internationally agreed timetables; there are set moments in which INGOs can engage and influence, and slow internal decision-making processes can lead to missed opportunities. Moreover, anyone who works in advocacy will comment on how you have to understand when and how to present an issue or try to influence a process in light of a range of contextual factors, often relating to national media and politics. This presented ActionAid with a challenge. The organisation wanted its structure and processes to enable the voices of the poor and excluded to be heard at the highest level of development debate, which suggested the need for participatory decision-making. And yet influential participation in these spaces necessitated ActionAid to respond quickly and efficiently to external contexts. This tension is neatly described in the idea of 'doing justice to people's voices'.

Doing justice to people's voices

In responding to these different pressures and timetables, many of the staff working in ActionAid's international offices believed that they were able – and even obligated – to make decisions on how to use and present the voices of the poor. They were committed to combating poverty and had access to certain fora that were typically beyond the reach of those living in poverty. It was therefore their responsibility to ensure good media attention and discussion of ActionAid's positions and understanding in a range of policy fora:

> The challenge has been ... the balance between participation and power and communication ... making sure that community voices are heard at all levels, and at a specific moment in time, an AGM or a report ... The Northern affiliates and the communications department ... view is that they become legitimate actors if they are doing justice to people's voices. Timing is an issue, external media opportunities can put pressure on participatory processes, and [there is] also a question of what to do about it if someone says something that you know won't appeal to the audience. Their argument is that to be legitimate and accountable we need to do the best we can by these people, which might mean putting a different spin on it. (Interview, Carroll)

But how you interpret and 'do justice to people's voices' is highly dependent on who you are and with whom you interact. Staff in ActionAid had policy backgrounds, and those interviewed in my research revealed how they spent more time with (and were thus more influenced by) external policy makers and senior management than those with direct connections to people living in poverty. Wilson

(2001) argues that knowledge is interpreted by what we already know, as well as our culture. This means that it is important to ask *who* decides which voices to do justice to? How are local voices interpreted and used? What is included or excluded? And – fundamentally – how can an INGO do justice to people's voices while also building a global alliance rooted in the goal of transforming power relationships? Beyond these questions, there is also a question of when 'doing justice' occurs:

> [the question] is not purely whether ActionAid is providing a platform for Africans to come to the G8, or whether it is collecting powerful stories of people living in poverty. The issue is who is setting those priorities and how are they are being collected and identified. (Interview, Watt)

This suggests a need to look beyond how poor people's voices are communicated in a policy agenda formulated in the Global North and to think through how those agendas are set in the first place and when and how grassroots voices are heard in this process.

Class and organisational culture

What did these shifts in staff orientation and the wish to participate in global advocacy mean for ActionAid?

An individual's background tells us very little – if anything – about their values or commitment to tackling poverty or promoting social justice. However, their class origins and current class position do have relevance. The shift from staff members who defined themselves as practitioners of community development to those who classified themselves as activists or professional policy experts and lobbyists was significant.

Organisations are influenced by socially defined norms and expected behaviour, but they are also created and recreated by human action (Giddens, 1986). The potential for action is influenced by an individual's 'habitus' (Bourdieu, 1984): their previous experience and current positionality. This suggests that the introduction of a significant number of different 'types' of person to an organisation is likely to influence the organisational culture and practice more generally. Moreover, the national policy staff recruits were being drawn from relatively elite social backgrounds:

> The policy voices that AA works with in the South tend to come from elites, from public policy or political backgrounds,

they are not necessarily any more programmatically rooted than anyone sitting in London. [The Africa Policy Coordinator] is no less a member of the globalised elite than [the head of the International Education theme],[3] for example. (Interview, Watt)

Win (2004) argues convincingly that her experience as a Zimbabwean woman needs to be understood at many different levels. For example, although she is a member of the national, middle-class educated elite her identity is more complex than this. Her family have certain expectations of her, and what she will do, and her relationship with them must be understood as factors which influence her thoughts, position and actions. Likewise, any individual staff member of ActionAid brings with them specific experiences, influences and positionality, which act in different ways to influence their approach to work. The expectations and experiences of a member of the elite in Zimbabwe will differ from a member of the elite in the UK; class is complex, and needs to be understood through an extensive range of interacting factors.

The shift in staff orientation described resulted in a shifting class identity (or 'habitus') of the organisation. If the individuals representing poor and excluded voices live their lives within a distant and distinct context with little connection to those who they are representing, it is unlikely that excluded voices are being 'empowered'. While organisational management and governance within ActionAid was designed to strengthen voices from the Global South, the voices that were actually being heard were not necessarily representative of people living in poverty. Although ActionAid was functioning with more equality between its northern and southern staff, questions remained regarding the extent to which these structures were actually enabling the voices and perspectives of those living in poverty to enter into and influence development debates. This situation was complicated even further by the nature of the global spaces in which much of the policy and advocacy work took place.

For ActionAid, there was a tension – and to some extent a contradiction – between how it built its capability in global alliance building and advocacy and its wish to sustain a local development programme deeply rooted in the local context and based on participatory principles. It valued both areas of work, but did not focus on creating an organisational structure and systems that would enable both areas to integrate well and complement each other. Consequently, although the overall organisational structure responded to a deep understanding of inequality, the detail of the practice was not coherent with this.

Participatory practice suggests a focus on 'bottom-up' development: on flexible and responsive systems that place process and empowerment at their heart and that build from the perspectives, voices and priorities of poor and excluded people. Power et al (2003) comment that bottom-up development requires an organisation:

> [t]o work for the liberation of those at the bottom by drawing its own sense of direction and priorities from this group ... [and] to adapt their internal structure, systems, and culture to the complex and evolving struggles of those in poverty, including even the choice not to be 'developed'. ... [t]o let go of the controls in community development. (Power et al, 2003, pp.26–7)

And yet, rights-based practice implies a focus on global standards: for example, using the discourse of universal human rights to ensure that governments and policy makers respect and fulfil their obligations. This skews attention upwards, to the power holders at national and international level.

Both the top-down and bottom-up practices described here are hugely relevant and important in the area of community development if it is going to move beyond alleviating poverty to actually engage with – and transform – power structures. But the ActionAid case study illustrates that, far from supporting and extending each other, the two approaches existed in tension and pulled the organisation in fundamentally different directions.

The first stage in addressing these tensions is to recognise that they exist and take active decisions in relation to the trade offs involved in managing them. This includes balancing a need to participate in spaces that have an externally set agenda with building collaborative working practices and mutual accountability – based on valuing different perspectives; positions; remits, skills and knowledge. It also means developing systems that enable the perspectives and voices from the grassroots communities that the organisation serves to influence organisational learning and understanding as well as wider development debates.

Conclusions

The ActionAid experience illustrates that, even for an INGO with a strong ideological position and understanding of inequality and power, the practice of shaping an organisation to respond to this analysis – and ensuring that day-to-day functioning aligns with the analysis – is complex. The research presented here suggests that it is not enough for organisations to invest in big structural change; it must also focus on who the staff are, how they interact, what language is used and how values and culture are experienced, created and recreated. Crucial to this is the application of a political power analysis inside an organisation as well externally.

Despite these challenges, ActionAid's experience provides many positive examples of how an organisation can work outside or beyond a mainstream technical approach to development, adopting a practice of community development that focuses on challenging and transforming power relations. Taking a rights-based approach to community development moved the focus beyond local engagement and service delivery, rooting the aims of community development within a structural analysis of power (and lack thereof). Increasing their focus on policy and advocacy, and partnering with social movements, enabled the organisation to take on a more political analysis based on understandings of equality and justice and to avoid the trappings of neoliberal management discourse. Moreover, the organisation has a deservedly good reputation for its radical analysis, activism and organisational structure.

The insights gained from this experience suggest a need to consider class and inequality in a much more sophisticated way than the traditional, populist view of a rich Global North and a poor Global South. More representation of the Global South in and of itself does not necessarily turn an INGO into an effective actor for challenging international power relations on behalf of the poor and excluded. Rather, it is necessary to understand how class interacts with context and how context can shape and amplify different class dynamics. This includes recognising that class differences have different implications *within* Southern and Northern contexts as well as *between* these contexts, and that spaces, associations, ideas and language – whether espoused by individuals or by community development theory – all contribute to the ways in which class manifests within a community development process.

Notes

[1] The Millennium Development Goals were agreed in 2000 at the Millennium Summit of the United Nations. They consist of 8 international development goals that the United Nation Member States committed to help achieve by 2015, and they span child mortality; maternal health; primary education; gender equality; environmental sustainability and combating diseases including HIV and malaria. Importantly, the final goal was to develop a global partnership for development – in order to achieve the seven other goals.

[2] The final statement from the 2005 meeting of the G8 Heads of State at Gleneagles, Scotland.

[3] Names referred to here have been removed and replaced with job titles.

References

ActionAid (2008) *Human rights-based approaches to poverty eradication and development*, ActionAid International, http://www.actionaid.org/sites/files/actionaid/the_rights_based_approach.pdf

ActionAid (2016) *Who we are*, ActionAid International, http://www.actionaid.org/who-we-are

Batliwala, S. (2002) 'Grassroots movements as transnational actors: implications for global civil society', *Voluntas*, 13(4), pp.393–409.

Batliwala, S. and Brown, L.D. (eds) (2006) *Transnational civil society: An introduction*, Bloomfield, CT: Kumarian Press.

Bourdieu, P. (1984) *Distinction: A social critique of the judgment of taste*, Cambridge, MA: Harvard University Press.

Eade, D. Hewitt, T. and Johnson, H. (eds) (2000) *Development and management: A development in practice reader*, Oxford/Milton Keynes: Oxfam GB in association with The Open University.

Giddens, A. (1986) *Constitution of society: Outline of the theory of structuration*, Berkley, CA: University of California Press.

Heyzer, N. (2005) 'Making the links: women's rights and empowerment are key to achieving the Millennium Development Goals', *Gender and Development*, 13(1), 9–12.

Jayawickrama, S. and Ebrahim, A. (2013) *Building and governing a democratic federation: The ActionAid international story*, Boston, MA: The Hauser Centre, Harvard Business School.

Johnson, H., Mosley, P. and Olsen, W. with Pearson, R. (2002) *Poverty and inequality*, Milton Keynes: The Open University.

Newman, K. (2011) *Challenges and dilemmas in integrating human rights-based approaches and participatory approaches to development: An exploration of the experiences of ActionAid International*, PhD Thesis, Goldsmiths, University of London.

Power, G., Maury, M. and Maury, S. (2003) 'Operationalising bottom-up learning in international NGOs: barriers and alternatives', in L. Roper, J. Pettit and D. Eade (eds) *Development and the learning organisation, a development in practice reader*, Oxford: Oxfam GB, pp 22–39.

Thomas, A. (2008) 'Whatever happened to reciprocity? Implications of donor emphasis on 'voice' and 'impact' as rationales for working with NGOs in development', in A.J. Bebbington, S. Hickey and C. Mitlin (eds) *Can NGOs make a difference?* London: Zed Books, pp 90–110.

VeneKlasen, L., Miller, V., Clark, C. and Reilly, M. (2004) *Rights-based approaches and beyond: challenges of linking rights,* A Joint Initiative of the Participation Group-IDS and Just Associates, International Development Institute Working Paper 235, Brighton: IDS.

Wilson, G. (2001) 'Technology, knowledge and development', in V. Desai and R. Potter (eds) *The Arnold companion to development studies*, London: Arnold.

Win, E. (2004) 'Not very poor, powerless or pregnant: the African woman forgotten by development', *IDS Bulletin*, 35(4), 61–4.

Yaziji, M. and Doh, J. (2009) *NGOs and corporations: Conflict and collaboration*, New York, NY: Cambridge University Press.

TWELVE

Transformative education and community development: sharing learning to challenge inequality

Anindita Adhikari and Peter Taylor

Introduction

At a time when economic forces continue to drive a global growth agenda and ever more imaginative approaches are introduced to alleviate the suffering of many millions – perhaps billions – of the world's citizens, enormous inequalities continue to exist. Since 2000, the Millennium Development Goals (MDGs) have been used as an important lever to help to address critical needs related to wealth, health and education. Now, writing in 2015, it is clear that many of the development goals set out in 2000 are unlikely to be met in numerous countries. A major global effort is underway to set out a series of 'Sustainable Development Goals' (United Nations, 2014), which seek not only to continue the efforts encouraged by the MDGs but also to address the massive inequities experienced in countries in the Global South as well as in wealthier nations in the Global North. These inequities are manifested in many different forms, including the fundamental gap between rich and poor, the difference in wellbeing between those who have access to resources and decision-making processes and those who do not and the continued absence of political voice for many citizens.

In addition to material inequities (including global, regional and national imbalances in wealth and access to resources), it is clear from the life experiences of social groups who experience identity-based marginalisation (such as women, children, the elderly and disabled people) that power differentials continue to persist. Others experience marginalisation on the basis of their membership or alignment with specific societal groups, which may be identified according to caste, ethnicity or religion. Class, meanwhile, is more closely tied to occupation and wealth. In many countries, decision makers attempt to address these differing forms of inequity through policy processes that seek to assure the rights of citizens.

Education is widely regarded as a hugely significant means of addressing such inequalities. As well as increasing the likelihood of employment for those who have access to education, it can lead to the imparting of a range of life skills that have been shown to help address major challenges such as decreasing rates of maternal mortality and improving child nutrition. However, formal education systems – and particularly schooling for children and young adults – have rarely sought to specifically address imbalances in power or the needs of societal groups who are discriminated against because of their class and/ or identity. Formal education systems may even reinforce dominant hierarchies and structural imbalances of power within society by socialising people into accepting their 'place' within existing systems of inequality.

This chapter aims to reflect on ways in which schooling can play a different role in society: as a transformative force that makes a real difference by empowering those who are marginalised due to their position and constructed role in society. Using case studies from India – a country of over a billion people and home to some of the greatest societal inequalities in the world – it presents examples of specific transformative educational approaches and methodologies that have helped communities to co-construct diverse forms of knowledge, which have led to practical, positive change in their lives. The chapter begins with some reflections on the relationship between knowledge, power and education; it then explores some of the opportunities that these approaches provide as well as some challenges in their application.

Knowledge, power and education

The relationship between education, learning and transformation has been explored widely to address power at different levels: from the individual to the structural, the social and the discursive (see, for example, Taylor and Fransman 2004). The absence of an analysis of the wider context of power in an individual's transformation of perspective has been considered broadly by writers on the sociology of education as a means of understanding the relationship between learning and social change. For example, education has been viewed as a primary transmitter of the values through which control and stability are maintained (Clark 1962; Durkheim 1972) and as something that therefore may be manipulated by dominant groups to legitimise certain kinds of knowledge and reproduce existing social inequalities (Illich,

1971; Apple 1978). Bourdieu (1977) has in turn argued that the nature of knowledge, and the manner in which it is transmitted (pedagogic action), plays a significant role in legitimising relations of power and social class structures outside institutions of learning. Pathways of change suggested by this broad approach range from a call for the 'de-schooling of society' towards entirely informal education (Illich, 1971) to adopting pedagogic practices that make students and teachers 'self-critical about both the positions that describe and the locations from which they speak' (Giroux 1993, p.38) and teaching that unveils oppression (Freire, 1970).

Observations of the limitations of transformation at the personal, social and institutional levels have led to an even more fundamental return to learning as a discourse. Foucault (1979), for example, furthered the notion that knowledge and power are intrinsically linked. He argued that, by creating meaning, knowledge controls conduct or action and therefore exercises power. In turn, this legitimises a certain structure of meaning or form of discursive practice. It is the rules that govern the reproduction and legitimisation of knowledge and power that Foucault refers to as 'discourse'. Changing power relations therefore requires engaging with the processes that form discourses – and their implications for action.

Attempts have also been made to explore the educative potential for transformation at the individual level. Mezirow (2000), for example, suggests that learning involves critical thinking that revises meaning structures and that this in turn leads to a transformation of perspective, which guides future action. A foundation may be laid by drawing on critical pedagogy school of thought (Freire, 1985; Giroux, 1993) and making connections with emerging understandings of transformative learning. This can help in analysing the connections between knowledge and power. Critical learning is therefore viewed as emancipatory because it offers learners 'voice' and 'language' for reimagining their realities as a means of challenging power.

How, then, can education help to promote transformation within communities? In particular, how might individuals or groups within a community be exposed – through structured learning programmes – to ways of imagining a significantly different set of life experiences from those that predominate in society, leading them to reconstruct their social realities and their life practices? Also, how can practitioners who seek to promote such transformation (educators, activists, community and political leaders) learn the skills and practice the behaviours that can help to facilitate positive change? In short, how can more transformative forms of education and learning help to tackle inequalities of class, race and gender by supporting the efforts of citizens who want to make a difference to their communities?

Merrifield (2002) argues that how people learn citizenship is dependent on a complex interrelationship between different forms of learning. Inclusive approaches (Johnston, 2003) are important if education is to address diversity and difference and highlight ways in which these are essential ingredients of civil society. Many educative approaches have engaged with issues of access, for example by engaging with people who are marginalised on the grounds of race, ethnicity, language, gender, or wealth – either as entire communities or within communities. Great gains have been made in this regard in many countries, and broader access to education has opened doors to more diverse learners, whose different needs must be met. At the same time, however, there is growing recognition that the world for which learners are preparing themselves is itself enormously complex. The idea that educational institutions can serve as repositories of knowledge and models required for professionalism and problem solving is increasingly doubtful.

Consequently, some (although by no means all) educational institutions are revisiting the context in which such learning approaches take place (Brennan and Lebeau, 2002; Mott, 2005). Participation and participatory approaches in education have emerged as a means of not only promoting inclusivity but also of recognising and shifting power structures, and ultimately contributing to social change and transformation. This includes the recognition that knowledge is a means of propagating power. Methods of popular adult education, participatory action research (PAR) (Fals-Borda 2001) and participatory learning and action (PLA) (Pretty et al, 1995) have been widely used in the contexts of community development and social movement organising, often with promising results; yet these approaches and their ability to address established relations of knowledge and power have not always been applied internally by the organisations that promote them with 'others'. This may raise questions about the real commitment of such organisations to the use of innovative processes and methodologies, and invite criticism of those who are reluctant to adopt them within their own ways of working while attempting to promote them elsewhere.

Understanding power differentials in the Indian context

A useful lens for understanding the layered ways in which exclusion and inequality in education manifests in India is through a framework proposed in the India Exclusion Report. Exclusion is defined here as 'the processes by which individuals and population groups face barriers in relation to their access to public goods, resulting in inequitable social attainments, capabilities, development, justice and dignity outcomes' (Centre for Equity Studies, 2014, p.4).

The report attributes exclusion primarily to access barriers that span the state, markets and civil society more generally. These barriers may remain as a result of neglect; discrimination; active or tacit denial; violence, cultural norms and practices or simply the faulty design and implementation of state policies and programmes. India makes for a challenging case in the study of education and inequality not only because of its sheer size and complex forms of social organisation but also because of the persistence of inequality at all stages of education, even with the massive expansion of the education system and the drive towards universalisation and provision of targeted strategies for marginalised groups.

In this chapter, the discussion on inequality and exclusion in education will focus on a particular context of class and how this affects children via access to schooling: the experience of socially and economically disadvantaged groups, including scheduled castes (*dalits*), scheduled tribes (*adivasis*) and socio-religious minorities. In India, class and caste are intertwined concepts that determine social formations and relations of power. While some argue that the significance of caste is slowly declining, caste as a structure of power continues to provide the ideological underpinning of material differences of class (Harriss, 2012). For example, the landed class in rural India will tend to be upper caste whereas a large proportion of sharecroppers and agricultural labourers (who are landless, or own very little land) will be from the scheduled caste community. A complete understanding of inequality in India therefore requires an analysis of the intersections of caste, class and power. There is insufficient space in this chapter to focus on the specific inequalities that relate to gender and disability, although it is important to state that these groups of children – as well as child workers, migrant children and children living in conflict areas – often face even deeper forms of exclusion.

Education, equality and the law in India

At the time of independence in 1947, education in India was seen as a means to nation building and development through which equity and social justice for socially disadvantaged groups could be achieved. This has been reflected in the number of constitutional safeguards that have called for enabling policies that promote equality based on caste, religion and gender. The constitutional mandate subsequently translated into a number of education policies, such as the National Policy on Education, which emphasised the 'removal of disparities to equalise educational opportunity by attending to the specific needs of those who have been denied equality so far' (Ministry of Human Resource Development, Government of India, 1986, p.7).

Interventions to address exclusion have included incentivising education for groups who have experienced poor education outcomes in the past, including women, religious minorities, *dalits*, *adivasis* and other groups who traditionally have been marginalised by formal education. Such interventions have included providing residential facilities for tribal children, opening schools in *dalit* and *adivasi* neighbourhoods, reforming curricula to reflect local cultures and providing scholarships for disadvantaged students. Initiatives to improve the learning outcomes of disadvantaged children were also stressed through schemes such as Sarva Shiksha Abhiyan (SSA) and the District Primary Education Programme (DPEP). Bandyopadhyay (2012, n.p.) views these policies and initiatives as part of a 'broader strategy (of the state) to reduce poverty and overcome social exclusion'.

The Right to Education Act passed by Parliament in 2009 affirmed universal elementary education as a right and, for the first time, laid down minimum quality standards for schools. Among other measures, the Act attempts to correct the divisive nature of the education system, calling for the reservation of a quarter of private school places for children from socially and economically marginalised communities. It is evident, therefore, that the twin goals of universalising education and promoting social equity have been relatively well recognised in India. However, while these policies and legislative measures have gone a long way towards improving enrolment across the country, they have fallen short of substantively addressing underlying issues of inequality. This failure becomes more evident when education figures are disaggregated by social group.

Access inequality

Inequalities persist at various stages of schooling post enrolment, as revealed in the attendance, dropout and retention figures. Studies (such as CREATE, 2011) indicate that children from poorer backgrounds such as *dalits* and *adivasis* have higher rates of absenteeism. Similarly, and in parallel, a study on school functioning (Bhattacharjea et al, 2011) found that children from higher castes were attending school more regularly than those of other caste groups. A similar trend can be seen for Muslim children, who belong to a religious minority. Overall, then, close associations have been identified between children's socioeconomic backgrounds on the one hand and their attendance records and learning outcomes on the other. Furthermore, the government's success in creating equal access to schooling has been offset by school dropout figures, which are significantly higher for the children of marginalised communities and even sharper for girls within these communities.

Hierarchies of access are also manifest in the creation of a parallel system of private schools that involve additional barriers such as school fees and admission tests. As such, children from socially and economically disadvantaged backgrounds continue to go to government schools with substandard facilities while better-off children use this exit option. Bandyopadhyay's 2012 study of the enrolment patterns of children from different caste groups demonstrates the extent of de facto segregation between children from poor and rich backgrounds.

Inequality inside schools and classrooms

While the previous section provides a narrative on inequalites relating to access to the school system, a second narrative around inclusion and exclusion in education looks at the ways in which teaching and learning are organised within the school and the socially constructed nature of school reality. Oommen (2012) refers to the result of the ways in which norms, values and messages are communicated in school curricula as ideological exclusion. Content analyses of textbooks have consistently highlighted the ways in which the perspectives of urban India have been privileged over those of rural India; male aspirations have been given greater attention than those of females; middle-class aspirations are promoted as those that contribute to the 'nation'; religious minorities are underrepresented, or even portrayed as anti-national; the culture and identities of *dalits*, *adivasis* and other marginalised groups face exclusion, how the religious history of India and secularism as a constitutional ideal becomes distorted in favour of the majoritarian religion, and so on. These values underly the content of most textbooks, thereby reproducing inequalities within and outside schools.

The study of how teaching–learning is structured within the classroom also offers insights into how inequalities are created and reinforced. For example, Sayed et al's (2007) study of government schools in two states in India (Madhya Pradesh and Rajasthan) found that the pedagogic style of the teacher and their interactions with students were heavily influenced by the teacher's perception of the student's socioeconomic background. Teachers' approaches were being shaped by stereotypical constructions of less advantaged students as 'ineducable'. Further, given that the teachers in these schools belonged to upper castes, *dalit* and *adivasi* parents found it hard to engage with the school space and tended to stay away. This further reinforced the teachers' stereotypes of their 'innate inability to take an interest in their children's learning' (Sayed et al, 2007, p.91). Ramachandran and Naorem's (2013) study on exclusion in state run schools found that there were also clear caste and gender distinctions in the chores assigned to pupils. Poor and marginalised children from tribal families were generally expected to carry out menial tasks such as sweeping the classroom and cleaning up after the midday meal, while the 'best and the brightest', who also tended to be from the upper castes, were called upon for education-related tasks such as leading the morning assembly. In these different ways, inequalities of caste, class and gender were routinely reinforced, with significant consequences for differential outcomes. In terms of learning outcomes, the variations between different social groups have been significant as a result of all these factors. Furthermore, schools have lacked the resources to provide adequate learning support to children form disadvantaged backgrounds to compensate.

Moving from universal access and quality to equity: the role of transformative education

While addressing persistent inequality in education in India remains a big challenge, there is nonetheless a strong policy commitment to promote inclusion, and some innovative efforts have been introduced drawing upon methodologies and practices perhaps more familiar to popular education practitioners. Even so, the focus has been almost entirely on cognitive achievement and test scores. Bivens et al (2009) argue that the current managerial discourse leads to students and educational institutions dissociating from local realities, intentionally or not. In any case, this approach fails to address the ways in which deep inequalities that are transmitted and reproduced intergenerationally need to be tackled through pedagogical processes.

In some cases, however, efforts are being made to go beyond merely looking at the needs of the learner as an individual. There have, in fact, been a number of exciting educative initiatives seeking to locate learners within their wider socioeconomic contexts. These examples aim to empower learners and to increase their potential to exert agency and challenge existing structures of power. Each of these examples is demonstrative of an effort to integrate education with wider struggles to develop more comprehensive, sustainable and empowering forms of community development that might challenge the dominant discourse of quality education in India.

Example 1: Mobilising communities through education volunteers

In the state of Bihar, which is highly stratified in terms of social and community identities, the Musahars – traditionally a rat-eating community – are from a sub-caste of *dalits* and constitute the most socially and economically deprived group among the poor. They are landless, live on the periphery of the village and are mostly engaged in menial labour. Their social exclusion was mirrored in the schools, with Musahar children facing barriers both in terms of access and within the schools themselves. To address this the government of Bihar has appointed *tola sevaks* (neighbourhood volunteers), who are selected from the Musahar community itself. The *tola sevak* plays the dual role of escorting children to school to ensure attendance and providing learning support to children who would otherwise not receive such reinforcement. This learning support is provided for two hours in the evening and aims to ensure these children do not lag behind in class. The role of *tola sevaks* also extends to ensuring that non-discriminatory practices are followed in the school. These *tola sewaks* are viewed as change agents, then, providing authentic voices on education-related issues within their communities. A similar initiative has also been introduced for Muslim children: the appointment of education volunteers for the Muslim community, called *Talim-e-Markaz*.

Ramachandran and Naroem (2013) have found that the *tola sevak* initiative has increased social inclusiveness and cohesion in schools. Initiatives like this, combined with the wider context of social mobilisations and political movements led by excluded castes over the last two or three decades, have gone a long way towards ensuring greater inclusion in school. In fact, the overarching findings of the study indicate that – contrary to what was originally expected – explicit caste-based discrimination was significantly lower in Bihar than in other comparable states.

Example 2: Strengthening the link between education and empowerment in residential schools

Residential schools have been introduced with the aim of addressing inequality of access and the absence of educational support for children from marginalised communities. Kasturba Gandhi Balika Vidyalayas are perhaps the best examples of government sponsored residential schools for girls from marginalised communities and poor backgrounds. Although the academic support and quality of the infrastructure in these schools may often be inadequate, they nonetheless fill an important educational gap for adolescent girls who are either unable to attend regular schools or are likely to discontinue their education after primary school.

There are also residential and non-residential bridging courses, which have been introduced by the government – both directly and in partnership with civil society organisations – to mainstream out-of-school children into state-run schools. Noteworthy interventions such as seasonal hostels and schools have been set up for migrant children at seasonal worksites such as brick kilns, sugar cane factory sites and stone quarries. Bridge courses are run in these worksite schools in the migrants' languages to facilitate their reintegration into mainstream schools in their home states when they return. In running these schools, dialogues with the employers and both the 'sending' and 'receiving' state governments have also led to wider impacts, such as ending child labour at these worksites, improving working conditions and increasing awareness about the health- and education-related problems that migrant children face.

Some non-governmental organisations have taken this idea of residential schools for adolescent girls forward by strengthening the link between education and empowerment. Janishala, a residential learning centre set up by the NGO Nirantar in Uttar Pradesh (one of India's largest and most populous states), seeks to build the capacities of adolescent girls in ways that extend beyond mainstreaming them into formal schools to deepening their critical understandings of the connections between different social dimensions such as gender, caste, religion and sexuality. This approach aims to help the girls to reconstruct their social realities via their educative experiences and exposure to different life skills and behaviours. The curriculum in these Janishalas is therefore based on the principles of transformatory education and feminist pedagogy. This is illustrated in their textbooks and educational materials, which aim to help young girls to build life skills that enable them to play more active roles in society, including stories centred around women in different roles (within and outside the household) and the provision of sexuality education.

Example 3: Embedding education in the community's wider struggle

Some innovative education initiatives have recognised the need to embed education in communities' wider struggles for survival, dignity and justice. For example, the Adharshila Learning Centre is based in a tribal-dominated area called Sheopur in the central Indian state of Madhya Pradesh. Adarshila is a residential school, set up in 1998 based on the belief that learning and knowledge are sources of empowerment for social change and that such empowerment must be achieved without alienating children from their social traditions. The school philosophy articulates the importance of providing children with the opportunities 'to become self-dependent through collective labour and social activism' (Adharshila Learning Centre, 2014). The school does not use textbooks; instead, children build collective knowledge and compile primers through activities such as interviewing village elders about the history of the land, writing down folk tales and songs and conducting scientific surveys on local plants, water resources, electricity consumption and other matters of common interest. Knowledge acquisition through labour and action is also stressed, with children spending two hours per day on organic farming and disseminating messages about new techniques through mobile radios. Importantly, all teaching takes place in Bareli: the local *adivasi* dialect. The school also aspires to instil the values of democratic participation in children through practices such as holding weekly student meetings to resolve disputes, having students make decisions on issues relating to school administration and running a regular newsletter. These practices instil within the children the habits of listening to each other and establishing principles of equality among themselves. The Adharshila form of work and education has even found mention in the National Curriculum Framework (NCERT, 2005), which guides textbook content and teaching practices across the country.

A second example is Agragamee: an experiment in education in seven tribal districts of Western Odisha, one of the poorest parts of India. Agragamee combines conventional learning and political education with developing new leadership styles amongst tribal children (Ramachandran, 2003). Teaching–learning in the Agragamee schools is informal, drawing on teachers from among the local youth. Timings are flexible and teaching content and practices draw on the everyday life, culture and language of the community. Adults from the community also remain fully involved in the running of the schools. Education in Agragamee schools combines general awareness and empowerment activities for adults through watershed development, food security and livelihood activities. The school's embeddedness in wider community development activities is demonstrated by the fact that the school is also used as an open forum for planning, with children participating in the process. Issues and processes related to community development are also included in the school curriculum (UNESCO, 2003). In addition to strengthening awareness around tribal rights, Agragamee has also succeeded in mainstreaming *adivasi* children into formal state-run schools.

The examples discussed here reflect, in some form, the intent of the National Curriculum Framework (NCF) of 2005, which sought to make equality an essential part of the drive for quality education. This framework laid out an expanded vision for school curricula, aiming to be responsive to local diversity and regional contexts, recognising different forms of knowledge construction and promoting citizenship and social and economic change through education. For example, the framework stated that students should 'connect knowledge to life outside school' and that teachers should 'ensure that learning is shifted away from rote methods', as well as calling for the abolition of caste and gender stereotypes in textbooks (NCERT, 2005, n.p.) This was radical in spirit and provided a philosophical base for redesigning curricula, classroom teaching and evaluation methods.

Concluding thoughts

This chapter has aimed to illustrate how, in India, some exciting innovations in schooling are drawing upon transformative educational approaches that seek to empower children and youth. By so doing, such innovations also support wider social empowerment in communities that until now have remained marginalised and disadvantaged due to their social class and caste positions. The examples cited reflect initiatives with different characteristics and approaches to addressing various kinds of inequality. The policy of using education volunteers to address the issue of access inequality experienced by marginalised communities contributes to bringing greater diversity into schools, together with a more inclusive idea of citizenship and entitlement to basic rights. In addition, the cadre of education volunteers helps to close the education gap between castes and classes; furthermore, the volunteers themselves also become agents for the promotion of more inclusive all-round development in the wider community.

The second example provided goes a step further by creating an institutional link between the local community and the existing school system. These educational institutions recognise the differentiated needs of learners from social groups that have historically been excluded from formal learning opportunities and development efforts. The outcomes of such recognition have been reflected in the use of language and the adaptation of textbook content to the specific contexts of the different learners involved.

The third set of examples demonstrates how participatory approaches can be applied to education with the aim of explicitly addressing issues of power and knowledge inequalities. The collective construction of knowledge and the empowerment activities that have been central to the learning agendas of these cases illustrate ways in which this approach to education challenges established class hierarchies. In addition, these approaches directly contribute to community development and strategies to promote social change.

It is clear that in a nation such as India, which has a huge population and deeply embedded inequalities, change will be difficult to achieve on a large scale – even with examples such as those cited in this chapter from which to learn. As many development interventions have demonstrated, the quest to 'scale up' involves taking a challenging road, even if it is paved with good intentions. However, as the examples suggest, there appears to be a growing recognition at the levels of the nation, the state and the community of the importance of improving the experience of education for all children: an ambition bolstered by the clarion call for a set of universally accepted sustainable development goals. Perhaps, as a consequence of such relatively experimental transformative educational innovations that link directly to change at the wider community level, important lessons can be learned. These lessons can, in turn, help to improve the life experiences of marginalised citizens and challenge the structural impediments posed by caste and class in India and beyond.

References

Adharshila Learning Centre (2014) *Annual Report 2013–14*, www. adharshilalearningcentre.org/2014/05/annual-report-2013-14. html#Introduction

Apple, M.W. (1978) 'Ideology, reproduction, and educational reform', *Comparative Education Review*, 22(3): 367–87.

Bandyopadhyay, M. (2012) 'Social disparity in elementary education', *Seminar*, 638, http://www.india-seminar.com/2012/638/638_ madhumita.htm

Bhattacharjea, S., Wadhwa, W. and Banerji, R. (2011) *Inside primary schools: A study of teaching and learning in rural India*, New Delhi: ASER Centre.

Bivens, F., Moriarty, K. and Taylor, P. (2009) 'Transformative education and its potential for changing the lives of children in disempowering contexts', *IDS Bulletin*, 40(1): 97–108.

Bourdieu, P. (1977) *Outline of a theory of practice*, Cambridge: Cambridge University Press.

Brennan J. and Lebeau, Y. (2002) *The role of universities in the transformation of societies: An international research project*, paper presented at the CHER 15th Annual Conference, 5–7 September 2002, Vienna, Austria.

Centre for Equity Studies (2014) *India exclusion report 2013–14*, New Delhi: Books for Change.

Clark, B.R. (1962) *Educating the expert society*, San Francisco, CA: Chandler.

Consortium for Research on Educational Access, Transitions and Equity (CREATE) (2011) *Absenteeism, repetition and silent exclusion in India*, CREATE India Policy Brief, www.create-rpc.org/pdf_documents/India_Policy_Brief_3.pdf

Durkheim, E. (1972) *Education and sociology*, New York, NY: The Free Press.

Fals-Borda, O. (2001) 'Participatory (action) research in social theory: origins and challenges', in P. Reason and H. Bradbury (eds) *Handbook of action research: Participative inquiry and practice*, London: Sage, pp 28–47.

Foucault, M. (1979) *Power/knowledge: Selected interviews and other writings, 1972–1977*, Brighton: Harvester Publishing.

Freire, P. (1970) *Pedagogy of the oppressed*, New York, NY: Seabury Press

Freire, P. (1985) *The politics of education: Culture, power and liberation*, translated by D. Macedo, London: Macmillan Publishers Ltd.

Giroux, H. (1993) *Living dangerously*, New York, NY: Peter Lang.

Harriss, J. (2012) 'Reflections on caste and class, hierarchy and dominance', *Seminar*, 633, http://www.india-seminar.com/2012/633/633_john_harriss.htm

Illich, I. (1971) *Deschooling society*, New York, NY: Harper and Row.

Johnston, R. (2003) 'Adult learning and citizenship: clearing the ground', in P. Coare and R. Johnston (eds) *Adult learning, citizenship and community voices: exploring community-based practice*, London: NIACE, pp 3–21.

Merrifield, J. (2002) *Learning citizenship*, Working paper 158, Falmer: IDS.

Mezirow, J. (2000) *Learning as transformation: Critical perspectives on a theory in progress*, San Francisco, CA: Jossey-Bass.

Ministry of Human Resource Development, Government of India (1986) *National policy on education, 1986*, Delhi: Government of India.

Mott, A. (2005) *University education for community change: a vital strategy for progress on poverty, race and community-building*, Washington: Community Learning Project.

NCERT (National Council of Education Research and Training) (2005) 'National curriculum framework', http://www.ncert.nic.in/rightside/links/pdf/framework/english/nf2005.pdf

Oommen, T.K. (2012) 'Ideology, culture and structure', *Seminar*, 638, http://www.india-seminar.com/2012/638/638_t_k_oommen.htm

Pretty, J., Guijt, I.,Thompson, J. and Scoones, I. (1995) *Participatory learning and action: A trainer's guide*, London: IIED.

Ramachandran, V. (2003) 'Backward and forward linkages that strengthen primary education', *Economic and Political Weekly*, 38(10): 959–62.

Ramachandran, V. and Naorem, T. (2013) 'What it means to be a *Dalit* or tribal child in our schools: a synthesis of a six-state qualitative study', *Economic and Political Weekly*, xlviii(44): 43–52.

Sayed, Y., Subrahmanian, R., Soudien, C., Carrim, N., Balgopalan, S., Nekhwevha, F. and Samuel, M. (2007) *Education, exclusion and inclusion: Policy and implementation in South Africa and India*, London: DFID.

Taylor, P. and Fransman, J. (2004) 'Learning and teaching participation: exploring the role of Higher Learning Institutions as agents of development and social change', *Institute of Development Studies Working Paper 219*, https://www.ids.ac.uk/ids/bookshop/wp/wp219.pdf

UNESCO (2003) *Six projects from rural India: Non-formal education for sustainable development*, Paris: UNESCO.

United Nations (2014) *Open working group proposal for sustainable development goals*, New York, NY: United Nations.

THIRTEEN

Community development and class in the context of an East Asian productivist welfare regime

Kwok-kin Fung

Introduction

This chapter argues that class analyses have been underdeveloped in community development studies in Hong Kong and that this has impacted on the ways in which community development services have developed. This paucity of class analysis is revealed through the findings of a study that the author conducted to exploring community development service organisations' approaches to service planning and delivery. In this chapter, the context of Hong Kong as a productivist welfare regime will be introduced to provide background for the subsequent discussion. Finally, the wider implications of these analytical lacunae will be considered.

Hong Kong as a productivist welfare regime

Hong Kong has been undergoing a form of economic globalisation, which has been restructuring the economy away from export-oriented manufacturing to service domination over the past two decades (Chiu et al, 1997). This process has testified to the government's de facto support for the financial and commercial complex and its associated neglect of manufacturing industries (Chiu, 1994). Concomitantly, continual inflows of foreign direct investment (FDI) to the finance and producer service sectors have reinforced the dominance of the financial sector and of Hong Kong as the key regional finance centre. Together with the growing importance of the real estate industry, the trade, finance and tourist industries have become the four main sectors of the economy (Enright et al, 1999). In addition, the economy of Hong Kong is renowned for its domination by giant corporations in most sectors (see Castells et al, 1990). For example, giant developers in the real estate industry and the giant commercial banks are powerful players, and they maintain close relationships with the government. Such state–business relations have, in fact, mediated these deindustrialisation processes (Chiu et al, 1997).

Following the end of the colonial era in 1997, the Basic Law, under the reign of China, constituted an executive-led government of the Special Administrative Region (SAR). The state's executive was to be chosen by a group of 1,200 electors by 2014: a group in which major business interests are overrepresented. The legislative council operates under an electoral arrangement through which the interests of businesses and related professionals are protected. The prevalence of neoliberal ideology within the government and among the middle class is all too evident in Hong Kong; it is under such a political–economic configuration that the government has promoted the characteristics of its status as a productivist welfare regime.

Studies focusing on welfare regimes highlight the main characteristics of Hong Kong as a developmental state (see, for example, Tang, 2000). Specifically, the colonial and SAR governments have both placed a high priority on economic growth as the main mechanism for the improvement of the welfare of its citizens. So the social policy provisions – which concern health; housing; education, personal social services and social security – are predominantly evaluated according to their productive functions or their contributions to economic growth. Services such as education and housing are regarded as particularly relevant in terms of their contributions to facilitating economic growth through ameliorating the quality of labour and so, in turn, contributing to the development of a more productive workforce (Tang, 2000). As a result, they receive remarkably higher levels of public resources than personal social services and social security, for example, as these mostly serve those who are out of paid employment – even though they also sustain social stability and legitimise the government (Gough and Wood, 2004).

As a whole, the middle class has been receiving higher levels of public resources than disadvantaged groups, while the government presumes that the family should shoulder the responsibility of care for young, old and disabled people, and the disadvantaged in general. In addition, the SAR government inherited the orientation of the colonial government towards the role of the community, since '[social welfare] objective(s) cannot be achieved without the support from the community through the establishment of networks of informal care and support provided by families, friends and neighbours' (Social Welfare Department, 1991, para.19). By emphasising the capacity of the community to cater for the needs of its members in the design of welfare services, the government actively made use of assumed caring capacities in the community – in addition to those of the family – thereby justifying its minimalist approach to the provision of personal social services.

Community development services since the 1980s

Community development services in Hong Kong include independent programmes alongside government-funded social welfare service programmes. The targets of these services are entire communities, defined mostly in a geographical sense. Since the 1980s, these have consisted mainly of Neighbourhood Level Community Development Projects (NLCDPs) and Community Centres (CCs). Non-governmental organisations (NGOs) employ separate teams of social workers to deliver these government-funded services. The subvention of these programmes fell under the ambit of the City and New Territories Administration Department in the colonial era before becoming the responsibility of the Home Affairs Bureau in the SAR era.

The programmes serve to facilitate the overall administration of Hong Kong through enhancing communication between the government and its citizens (Home Affairs Bureau, n.d.). However, the actual management of these programmes has been the domain of the Social Welfare Department (SWD) more specifically, and this has been the case during both the colonial and SAR eras. The manifest objectives of these programmes has been – and continues to be – to build community strengths, promote mutual help, encourage community cohesion and participation and serve the needs of disadvantaged groups (Home Affairs Bureau, 2005). The NLCDPs focus on transient communities in particular, including communities in squatter areas, temporary housing areas (THAs) built by the government, rural villages and public housing estates under redevelopment. The CCs, in contrast, are services provided to stable communities in a larger area, and serve a population of 100,000 to 150,000.

Despite being funded by government, having the official goal of managing communications between the government and its citizens and being in a context that lacks formal democratic structures, the actual implementation of these services involves conflict (Mok and Kam, 1994). Some emphasise the structural causation of the presenting social problems and the associated conflicts of interest, pointing to the significance of social movements in fostering the structural changes needed. Others, in contrast, adopt the type of confrontational tactics more associated with social action (see, for example, Alinsky, 1972) but without attending to the underlying structural causes (Fung et al, 1994). Despite these differences, though, community workers generally share the goal of empowering community members, using conflict approaches to foster policy changes when necessary. This has actually been the case from the 1970s onwards, as the popularity of protest actions during the colonial era of Hong Kong illustrates. Wong (1989), for example, identified resource allocation processes as key factors in limiting government control over such protests. As resources have been given to NGOs to deliver such programmes, the government has so far lacked the mechanisms through which to regulate the projects and centres, even if it would have liked to do so. This provides a framework for understanding the continued proliferation of conflict approaches in community empowerment in Hong Kong.

Since the mid 1980s, the NLCDP programme has been affected by the demolition of transient communities' informal settlements, as the government gradually cleaned up the squatter areas and THAs without replacing them with community development projects. As the communities serviced by the CCs have been larger and more stable communities in contrast, programmes should be better able to survive in these areas. However, the SWD proposed to merge CCs with family service centres following the 2003 interim review of the Integrated Family Service Centres, thereby posing a different threat to their continued independent existence. Through the late 1990s and early 2000s, these government attempts to terminate the NLCDP and CC programmes were met with large-scale mobilisations of community workers, service recipients and academics in tertiary social work training institutes. Together they succeeded in keeping the 13 CCs open, which they remain today. For the NLCDPs, meanwhile, there are 16 projects remaining, serving mainly rural communities.

There are other community development projects of short duration relying upon time-limited government funding, too. Under the influence of its neoliberal orientation, since the turn of the century the SAR government has followed 'new public management' principles and initiated a series of related welfare reforms. These have included competitive tendering for funds to provide short-term projects to meet the needs of disadvantaged communities. CCs and NLCDPs have increasingly counted on successfully bidding for such additional funds (Tsui et al, 2013). As a result, NGOs have become concerned not to jeopardise their relationships with government and funding departments have been accused of highly regulative behaviour towards the service provision delivered by project workers (Fung, 2014b; Fung & Wong, 2014).

Introducing the study

The research upon which the analysis of this chapter is based is a qualitative study conducted in the latter half of 2014 (Wong and Fung, 2014). The study aimed to explore the factors affecting the decisions of mainstream community development services in Hong Kong in relation to planning and delivering services. The research consisted of in-depth interviews with community workers involved in 15 community development projects together with analysis of secondary data including project reports and publications. Curricula of the courses on community work and community development, provided by five educational institutions, were also studied to explore how these forms of training might have impacted on community workers' perspectives and understandings.

Following purposive sampling, 15 CC and NLCDP projects were selected for study, covering a diversity of services aimed at various target groups with varying sources of funding. This enabled the views of the range of social workers who work for mainstream community development services to be captured.

Limited class studies in the social sciences and community development fields

Class had been at best a minor theme in social sciences disciplines in Hong Kong before the 1990s. An academic opined at the time:

> Indeed, 'class' seems to be ruled out in most discourses. In most studies, not only is there a systematic shirking of the task of constructing class maps capturing the post-war development of the society, there is also, in my view, a premature verdict on the irrelevance of class either as a socio-political force or as consciousness. (Wang, 1993, p.277)

Of the few studies adopting a class perspective, most favoured a gradational approach (see Crompton, 2000). In this way, they focused on the income, wealth and/or educational level attained by individuals or household heads. The analysis was therefore mostly concerned with the resulting differential outcomes or living conditions between individuals or families possessing different levels of resources (see, for example, Lee, 1976; Cheung & Yuen, 1987; Drakakis-Smith, 1979). The popularity (if not the dominance) of a consensus model in the social sciences disciplines could partly account for such a trend. This can be understood in the political context of Hong Kong as a capitalist economy under British rule, with the Socialist state of China across the border. Political and economic elites at that time did not favour a conflict approach in general, or in relation to class analysis in particular.

By the 1990s, drawing upon both Goldthorpe's concept of class on the one hand and the neo-Marxist version developed by Eric Olin Wright and others on the other (see Crompton, 2000), studies adopting similar approaches emerged in Hong Kong (Cheung, 1988; Wong & Lui, 1992a, 1992b). Most of these studies adopted Goldthorpe's approach to identify the existence of different social classes and class mobility patterns, their different political cultures and ways of life. These studies concentrated mostly on the new middle or 'service' class, finding them more socially mobile, valuing political participation and exhibiting particular lifestyles. In addition, there were studies on the differential social outcomes of social classes (Chan, 1994; Lui, 1997). Examples include studies of the educational performance of students of different classes, for instance, demonstrating how middle-class children were attaining higher levels as a result of their well-resourced family background (Tsang, 1993). There were also debates on differing methodological approaches (Wong & Lui, 1992b; Chan, 1995).

Democratisation processes in Hong Kong – as a result of decolonisation – provided further stimulus for critical social science research drawing upon political economy perspectives. Examples of such studies include research that countered the then-dominant view of Hong Kong's economy as a free market with limited government regulation, exposing the active role that had been played by a state committed to sustaining the reproduction of the colony's capitalist economy (Tang, 1998). There were also studies revealing how changes in the political economic environment (including the migration of capital and labour from mainland China following the Communist Revolution of 1949) had facilitated the economic development of Hong Kong (Castells et al, 1990). And there were studies focusing on economic growth in relation to land, housing and urban processes (Appelbaum & Henderson, 1992). In addition, there were critical studies documenting the difficulties being faced by disadvantaged communities and the persistence of social inequality (Chui et al, 1998; Fung & Hung, 1999). In relation to the field of community development more specifically, there were local academics who were arguing for the importance of class analysis, drawing upon a political economy perspective as among the core theories of practice for community workers (Fung et al, 1994). The 1990s was the era, then, which witnessed the development of these critical perspectives as indispensable themes in the social science disciplines in Hong Kong.

However, subsequent theoretical developments in the UK and the US have few counterparts in class analysis in Hong Kong. This diminishing interest has been reflected in the number of publications in which class remains – at most – an aspect of identity, rather than a central theme to be explored in the social sciences. The few available studies have included research into the ways in which cultural capital is reproduced (Waters, 2006) and studies examining the educational difficulties of children from lower-class families (Tam & Chan, 2009). Other examples include studies of the attitudes of different social classes towards social welfare, social order and voting rights (Wong et al, 2009) along with studies examining working-class communities' limited access to home purchase and poor living environments (La Grange, 2011; Fung, 2014a). Few class studies have seriously addressed the overall context of increasing social inequality in Hong Kong, however, despite the fact that the Gini coefficient has been worsening since the 2000s and attained a record high of 0.537 in 2006.

Underdevelopment of class perspectives in the community development field

The preceding discussion provided the sociopolitical and academic context within which community development theory and practice are located. An examination of the community work and related curricula of five social work training universities in Hong Kong revealed that they were all covering topics relating to class or drawing upon political economy perspectives. The theoretical components of community work have also included such courses as 'principles and values of community work'; 'ideology and community work'; 'community organising'; 'advocacy and social action'; 'conflict approach and social action', 'structural social work' and 'radical social work'. Conflict approaches and social action have also been included in the common core of practice skills. In addition, references showing clear preferences for class or political economy perspectives have been included.

Class perspectives: conflict- and service-based approaches

Despite all this, and taking account of the ways in which class or political economy perspectives have been embedded in social work education on community development, it appears that community workers have rarely adopted such perspectives when it comes to making decisions in practice. In fact, the findings of the research study reveal that class analysis has not been significant in informing the services that they provide. For example, when prompted, nine out of 16 interviewees preferred the term 'grassroots' to 'social class'. Although they rarely referred to the movement of capital or adopted political economy perspectives, however, those interviewed were still aware of the critical role of government in furthering or inhibiting the interests of the 'grassroots'.

The increasing dominance of direct service provision was confirmed by the research. Social recreational (8 out of 8 centres; 7 out of 7 projects), educational (8 out of 8 centres; 7 out of 7 projects) and volunteer development programmes (4 out of 8 centres; 6 out of 7 projects) emerged as predominant across the board. Community economic initiatives were similarly numerous (7 out of 8 centres; 6 out of 7 projects). Individual counselling services were also found in both CCs (5 out of 8) and NLCDPs (7 out of 7). This is a distinct change from the 1990s, when counselling and family support services were considered as core to conventional social work rather than to community development projects and programmes. In contrast, community organising work, which involved mainly conflict approaches in the 1990s, now emerged as relatively less significant (4 out of 8 centres; 4 out of 7 projects).

This prevalence of community economic initiatives and volunteer development programmes, conventionally involving the facilitation of mutual self-help, was also echoed in the pattern identified from the webpage analysis. As a whole, the increasing popularity of direct service provision, involving mainly consensual approaches and the facilitation of community mutual help, is evident.

A further analysis of the reasons provided by interviewees for their choices of work approaches reveals their differential conceptions of community development. In general, these can be broadly classified into two groups: those regarding community organising as essential (the conflict approach group) and those emphasising service provision (the consensus approach group). The balance of approaches among the groups interviewed was more or less equal.

A typical commitment to 'community organising' among those who adopted a conflict approach is suggested in the following comment: 'Our major services are of different kinds and organising work must be included. As everyone knows, community development must take organising work as its top priority.' For this group, a conflict approach was treated as an intrinsic feature of community development.

For those who primarily adopted a consensus approach, in contrast, the following view was typical: 'If I can help, I will. If I cannot, I will refer [them] to other service organisations that can offer help. This is actually what all community centres typically do.'

This second group of seven projects was mainly adopting a consensus approach, then, providing various social, recreational, and educational projects and programmes. These workers were effectively embracing the identities of conventional social workers, as reflected in the views of one worker:

> [A]ctually these activities are what social workers do. Through group and case [work] ... and delivering programmes ... these are the three typical intervention methods. Of course, case work is the least as it is not the core work of community centres.'

What this suggests is that an increasing number of community workers appear to be taking on a social work identity, which relates – at least partly – to their adoption of mainly consensual approaches. It is of course significant that of this group four projects relied mainly upon short-term project-based funding. The constraints and tensions that this creates are captured well by an one of the interviewees in this group: 'Our funding is all project-based. It means that we have to solicit funding for the project in order to keep a staff member here and get another project funded to keep one more colleague there.'

This clearly relates, in turn, to concerns about jeopardising relationships with funders and thereby limiting their choices of work approaches even further.

As mentioned earlier, the continual marginalisation of the community development field and the bidding process in allocating welfare service resources have arguably contributed to this tendency to submit to the preferences of funders and the government. One interviewee, for example, recounted an incident in which their team had been helping residents to protest against the government, and speculated that 'maybe we have already been blacklisted by the government. It might explain why we always lost in bidding for new social service projects.' It is clearly the case that funding concerns pose great constraints on the use of conflict approaches.

The reduction of conflict-based approaches in community development

Further analysis of the responses of workers in the conflict-based approach group confirms the diminishing number of incidents of social action in recent years. Thus one social worker explained: 'when I review the past 15 years, my impression is that in the past, residents felt like fighting for their rights more.' Another worker suggested that '[t]here are recently no longer those CD work[ers] adopting conflict-based approaches'. Another made a similar observation: 'the use of this kind of strategy [conflict approach] is less [frequent] in recent years'. Such comments reveal a reduction in social action in recent years.

It is relevant that interviewees who did adopt conflict approaches highlighted the significance of coalition building in facilitating social action. The view expressed by one worker was representative here: 'If only our residents fight for changes, the whole issue cannot be raised to a higher level [societal concern] … [Through coalition building] we can join with more participants, academics or residents from different communities.'

However, some of these projects also testified to the diminishing number of coalitions, and social actions involving coalitions, in recent years. The observations of one project echoed those of others: '[i]n the recent few years … we experienced great difference from the past. We find it difficult to initiate coalition activities.'

It has become clear that this downward trend of coalition development has reinforced the diminishing effectiveness of conflict approaches in the field.

Given the seriousness of current rates of income inequality, it is unsurprising that some interviewees highlighted the ways in which residents felt constrained from participating in social actions. In particular, they highlighted the adverse impact of long working hours as a major obstacle. It is ironic, then, that increasing income inequality creates the very conditions that limit the capacity of disadvantaged communities to resort to conflict approaches, thereby reinforcing the current emphasis on community mutual help initiatives.

The increasing popularity of consensus approaches has been linked to a number of factors, then, including increasing emphases on service provision and community mutual help initiatives and declining incidents of social action, with fewer policy-focused coalitions in recent years. Such factors have also constrained the use of conflict approaches. Because class analyses have become increasingly marginalised in practice, there is less scope for the development of holistic strategies for structural change. And conversely, the increasing popularity of consensus-based approaches has been associated with the weakening of the community development field's capacities for empowering the most disadvantaged communities to pursue agendas for social change.

The impact of the under-development of class analyses in the social sciences and community development field in general has also emerged from this research. For example, community development workers have paid scant attention to the dynamics of global finance capital in spite of the fact that the banking sector is one of the four clusters sustaining the economic growth of Hong Kong. As a result, there have been few – if any – examples of the types of protest actions that characterised responses elsewhere in the wake of the financial crisis of 2008. Furthermore, the ways in which commercial banks have passed the debts that led to the financial crisis on to the working class have not been publicly denounced in Hong Kong as they have been elsewhere. Last but not least, the opinion expressed by the SAR governor at the height of the Occupy movement in Hong Kong (late 2014), regarding how popular sovereignty inevitably generated policy favouring the working class, has received neither criticism from a class perspective nor protest actions within the community development field.

Conclusion

Class analysis has been underdeveloped in Hong Kong; this has been the case since the colonial era. The 1990s witnessed a flowering of interest in class analysis and the proliferation of studies adopting a political economy perspective in different social sciences disciplines. However, by the 2000s, this interest had subsided. This declining interest in class studies has been evident despite – or perhaps also partially because of – the wider context in which Hong Kong has been experiencing worsening social inequality and declining welfare for the most disadvantaged communities. This is particularly alarming because Hong Kong has been pursuing a productivist welfare regime, which combines reliance upon economic growth with limitations on welfare provision for the poorest. Meanwhile, the paucity of class analysis reinforces the popularity of the consensus approach and its implications in terms of the promotion of competitive tendering to provide services and the promotion of community mutual help initiatives. These parallel shifts have been accompanied by declining incidents of social action and fewer social action coalitions. Community development has, therefore, experienced continuing marginalisation, while social inequality has continued to increase. Even though the curricula in most of the Hong Kong's community development training institutions in Hong Kong haves included afforded attention to class perspectives, the paucity of class analysis apparent in community development theory and practice deserves continual attention and further research.

References

Alinsky, S.D. (1972) *Rules for radicals: A practical primer for realistic radicals*, New York, NY: Vintage Books.

Appelbaum, R.P. and Henderson, J. (eds) (1992) *States and development in the Asian Pacific rim*, Newbury Park, CA: Sage Publications.

Castells, M., Goh, L. and Kwok, R.Y. (1990) *The Shek Kip Mei syndrome: Economic development and public housing in Hong Kong and Singapore*, London: Pion.

Chan, T. (1994) *Social mobility in Hong Kong*, Oxford: Oxford University Press.

Chan, T. (1995) 'Optimal matching analysis', *Work and Occupations*, 22(4): 467–90.

Cheung, B. (1988) 'Political impact of the Hong Kong new middle class', in B. Cheung, D. Lui, M.H. Chan and W.B. Wong (eds), *Class analysis and Hong Kong*, (in Chinese), Hong Kong: Ching Men, pp 9–26.

Cheung, F.M. and Yuen, R. (1987) *Psychological and social characteristics related to social participation among working-class housewives in Hong Kong*, Hong Kong: Centre for Hong Kong Studies, Institute of Social Studies, Chinese University of Hong Kong.

Chiu, S.W. (1994) *The politics of laissez-faire: Hong Kong's strategy of industrialization in historical perspective*, Hong Kong: Hong Kong Institute of Asia–Pacific Studies, Chinese University of Hong Kong.

Chiu, S.W., Ho, K.C. and Lui, D. (1997) *City-states in the global economy: Industrial restructuring in Hong Kong and Singapore*, Boulder, CO: Westview Press.

Chui, E.W.T., Wong, Y.C., Ip, F., Lo, E. and Chi, I. (1998) 'Community support for frail elderly in public housing', *Hong Kong Journal of Gerontology*, 12(1): 34–42.

Crompton, R. (2000) *Renewing class analysis*, Malden, MA: Blackwell.

Drakakis-Smith, D.W. (1979) *High society housing provision in metropolitan Hong Kong, 1954 to 1979: A jubilee critique*, Hong Kong: Centre of Asian Studies, University of Hong Kong.

Enright, M.J., Scott, E.E. and Leung, H.K. (1999) *Hong Kong's competitiveness beyond the Asian crisis: An overview*, Hong Kong: Hong Kong Trade Development Council.

Fung, K.K. (2014a) 'Financial crisis and the developmental states: A case study of Hong Kong', *International Journal of Social Welfare*, 23(3): 321–32.

Fung, K.K. (2014b) *Exploration on the welfare bidding system of Hong Kong* in Chinese), Hong Kong: Hong Kong Social Workers' General Union.

Fung, K.K. and Hung, S.L. (1999) 'Rethinking services for new arrival women from Mainland China', in K.K. Fung (ed), *Convention and innovation, community development into the 21ˢᵗ century*, (in Chinese), Hong Kong: Community Service Division, Hong Kong Council of Social Services, pp 53–72.

Fung, K.K. and Wong, K. (2014) 'Neoliberalisation and urban redevelopment', *Proceedings of global social sciences conference 2014*, 7–9 April, Hong Kong Baptist University.

Fung, K.K., Wu, M.L. and Chui, W.T. (1994) 'The theoretical foundation of community work', in B.K. Kam, J. Leung, L.W. Chan, H.S. Lam, M.L. Wu, K.K. Fung and M.T. Wong (eds), *Community work theory and practice*, (in Chinese), Hong Kong: Chinese University Press, pp 79–116.

Gough, I. and Wood, G.D. (2004) *Insecurity and welfare regimes in Asia, Africa, and Latin America: Social policy in development contexts*, Cambridge and New York: Cambridge University Press.

Home Affairs Bureau (n.d.), *Home Affairs Bureau website*, www.hab.gov.hk

Home Affairs Bureau (2005) *Position paper on community development policy*, Hong Kong: Government Printer.

La Grange, A. (2011) 'Neighbourhood and class: A study of three neighbourhoods in Hong Kong', *Urban Studies*, 48(6): 1181–200.

Lee, R.P. (1976) *Sex and social class differences in mental illness: The case of Hong Kong*, Hong Kong: Social Research Centre, Chinese University of Hong Kong.

Lui, T. (1997) 'The Hong Kong new middle class on the eve of 1997', in J. Cheng (ed), *The other Hong Kong report 1997*, Hong Kong: Chinese University of Hong Kong, pp 207–26.

Mok, H.L. and Kam, B.K. (1994) 'Social action', in B.K. Kam, J. Leung, L.W. Chan, H.S. Lam, M.L. Wu, K.K. Fung and M.T. Wong (eds), *Community work theory and practice*, (in Chinese), Hong Kong: Chinese University Press, pp 135–70.

Social Welfare Department (1991) *White paper: Social welfare into the 1990s and beyond*, Hong Kong: Government Printer.

Tam, V.C. and Chan, R.M. (2009) 'Parental involvement in primary children's homework in Hong Kong', *School Community Journal*, 19(2): 81.

Tang, K. (1998) *Colonial state and social policy: Social welfare development in Hong Kong 1842–1997*, Lanham, MD: University Press of America.

Tang, K. (2000) *Social welfare development in East Asia*, Houndmills and New York, NY: Palgrave.

Tsang, W. (1993) *Educational and early socioeconomic status attainment in Hong Kong*, Hong Kong: Chinese University of Hong Kong.

Tsui, V., Lee, A. and Chui, E. (2013) 'Social welfare in Hong Kong', in S. Furuto (ed), *Social welfare in East Asia and the Pacific*, New York, NY: Columbia University Press, pp 67–86.

Wang, T. (1993) 'The new middle-class in Hong Kong: Class in formation?', in H.M. Hsiao (ed), *Discovery of the middle classes in East Asia*, Taiwan: Institute of Ethnology, Academia Sinica, pp 273–306.

Waters, J.L. (2006) 'Geographies of cultural capital: education, international migration and family strategies between Hong Kong and Canada', *Transactions of the Institute of British Geographers*, 31(2): 179–92.

Wong, C.K. (1989) *Social action and Hong Kong*, (in Chinese), Hong Kong: Ching Men.

Wong, K. L. and Fung, K.K. (2014) *Exploration of community development projects in Hong Kong*, unpublished research report.

Wong, T.W.P. and Lui, D. (1992a) *From one brand of politics to one brand of political culture*, Hong Kong: Hong Kong Institute of Asia–Pacific Studies, Chinese University of Hong Kong.

Wong, T.W.P. and Lui, D. (1992b) *Reinstating class: A structural and developmental study of Hong Kong society*, Hong Kong: Social Sciences Research Centre, University of Hong Kong.

Wong, T.K., Wan, S.P. and Law, K.W. (2009) 'Welfare attitudes and social class: The case of Hong Kong in comparative perspective', *International Journal of Social Welfare*, 18(2): 142–52.

FOURTEEN

Community organising for social change: the scope for class politics

Marilyn Taylor and Mandy Wilson

Introduction

In 2010, as part of its commitment to creating a 'Big Society', the newly elected UK Coalition Government announced a four-year programme to train a new generation of Community Organisers in England. After a period under the previous government in which, it argued, community programmes had been top-down and government-led, this was one of a number of initiatives claiming to put power back in the hands of people and to encourage them to take a more active role in their communities.

However, these initiatives were introduced against a background of austerity policies, which were to have a disproportionate impact on low-income and working-class households (Browne and Elming, 2015). In this context, the Coalition's community programmes have been strongly criticised for expecting communities to substitute for a declining public sector and failing to address the root causes of disadvantage. Nonetheless, it is claimed that community organising, based on the work of Saul Alinsky (1971), has the potential to provide a more radical approach. The question is whether it has delivered on this promise and to what extent it offers the kind of class-based approach for which this book argues.

This chapter looks at community organising through the lens of the government-funded England-wide programme, which ran from 2011 to 2015, and explores the extent to which its approach has the potential to reintroduce a class dimension to community development practice in England. Much of its content is informed by interviews with a range of people who have direct experience of the programme.

The context

Some commentators (such as Carley and Smith, 2001, p.87) argue that traditional movements built around class cannot articulate the increasingly diverse interests in society today. The advance of the market, consumerism and individualism has redefined allegiances and identities and undermined solidarity. The changing structure of the labour market has fragmented workforces and destabilised working practices. Communities and the workplace are no longer bound together as they once were, and the organisations of the working class reflect these changes. The nonconformist chapels, the working men's clubs and the mechanics institutes, in which working-class culture was forged and reproduced and where working-class people got their political education (Thompson, 1963), scarcely exist. More recently, libraries and community centres have also disappeared. These successive losses leave many people without any anchor or voice in a rapidly changing society.

Class identities have also been affected by the increasing demonisation of the poor, fanned by politicians and the media. 'Strivers' are compared to 'scroungers' and 'hard-working' families are contrasted unfavourably to those that are 'dependent' on benefits (Jones, 2011). Disadvantaged communities are often marked by ethnic division too, as the poor compete with each other for the crumbs that society appears increasingly reluctant to give them. There is a particularly potent rhetoric around immigration, with the rise of far-right politics in some working-class communities. But the racism and ethnic stereotyping attached to debates on immigration is increasingly matched by a vilification of white working-class communities: 'Typically [white working-class] communities are viewed as being problematic, dysfunctional and occupying annexed council estates. Fixed attributes are ascribed rather than recognising individuals residing in different areas with composite identities' (Beider, 2011, p.6).

Community development and class

Finding the points of solidarity within this context of diversity and change poses major challenges for community development. Of course, historical analysis tells us that community development in the UK has a patchy history when it comes to understanding the dynamics of class and challenging the causes of inequality (see, for example, CDP, 1977; Corkey and Craig, 1978). The term community development itself famously encompasses a wide range of values, ideologies and approaches (Taylor, 2011). While the authors understand the term to cover a variety of methods and skills employed through the practice of both paid community workers and unpaid activists, it is also defined here as a practice that supports leadership and collective action by those seeking social justice, and one that should be strategically focused on transforming the political, social and economic relationships between people and the state.

A commitment to this kind of transformative or radical practice has ebbed and flowed over the decades. The dominant practices of the postcolonial era in the UK, and the community programmes introduced by successive governments in the 1970s, were increasingly challenged over time by the more radical practices of class-conscious community action and alliance-building in the National Community Development Project and elsewhere (Loney, 1983). But this in turn was challenged in the 1980s by the politics of identity and a recognition that spatial communities, far from being a source of shared interest, could also be the site of division, discrimination and competition (Meekosha, 1993). In a globalising world – and under an increasingly neoliberal state formation – a post-industrial class emerged from the 1980s on, characterised by its marginalisation from sources of power but also by its different individual and collective identities (Waddington, 1979).

Meanwhile, political parties of all persuasions were latching onto the communitarian ideologies of the 1990s, emphasising the need for citizens to understand their responsibilities and obligations as well as encouraging them to be more internally resourceful. The communitarian belief in shared values and the common good permeated the policies of the New Labour administration (elected in 1997), whose 'Third Way' discourse has been described as 'a political vocabulary which eschews market individualism, but not capitalism; and which embraces collective action, but not class or the state' (Driver and Martell, 1997, p.33). While the New Labour government introduced a raft of community programmes that rekindled investment in community development, a growing body of opinion argued that its embrace by an increasingly managerial state had squeezed the life – or at least its independence – out of it (Taylor, 2007).

By the end of the New Labour era in 2010, there was a growing interest in doing things differently – both within the community sector and at national policy level – and this is where community organising came in. It wasn't a new model, but in the US its populist methods had been successful in mobilising huge numbers of people in Barack Obama's US election campaign, while in the UK an organisation called Citizens UK was using community organising to mobilise impressive numbers in support of its campaigns (Bunyan, 2010), several of which were very successful. A notable example is the Living Wage Campaign, which has won over £210 million worth of additional wages, lifting 40,000 families out of working poverty.[1] It is significant that community organising has been embraced across the political spectrum, attracting interest from the churches (Changemakers), the Labour Party (the Labour-affiliated Movement for Change) and the trade unions (Unite, Unison and GMB). In 2010, the newly elected centre-right Coalition Government announced its intention to train 500 paid Community Organisers and, through them, to recruit 4,500 more volunteer organisers. The contract to deliver this ambition was awarded to Locality, a community-sector support organisation.

Community organising: an introduction

Community organising is commonly associated with the work of Saul Alinsky in Chicago (Alinsky, 1971). It builds power through alliances of organisations with interests in common – typically community associations, tenants' groups, churches and unions – in order to change policy and practice within government and other institutions. Approaches vary from negotiation through to more confrontational tactics. It has variously been characterised in classifications of community development as community action (Glen, 1993; Rothman with Tropman, 1993), a power-based approach (Smock, 2003) and a 'radical' model (Gilchrist and Taylor, 2011). But since its introduction, it has developed in a number of different directions, of which the Industrial Areas Foundation, ACORN (Associations of Community Organisations for Reform Now) and Slum Dwellers International are perhaps the best known versions (Beck and Purcell, 2013).

The Community Organisers Programme was a one-year training programme (although with scope for continuation) leading to a practice-based qualification for 500 paid Organisers, who were hosted by existing local organisations. The model adopted by Locality was Roots Solution Listening Matters (RSLM): an approach developed by ReGenerate, its training partner. As its name suggests, this model places considerable emphasis on 'listening' as the root of subsequent action, with the impetus for that action placed firmly with the community rather than with the Organiser. As such – and given its parallel emphases on reflection and experiential learning – it is an approach that draws on the 'conscientisation' work of Paulo Freire (1972) as much as the work of Alinsky (Little, 2011).

Community organising and class

As suggested earlier, the relationship between community politics and class politics has been the subject of long-running debates in community development, whatever the approach deployed. This section discusses the scope for a class-based approach in the programme in relation to three particular aspects: government funding, characteristics of Organisers and the emphasis on a community-led approach. The subsequent section goes on to discuss the key challenges that a class perspective on community organising raises in relation to leadership, time and identity.

Community organising: government funding

> 'Government was never going to fund anything that would threaten class war!' (Community Organiser)

There was considerable scepticism about the Coalition government's commitment to a radical community-organising approach (Little, 2011), let alone one that could be class-aware and challenge inequality. Most other community organising programmes follow Alinsky's (1971) lead in staying resolutely independent. Thus for many critics government support was incompatible with any form of serious challenge to neoliberal government policies, which were simultaneously creating conditions that produced ever-rising inequality between the 'haves' and 'have nots', and in which unaccountable private sector companies were fast replacing services provided by the state. These developments have had serious consequences for local democracy. As Goode and Maskovsky (2001, p.9) argue, 'Privatisation removes the poor from a direct relationship to the state, a relationship that historically has been essential to the expression of collective agency for poor communities.' Debates about whether community development in general is simply a sop to the poor and 'part of the software of capitalism' (Bryant and Bryant, 1982, p.142) or whether it has the potential for transforming society are certainly not new. For example, detractors argue that the kind of community organising that has attracted cross-party support is one that is entirely consonant with neoliberal management of the inequalities that arise from a capitalist system and the need to ameliorate the social consequences of an ever-widening gap between the rich and the poor. Alinsky's (1971) mantra, 'don't do for the poor what they can do for themselves', was interpreted by some as suggesting that communities could solve their own problems without the need for state intervention (Mills and Robson, 2010, p.13).

Nevertheless, as reported earlier, Locality wanted to drive a new approach; one in which communities were in the lead, not managed or suffocated by professionals. As well as summoning Alinsky (1971) and Freire (1972) to support its arguments, its successful bid emphasised the importance of 'speaking truth to power' and its methodology championed self-determination, collective action and political influence.

Characteristics of the Organisers

There have been class-based, feminist and anti-racist critiques of Alinsky's (1971) model. These have been partially on the basis that it ignores the structural dimensions and social constructions of race and gender, and that the 'expert' Community Organisers trained were middle-class – and predominantly male – students and professionals, whose task was then to 'go into' communities and train up local leaders (Stall and Stoecker, 1998; Delgado, 1999; Sen, 2003). Within the Community Organisers Programme however, several 'host' organisations made it their mission to 'grow' their staff from the locality, seeing it as essential that local people had the opportunity to train as Community Organisers. To some extent it might be argued that the background of Community Organisers is immaterial; for a class-based approach, it may be more important that they bring a structural analysis to community issues so that class-based alliances can be formed and inequalities challenged. Alternatively, it could be argued that the legacy of the Programme should lie not so much in the 500 paid Community Organisers who it has supported but rather in the 4,500 local leaders who they recruited and trained, and that the programme's success should be judged on the latter.

A community-led approach

The Programme's theory of change concentrated on working with people who are 'disillusioned with government'; who 'feel they are not listened to and have no voice' (Pearce et al, 2011). It also stressed the importance of ensuring that local people define the issues to be addressed. One-to-one listening was therefore a basic tenet of the approach used. This was to ensure that the results of extensive listening programmes were owned by local groups and formed through the listening process rather than by the Organisers – much less the host,

Locality or other funders. This was in reaction to previous programmes in which, Locality felt, government and professionals largely defined the issues and how they were to be addressed.

Community Organisers talk about working without an agenda, listening to residents' concerns and facilitating people to come together to decide their own course of action. Their focus on listening has proved to be essential. People value being listened to – it is an all-too-rare occurrence. Many hosts testified to the value of this approach within their local communities, saying that although the principle of listening to the community had always informed their work, successive regeneration programmes, cuts and the demands of contract work meant that they had gradually lost the capacity for this basic outreach. They also commented on the way that the practice of going out and knocking on doors, listening to people in cafes and other natural gathering places had extended their reach to a more diverse group of people: different ethnic groups in some areas, children and young people in others.

However, starting from community concerns does not necessarily imply tackling inequality or promoting social justice – or, indeed, a class-based approach. It is often the cleaner, greener, safer agenda that emerges as a priority on the doorstep. People focus on the things that they can see in the here and now and often struggle to come up with ideas about what might make their lives better. In addition, their points of reference are often framed by dominant norms and debates in society. As such, they may follow the lead offered by the media and blame the immigrant or 'benefit scrounger' a few doors down rather than the external, structural and more difficult to tackle causes of their problems.

From listening through dialogue to action

Some Community Organisers felt that the type of questions that they were encouraged by RSLM to ask on the doorstep framed residents' responses:

> 'The questions encourage an individualised response: "What can *you* do about it?"' (Community Organiser)

> 'In my imagination, Freire and Alinsky would not have asked people who were concerned about the cuts to local services to volunteer to replace them.' (Community Organiser)

Indeed, the programme has much loftier aspirations:

> We believe that community organising has the potential to establish a new and much healthier social contract between people and power. Community organising, grounded at local level, provides the means for people – above all those who are most excluded from the inner circles of power and privilege – to combine and be counted, to discover their ability to identify those changes which will mean most to them and, on their own terms, take action to tackle vested interests. (Locality funding bid)

The job of the Organiser, one Community Organiser argued, is to turn (personal) problems into (political) issues and to explore why things are as they are. That means extending listening into a dialogue, which needs to be underpinned by further questioning in order to facilitate a deeper critical awareness (in keeping with Freire's process of 'conscientisation', 1972). For some Organisers, the question on the doorstep should not only be 'What can *you* do?' but also 'Who is responsible, and how can we get *them* to sort it out?'. For example, one organising team asked residents if they thought that another, more affluent area had similar problems. When the answer was 'no', they asked why that was the case. Another organising team, faced with the problem of moving from listening to action, decided to organise an exhibition in a public space in which they were working. They created two 'word clouds' – one of residents' positive feelings and one of their concerns – and placed them next to each other. There often seemed to be contradictions. For example, one resident commented that the high levels of security in the tower block, which made people feel safer, also bred isolation among residents. This prompted an interesting conversation about fear of crime. Equally, the word 'community' appeared on the positive list and 'segregation' on the concerns. This led to a discussion between residents of different races and cultures and a recognition that, just by coming together to take action, barriers were being broken down.

As such, the ways in which Community Organisers enter into dialogue with residents, how they frame that dialogue and how they understand the fine balance between helping someone to sort out an immediate problem and enabling them to join with others to take public action may depend on political starting points. There is a tension between on the one hand ensuring that issues are raised by residents themselves and on the other encouraging residents to see beyond the immediate symptoms to the wider causes of the problems that they raise: between 'fishing' and 'pushing', as one Organiser put it. This tension is even sharper when it comes to moving towards action. For example, if several residents want a community allotment, should the Organiser be asking 'why is this necessary?' This might lead to residents knocking on the door of the Town Hall to discuss equity in environmental services or confronting those implementing the welfare reforms that make the ability to buy decent food an everyday struggle.

A further argument is that community organising cannot reach the structural causes of inequality 'if the questions are based around perceptions of the locality alone' (Community Organiser). The challenge of moving from neighbourhood awareness to a broader class-consciousness is hardly new. In the 1970s, Cowley et al (1977), for example, noted how the UK workshop model of organising (which was popular at the time) struggled to move beyond recognition of the problem to effectively challenge the systemic causes of inequality: 'when it comes to the specific tasks of organising, all this is easier said than done. Finding the issue with an immediate appeal is difficult enough, let alone finding the immediate issue which also has clear class dimensions' (Cowley et al, 1977, p.238).

Ultimately, building an effective challenge to the systemic causes of inequality entails making alliances and scaling up. The recognition that change needs to happen beyond the neighbourhood is likely to take time, although it can be developed through small-scale local activities while relationships between people are being built. As one Organiser remarked: 'some people will join with a big end in mind, but others will take it step by step'. The programme only ran for four years in total and Community Organisers were taken on in waves, with the latest cohorts only finishing their first year of training towards the end of the Programme. However, campaigns were beginning to emerge: sometimes within the programme and sometimes initiated by Organisers who had moved on from the programme to create their own initiatives. These included, for example, campaigns on transport and road safety, and on availability and access to decent, secure and affordable housing. In the latter case, one successor initiative had 1,600 people signed up in the area of the city in which it was based and has since gone citywide, while another was building national awareness and harnessing widespread support through social and mainstream media. As one journalist put it: 'The year the grassroots took on the powerful – and won. Ignored communities have forced the elites to listen by getting organised' (Jones, 2014).

Barriers to action

Leadership, time and energy

Community Organisers actively look for local leaders; but research by Pearce and Milne (2010) illustrates how hard-working activists can be sidelined by those around them. In communities that are already suffering from disadvantage and social exclusion, many residents fear that simply raising their heads above the parapet will alienate friends and neighbours. For example, one Community Organiser told of how a woman who was showing real leadership in a community was being accused of 'not being a proper Muslim'. There are many practical barriers too. Economic, social, human and cultural capital are strongly linked (Harflett, 2014), and poverty – along with the stigma it often attracts – is a powerful barrier, both practically and psychologically, to being part of effective and influential social networks. Crisp et al (2014, p.83) suggest that it may be a 'leap of faith' to expect residents who are facing considerable economic pressures to work with others to transform their neighbourhoods (see also Taylor, 2011).

A lack of time and energy are also significant barriers to getting involved in action. One Organiser commented that 'organising the poor is a nightmare'. The current structure of the labour market, with its reliance on zero-hours contracts[2] and part-time working, removes not only the emotional energy required to be involved but also control over free time. Increasingly punitive regulations surrounding benefits and availability for work also limit claimants' capacity to be involved.

Identity and solidarity

> 'The working class today may not work in a factory, be male, or white. They may be a migrant on zero-hours contracts, someone who works in a call centre who is borrowing money to pay the rent, they might be housewives dealing with cuts to the 'social wage' – which means childcare is more expensive, or local play facilities are reduced – or someone being sent on enforced workfare via the Jobcentre for work experience stacking shelves, under threat of sanction.' (Community Organiser)

As argued earlier, global capitalism has fragmented and complicated class identities. The rise of identity politics and crosscutting allegiances poses challenges for locality-based organising. Thus one Organiser, reflecting on the fact that many of those getting involved were white in an ethnically diverse area, commented that this might be because many Black and Minority Ethnic (BME) residents already had their own community groups: 'the different BME groups are already more organised. They have much more of a collective identity. They are aware of class issues but these find expression through their existing organisations. You can only belong to so many [groups].' The introduction to this chapter highlighted the potential for division at local level. As Marris (1998, p.14) argues: 'The more uncertainty we generate, the more we provoke a politics of defensive exclusion, scapegoating and cynicism'. Being someone's neighbour doesn't necessarily lead to social interaction. In their studies of disadvantaged neighbourhoods, Forrest and Kearns (1999) found that many BME residents at that time tapped into wider networks across the city. More recently, Blake et al (2008, p.69) challenged the 'assumption that communities can be identified in terms of particular geographical neighbourhoods, with relative stability, enabling shared interests and priorities to be identified as the basis for continuing engagement over time'. People have multiple attachments and the 'local' isn't the only focus for many.

In this regard, Sondhi (2008, p.253) comments that: 'The most powerful "new" social movements of modern times are those that have used race, religion, culture and nationalism as a basis for radical grouping.' He goes on to describe those who are left behind:

> A whole class of people that is not so much under as out ... the poorest sections of our communities ... [who] scrabble over the leftovers of work, the rubble of slum housing and the dwindling share of welfare ... This is precisely where the challenge lies. To work ... with the most disadvantaged, disenfranchised, dispossessed. (Sondhi, 2008, p.261–2)

However, as one Organiser commented:

> maybe by using a class analysis, we can draw parallels between the roots of all exploitation, whether gender or race. ...I believe the most successful anti-racist organising I have seen has been one that also embraces questions of class. Racism viewed not as an inbuilt tendency that can be 'educated' out – but is a means of divisive 'othering', which can be made worse by particular economic situations – as a structural expression of a class relationship.

Similarly, Franklin (2014, p.193) argues that while the lessening significance of workplace organisation and the rise in other identity-based activism through new social movements (NSMs) mean that Community Organisers need to find different 'ways in', this doesn't negate the centrality of economic inequality: 'The emergence of NSMs does not reduce the influence of class-based grievances. ... these factors can accentuate concerns about economic disparities, while calling into question ascriptive hierarchies external and internal to community organizations.' The same Organiser spoke of challenging racist behaviour on the doorstep, but also consistently asking probing 'why' questions to continue a dialogue rather than condemning. He also described how complaints about the use of local services had initially brought racial tensions to the surface but that, once residents realised that they shared the same concerns, they were able to work together to resolve the issue and campaign for better provision from the council:

> Some white residents were talking about 'the Somalians' misusing communal facilities in their block. When pressed they would describe it as a behaviour of 'some' people, and when it came down to it, they were able to work with those Somalis who also viewed the behaviour as something they wanted to take action on. This was a light-bulb moment, witnessing this transformation of how creating a shared interest can transcend cultural differences.

Conclusions

This book has made a strong case for returning to ideas of class in community development today. This chapter has focused on the Community Organisers Programme, set up by the government and run by Locality. The Programme came to an end in 2015 and it remains to be seen what legacy it will leave behind. Some Community Organisers are branching out in new ways: at the time of writing, for example, there are four ACORN chapters developing local campaigns. A number of hosts have managed to find alternative funding for their Community Organisers, and other organisations have also come into the picture, employing Organisers who want to progress beyond their training year. The programme has also trained a significant number of volunteer local leaders across England. And it has a successor body – COLtd – which will continue to promote and train people in its evolving model of organising.

There have been ups and downs – as might be expected in a pilot programme – and there has been a lot of learning along the way. Whether or not the Programme will confound the criticisms of those who saw it as a creature of the government and the neoliberal agenda remains to be seen. Its adherents would no doubt strongly dispute this. But meanwhile, the Programme has demonstrated the importance of grounding Community Organising in a clear understanding of the experiences and concerns of residents in the most marginalised neighbourhoods. It has reminded us that there is a space for organising at the grassroots as the foundation for wider action. Finally, its experience echoes familiar debates from the 1970s and 1980s about the motivations of those working in communities and the extent to which they are engaged in facilitating 'community' or 'class' struggle.

Notes

[1] www.livingwage.org.uk

[2] Zero-hours contracts are arrangements whereby workers have no guaranteed weekly hours, nor regular times when they will be required to work.

Acknowledgements

The authors would like to acknowledge the contribution of the following Community Organisers: Nick Ballard; Steve Crozier; Louie Herbert, Ruby Orton and Paulette Singer, and host Kamila Zahno (trustee at Selby Trust, Tottenham), who were interviewed for this chapter. The chapter also draws on a much larger range of interviews carried out by the authors and Tricia Zipfel in their roles as learning advisors to the programme. However, responsibility for the final chapter lies solely with the authors.

References

Alinsky, S. (1971) *Rules for radicals*, New York, NY: Random House.

Beck, D. and Purcell, R. (2013) *International community organising: Taking power, making change*, Bristol: Policy Press.

Beider, H. (2011) *Community cohesion: The views of white working-class communities*, York: Joseph Rowntree Foundation.

Blake, G., Diamond, J., Foot, J., Gidley, B., Mayo, M., Shukra, K. and Yarnit, M. (2008) *Community engagement and community cohesion*, York: Joseph Rowntree Foundation.

Browne, J. and Elming, W. (2015) *The effect of the Coalition's tax and benefit changes on household incomes and work incentives*, London: Institute for Fiscal Studies.

Bryant, B. and Bryant, R. (1982) 'Change and conflict: a defence of local community action', in G. Craig, M. Mayo, K. Popple, M. Shaw, and M. Taylor (eds) (2011) *The community development reader: History, themes and issues*, Bristol: Policy Press, pp.137–46.

Bunyan, P. (2010) 'Broad-based organising in the UK: reasserting the centrality of political activity in community development', *Community Development Journal*, 45(1), pp.111–27.

Carley, M. and Smith. H. (2001) 'Civil society and the new social movements', in M. Carley, P. Jenkins and H. Smith (eds) *Urban development and civil society: The role of communities in sustainable cities*, London: Earthscan, pp.192–200.

Community Development Project (CDP) (1977) *Gilding the ghetto: The state and poverty experiments*, London: Community Development Project.

Corkey, D. and Craig, G. (1978) 'CDP: Community work or class politics', in P. Curno (ed) *Political issues and community work*, London: Routledge, pp. 36–66.

Cowley, J., Kaye, A., Mayo, M. and Thompson, M. (1977) *Community or class struggle?* London: Stage 1.

Crisp, R., Gore, T., Pearson, S. and Tyler, P. (2014) *Regeneration and poverty: Evidence and policy review, final report*, Sheffield: Sheffield Hallam University.

Delgado, G. (1999) *Beyond politics of place: New directions in community organizing*, Berkeley, CA: Chardon Press.

Driver, S. and Martell, L. (1997) 'New Labour's communitarianisms', *Critical Social Policy*, 17(3): 27–46.

Forrest, R. and Kearns, A. (1999) *Joined-up places: Social cohesion and neighbourhood regeneration*, York: Joseph Rowntree Foundation.

Franklin, S. (2014) 'Race, class and community organising in support of economic justice', *Community Development Journal*, 49(2), 181–97.

Freire, P. (1972) *Pedagogy of the oppressed*, Harmondsworth: Penguin.

Gilchrist, A. and Taylor, M. (2011) *The short guide to community development*, Bristol: Policy Press.

Glen, A. (1993) 'Methods and themes in community practice', in H. Butcher, A. Glen, P. Henderson and J. Smith (eds) *Community and public policy*, London: Pluto Press, pp.22–40.

Goode, J. and Maskovsky, J. (2001) 'Introduction', in J. Goode and J. Maskovsky (eds) *New poverty studies: The ethnography of power, politics and impoverished people in the United States*, New York, NY: NYU Press, pp.1–34.

Harflett, N. (2014) *For ever, for everyone? Patterns of volunteering: The case of the National Trust*, Unpublished PhD thesis, Southampton University.

Jones, O. (2011) *Chavs: The demonization of the working class*, London: Verso Books.

Jones, O. (2014) 'The year the grassroots took on the powerful', *The Guardian*, 28 December.

Little, M. (2011) 'Analysis: why Alinsky's supporters lost out', *Third Sector*, 8 March, www.thirdsector.co.uk/analysis-why-alinskys-supporters-lost/infrastructure/article/1058293

Loney, M. (1983) *Community against government: The British community development project, 1986–78*, London: Heinemann.

Marris, P. (1998) 'Planning and civil society in the twenty-first century', in M. Douglass and J. Friedmann (eds) *Cities for citizens*, Chichester: John Wiley, pp.9–17.

Meekosha, H. (1993) 'The bodies politic: equality, difference and community practice', in H. Butcher, A. Glen, P. Henderson and J. Smith (eds) *Community and public policy*, London: Pluto Press, pp.171–93.

Mills, J. and Robson, S. (2010) 'Does community organising empower or oppress?' *CDX magazine*, Winter: 12, pp.12–14, www.corganisers.org.uk/sites/default/files/does_community_organising_empower_or_oppress.PDF

Pearce, J. and Milne, E. (2010), *Participation and community on Bradford's traditionally white estates*, York: Joseph Rowntree Foundation.

Pearce, J., Taylor, M., Wilson, M. and Zipfel, T. (2011) *Interview transcripts to inform theory of change*, Unpublished internal document.

Rothman, J. with Tropman, J. (1993) 'Models of community organizations and macro practice perspectives: their mixing and phasing', in F. Cox, J. Erlich, J. Rothman and J. Tropman (eds) *Strategies of community organization*, 4th edition, Itasca, IL: F.E. Peacock, pp.3–26.

Sen, R. (2003) *Stir it up: Lessons in community organizing and advocacy*, San Francisco, CA: Jossey-Bass.

Smock, K. (2003) *Democracy in action: Community organizing and urban change*, New York, NY: University of Columbia Press.

Sondhi, R. (2008) 'The politics of equality or the politics of difference? Locating Black communities in western society', in G. Craig, K. Popple and M. Shaw (eds), *Community development in theory and practice: An international reader*, Nottingham: Spokesman, pp.253–63.

Stall, S. and Stoecker, R. (1998) 'Community organizing or organizing community? Gender and the crafts of empowerment', *Gender and Society*, 12(6), 729–56.

Taylor, M. (2007) 'Community participation in the real world: opportunities and pitfalls in new governance spaces', *Urban Studies*, 44(2), 297–317.

Taylor, M. (2011) *Public policy in the community*, 2nd edition, Bristol: Policy Press.

Thompson, E.P. (1963) *The making of the English working class*, London: Victor Gollancz.

Waddington, P. (1979) 'Looking ahead: community work into the 1980s', *Community Development Journal*, 14(3), 224–34.

Community unionism: looking backwards, looking forwards

Marjorie Mayo and Pilgrim Tucker, with Mat Danaher

Introduction

This book set out to explore ways in which community development workers can enhance their contributions to social justice agendas by developing strategic approaches that take account of the contested concept of social class together with the ways in which class intersects with gender; race; ethnicity, caste and faith, among other forms of social division. Community development itself cannot, of course, resolve the challenges posed by neoliberal globalisation. But as Shaw and Martin have argued (2008, p.305), community workers can make significant contributions, enabling people in communities to pursue their interests democratically as part of wider strategies for social justice.

The aim in this chapter is to reflect upon strategies and experiences of aiming to build bridges between community-based and grassroots organisations on the one hand and workplace-based organisations on the other. While the chapter focuses primarily upon British examples, there seem to be a number of potentially wider implications, too. For example, how might such reflections inform community development more generally, drawing upon critical understandings of social class and inequality to build effective and sustainable alliances with wider movements for progressive social change?

Alliances based on addressing shared community and union concerns constitute a theme that runs through many of the preceding chapters. For example, Gary Craig's chapter (Craig, chapter Three) includes reflections on experiences of strategic alliance building in the past. The more recent experiences of the MST in Brazil illustrate the potential for building alliances between rural workers and urban workers (*Martínez-Torres and Firmiano*, chapter Ten), while the chapter on environmental struggles in Italy demonstrates the scope for linking workers and their communities in struggles against industrial pollution (Barca and Leonardi, chapter Four). Similarly, other chapters reflect on the opportunities and challenges involved in working alongside formal political structures, including political parties and movements of the Left (Franklin, chapter Five; Geddes, chapter Six; Hicks and Myeni, chapter Seven).

This chapter starts by reflecting upon further examples of community–trade union organising in Britain. This sets the framework for summarising some potential implications for alliance building for the future. Trade unions have a long history of engagement with movements for progressive social change, the significance of which has not been lost on governments with very different political agendas. Curbing the power of the trade unions has been a major theme within neoliberal policy agendas over past decades; indeed, has been a central component of wider strategies to shift the balance of power away from working people and their communities more generally. There are common interests to be addressed as a result, cutting across community–workplaces divides, in the pursuit of alternative agendas for social justice.

Building alliances: community organising and community unionism in Britain

Although alliances between communities and trade unions have featured in the history of community development over time, this approach has taken on a new urgency more recently. This is in the context of regressive shifts in patterns of work and the power of labour together with regressive shifts that have taken place for communities – as a result of neoliberal strategies in general and austerity policies more specifically – following the international financial crisis of 2008–09. While these processes have been global in scope their impact can be traced particularly clearly in Britain, which has stimulated trade union and community activists to develop joint strategies in response. These responses have consciously drawn upon previous experiences elsewhere – including Australia, Canada and the USA – in order to learn what works most effectively in which types of circumstance (Holgate, 2015).

The recent impetus for developing these types of alliances in Britain has been the necessity to respond to significant contemporary challenges. From 2010, the Coalition Government pursued austerity policies that compounded previous trends, including the shift towards increasing financialisation, promoting the interests of finance capital as part of wider global trends (Lapavitsas, 2013). In parallel, that government was committed to increasing the marketisation of public services and undermining public service jobs, pay and conditions of employment while further stigmatising those relying on social security – whether such reliance was a result of being unable to undertake paid work or, more typically, because of being trapped in insecure, low-paid employment (Standing, 2011). These welfare myths – 'strivers' versus 'skivers' or 'scroungers' – have been significant factors in exacerbating divisions within and between communities, and increasing fragmentation within and between workplaces, further undermining traditional solidarities. Since the election of a Conservative Government in 2015, these challenges have been exacerbated, with further legislation being introduced to curtail the power of trade unions and further reductions in the provision of welfare.

While the state was actively reinforcing inequalities and promoting the interests of the richest 1% (Weeks, 2014) at the expense of the rest of the population, the need for an alternative approach was becoming correspondingly more pressing, and potentially more plausible. As Hills (2015) has argued (among others), there has been increasing scope for identifying common interests among the 99% as the basis for building shared understandings: 'There is no "Them and Us" – just us' (Hills, 2015, p.266). Austerity has been affecting living standards for the so-called 'squeezed middle' too, just as casualisation has been impacting upon those with professional occupations as well as those in manual occupations, with particularly devastating effects upon young people and women (TUC, 2014). Groups that have been pitted against each other in the past might be brought together across previous divides, then, constructing alliances around issues of common concern.

The research upon which this chapter draws consists of semi-structured interviews with a number of those directly concerned: as organisers and activists. Although this includes a disproportionate weighting of interviews with activists and organisers based in London, these experiences do offer illustrations of wider trends. As the capital city and a global finance centre, London has been experiencing the impact of neoliberal globalisation in extreme forms, with an increasingly casualised labour market, widening inequalities and increasing social fragmentation. The accompanying pressures on the housing market have compounded these trends, as have the so-called 'reforms' of social welfare benefits – including housing benefits – which have squeezed low- and middle-income residents out of Inner London altogether (Dorling, 2014; Mayo and Newman, 2014). These combined pressures highlight the challenges to be faced more generally in terms of trade union and community-based organising.

The concluding section of this chapter considers some of the implications for community development workers in terms of building alliances in the pursuit of social justice agendas at different levels: locally, nationally and beyond.

Community unionism: contested concepts and practices, past and present

As previous chapters have already established, the concept of 'community' has been notoriously slippery, causing earlier sociologists to question the extent to which this notion could usefully be employed at all (Stacey, 1969). There have, in addition, been comparable questions about the concept of 'community unionism' and the varying ways in which the term has been used in different contexts (Stewart et al, 2009). In summary, these have included a range of trade union–community relationships at local, national, regional and international levels, typically concerned with revitalising trade union and progressive movements in the face of increasing challenges: both locally and globally. As will be suggested subsequently, however, these alliances have had to take account of the differing priorities and objectives of the different partners concerned, and to address the resultant tensions produced.

Given that trade unions represent the largest section of civil society (with some six million members), community unionism might seem to be an obvious and positive development for all concerned. But the realities of previous experiences illustrate some of the complexities, which have continuing relevance for those concerned with community development in the contemporary context. As will also be suggested, a critical understanding of the concept of social class has particular relevance here, offering ways of identifying common interests between partners with differing traditions and structures.

Previous accounts of community unionism in Britain can provide illustrations of its potential contributions to community development, although it is important to recognise that there have also been longstanding differences and division even within relatively homogenous working-class communities. These have included divisions between those employed in different sectors – whether in skilled or unskilled work, for example – as well as between women's and men's priorities and in terms of ethnicity and identity.

For example, reflecting on the links between active trade unionists and tenants in Glasgow during the First World War and subsequently, a tenants' leader explained that a large number of the people involved in tenants' organisations were also trade unionists, 'in the sense of being members of trade unions' (Liddell and Bryant, 1974, p.92). But, as he went on to explain, 'there's more to it than just being trade unionists. Because invariably active trade unionists are probably active ... out of a sort of class consciousness and the same class consciousness can find its expression in tenants' organisations' (Liddell and Bryant, 1974, p.92). The results of this concerted – and class conscious – campaigning often resulted in progressive legislative change, spearheading the development of social housing (and tenants' rights more widely) for the future. But even here, in Glasgow, there were organisational challenges to be faced in subsequent years, including those that resulted from processes of fragmentation arising particularly from the increasing privatisation of public housing. This fragmentation was felt especially among tenants with different landlords, as social housing was increasingly being managed by housing associations and New Town corporations as well as by local government authorities. As this tenants' activist acknowledged, it took time and conscious effort to build the type of solidarity that was needed, taking account of continually changing circumstances and challenges for tenants as well as the differences between tenants' organisations and trade unions in terms of their organisational traditions and structures.

Similar examples of the potential for community unionism emerged from the history of organising unemployed workers in Britain in the 1920s and 1930s through the National Unemployed Workers Movement (NUWM). As local activists reflected at the time, local struggles were part of wider national struggles (Edwards, 1979). Those local struggles included community-based campaigning over issues such as rents and community-based resistance to evictions when tenants were refusing, or simply unable, to pay the rent (Edwards, 1979). As previous cases have also illustrated, these struggles had very local bases, particularly in localities in which the links between working-class experiences (at work, out of work and in the community), such as experiences as tenants, were relatively overt. Despite these links between different aspects of working–class experiences, there were still tensions between the NUWM and the rest of the trade union movement, illustrating the complexities involved in developing common understandings even in these relatively non-fragmented contexts. In recent times, critical understandings of class, and shared class interests have correspondingly become more crucial.

In the case of joint union–resident action campaigning around 'green bans' in Australia, this critical consciousness included questioning the nature and purposes of the work that trades unionists do, raising wider questions of workers' control for the longer term (Mundey and Craig, 1978). For example, how should neighbourhood spaces be developed

– taking account of environmental issues as well as community needs – and how should construction workers organise around these types of issues? There are resonances here with longstanding theoretical debates about the nature of trade unions and their contributions to wider movements for social justice: confined to bargaining around immediate issues of pay and conditions in the workplace, or locating these struggles within wider strategies for social change in the longer term. There are further resonances with social movement theorists, who envisaged urban social movements as the equivalents of trade unions within communities: mobilising around immediate issues of collective consumption such as housing and planning issues within the framework of existing social relations, although with similar potential for contributing to wider movements for social change as well in the longer term.

As Craig (1998) has so clearly pointed out, in reality, 'Community workers are often called on by government to contribute to the peaceful management of the process of economic change ... to help people adjust to the insecurity and fragmentation of their lives'. Trade unions can adopt similarly adaptive roles: managing rather than challenging processes of economic restructuring and social change in increasingly managerial cultures in the context of neoliberalism more generally. But conversely, they can also contribute to the development of alternative agendas. As the British Trades Union Congress (TUC) report *Swords of Justice and Civic Pillars* (TUC, 2010) demonstrated, community unionism can enable trade unions to organise vulnerable, fragmented sections of the workforce while also strengthening community organisations and promoting active citizenship, empowerment and social solidarity. These initiatives need to be rooted in critical understandings of social class and the class interests that can be shared between activists: for example, crossing boundaries between those who provide services and those who need them; between professional employees and manual staff, between activists across different housing tenures and between working and unemployed people. As the following section illustrates, these analytical understandings are essential, along with the more practical understandings that relate to the very different organisational traditions and structures that underpin trade unions and community organisations respectively.

Contrasting approaches to building community unionism

Community unionism has been broadly defined as a concerted effort to partner unions with community actors in order to reach a common goal, rather than reaching said goal through industrial activities conducted by trade unions alone (Stewart et al, 2009). Drawing on models developed internationally, a number of trade unions – including the two largest: UNITE (active in all sectors of the economy) and UNISON (which organises largely among those who provide public services, whether these are funded from the public purse directly or indirectly) – have formally adopted this as a strategy in recent years. For example, UNITE launched its strategy towards the end of 2011, with the appointment of regionally dedicated staff taking place some months later. (The original remit was for just one year, which was subsequently extended). UNISON's Community Organising Coordinator was similarly appointed in 2012.

However, while there are parallels in terms of their overall goals, these unions have developed different models of engagement. In UNISON, the Community Organising Coordinator's remit focuses upon supporting and enabling the union membership – particularly the activists – to engage with communities, whether these are communities of locality, identity or faith. The broad aim has been to spread the lessons of what works most effectively: through preparing training materials and organising training events, for example. The union works in partnership with a wide range of national organisations, including established voluntary sector and faith-based organisations, as well as with locally-based community organisations and groups.

In contrast, the UNITE model involves building a new type of organisation, bringing wider communities into union membership. This new type of membership was initially made available to those who would not otherwise be able to access workplace trade unions: unemployed people, students, retired people and those in irregular, precarious employment (a significantly increasing section of the workforce in the context of neoliberal austerity policies in Britain). The project has a number of aims:

- to reach people who may feel disenfranchised and disengaged, providing them with the knowledge, confidence and skills to (re) engage and to take part in collective action on issues of mutual concern;
- to bring the strengths and values of trade unionism, such as the importance of collective action and social solidarity, into communities suffering from the impacts of austerity;
- to increase awareness and understanding of trade unionism among working-class people who have little or no knowledge of the

importance of trade unions: both for workers' rights and for progressive social change more broadly.

For example, the crisis in the availability of genuinely affordable housing in London – with rocketing house prices and rapidly rising rents – has been a key focus for community organising. These housing pressures have been compounded by cuts in social welfare benefits, which have had the most severe impact on the most disadvantaged in society, including those in low-paid work as well as those outside paid work altogether. As a result of these combined pressures, local struggles to resist dispersal have the potential to bring tenants' and residents' organisations together alongside trade union and community activists more widely.

These differing approaches each have their own distinct rationales, taking account of the varying contexts that impact upon trade unions' approaches more generally. For example, the UNITE model enables those without access to workplace-based organisations to become directly involved, including those living in socially fragmented neighbourhoods such as those with very high levels of population churn in Inner London. This type of community fragmentation has become a major issue in areas in which a third of the population moves every year, for example (typically, areas characterised by disproportionate amounts of very insecure tenancies in the privately-rented housing market). As has already been suggested, such areas in the global city of capital illustrate the impacts of neoliberalism in extreme forms: both in the workplace and in neighbourhoods and 'communities'.

The UNISON approach, meanwhile, places more emphasis on building alliances between those who provide public services and those who use them – or would like to use them, were it not for the austerity agendas that have severely depleted them. There are, of course, examples of very successful campaigns in varying international contexts over time that demonstrate the potential for building precisely such alliances, resisting privatisation and defending public services more generally (see, for example, the Public Services International and the Transnational Institute report, *The Tragedy of the Private: The Potential of the Public*, 2014). A similar example in the British context is the support provided to UNISON's members in the health and social care sectors by carers' organisations, which recognise their common interests in campaigning to improve the availability and quality of care more generally.

Conversely, however, it has also been pointed out that service users do not always or necessarily identify with the interests of service providers. On the contrary: social workers can be blamed by parents when their children are taken into care, and mental health workers blamed by patients when they are hospitalised against their will. Local authority housing staff can be blamed when they are unable to respond to applications for housing provision in the context of rising demand for a shrinking supply of genuinely affordable housing. These tensions have been exacerbated as a result of austerity policies, increasing the tensions to be addressed whichever approach is being adopted.

Reciprocal community unionism: tensions and challenges

These contrasting approaches each have success stories to share. Despite the particular pressures in London, for example, community organising has been reaching those outside the framework of stable employment: including those with no previous experience of trade unions, no shared family memories of trade unionism and little (if any) experience of advocacy and campaigning more generally. Through training in community organising, media skills, specific campaign issues and rights, community members have been supported in becoming generally more active in civil society. Housing has probably been one of the most successful mobilising issues for these newly engaging activists, particularly young activists: perhaps unsurprisingly, given the scale of the housing crisis in London.

Community organising has also succeeded in strengthening trade union activists, enabling them to identify the scope for building alliances. Some 80% of trade unionists are also active in their communities,in any case, but members do not necessarily perceive the links between their different spheres of activism until these are drawn to their attention. There are particularly relevant links for women members, as women have been especially vulnerable to the impacts of austerity: both as public service workers and as the users of public services for themselves and those for whom they care, at home and in their communities (TUC, 2014). Women have been particularly seriously affected by austerity generally (Karamessini and Rubery, 2014) as well as more specifically by casualisation: a process that impacts upon women in different sections of the labour market, including professional women as well as women in less highly-skilled jobs (TUC, 2014).

With appropriate training, trade union activists have also been enabled to engage more effectively with minority communities; for example, Polish and Philippino communities, both of which have substantial numbers of members working in the health and social care sectors. More generally, training can also stress the importance of developing links and building relationships of trust before attempting to create joint campaigns: 'You can't just go in there and expect them [communities] to work with us' before building such relationships, as one organising coordinator emphasised.

However, while there have been notable successes there have also been significant challenges. For example, trade unions are concerned with recruiting and retaining members; understandably so in a period of declining membership as a result of deindustrialisation, job cuts and casualisation. These processes have been especially marked in the public sector, in which trade union organisation has traditionally been denser. It has been argued that community organising has indeed produced some results in terms of the recruitment of trade union members, if not so significantly in terms of increasing trade union density (that is, the proportion of the workforce that is unionised) (Simms et al, 2013). But this has by no means been the only aim, as those directly involved evidently appreciate, understanding as they do the importance of enhancing the agency of working-class communities and achieving wider social change starting from people's own issues and priorities. 'Reciprocal community unionism', as Wills and Simms explain, 'means sustaining relationships with community groups to help improve local life *as well as* fostering trade union growth' (Wills and Simms, 2004, p.66, emphasis in the original).

Such potentially beneficial synergy has not necessarily been experienced or appreciated by community organisations, however; on the contrary, research evidence suggests that community organisations have tended to perceive trade unions as primarily interested in recruiting members, with little interest in pursuing wider strategic goals (Simms et al, 2013). There have been potential sources of tension here, then, as those directly involved in trade union community organising have clearly been recognising.

There have also been challenges relating to different organisational forms and approaches to the issue of democratic accountability, as Holgate (2009) has illustrated in her study of the London Campaign for a Living Wage. Although this campaign achieved considerable success in terms of persuading employers to improve pay and conditions for low-paid employees in some sectors, it was not without its inherent tensions. Many – if not all – of those based in the community organisation involved in this specific campaign perceived the trade unions as being overly bureaucratic and slow: incapable of responding rapidly as the campaign developed. Conversely, the trade unions perceived the community organisation in question as being fundamentally undemocratic in its ways of operating. In particular, they did not recognise the community organisation's annual open assemblies as providing for effective democratic accountability, or indeed as democratic structures at all. There are striking parallels here with more general debates between so-called 'horizontal' and 'vertical' approaches to community organising and building social movements (Della Porta and Rucht, 2013): debates that continue to have relevance in the context of community unionism.

Trade unions and community organisations tend to have different cultures in any case, with widespread misconceptions on either side. So, for example, trade unionists have been stereotyped as 'pale, male and stale', while community activists have been characterised as too often lacking any understanding of trade unions – let alone of the differences within and between trade unions – and their varying perspectives at regional and national levels. Negative portrayals of trade unions in the mass media can exacerbate these problems. Such misconceptions can be further compounded when activists come from different cultural backgrounds – in terms of socioeconomic position, ethnicity or faith – each with their own ways of communicating. The extent to which there is an understanding of the daily lives of the 'other' (or not) is also significant. As a result, there are major – but by no means insurmountable – challenges to be addressed.

Political structures, strategies and roles

Before moving on to the wider implications, there are two remaining sets of issues and challenges identified in the research. The first of these relates to working within political structures and frameworks. A number of chapters in this book point to the importance of formal political structures as a critical factor in the degrees of success to be achieved (Franklin, chapter Five; Geddes, chapter Six; Martinez-Torres and Firmiano, chapter Ten; Taylor and Wilson, chapter Fourteen). As Tattersall (2010) has pointed out, political contexts are centrally important to community trade unionism; for example, when relatively progressive parties are in power, spaces can be opened up, enabling community trade union coalitions to be heard. In her view, coalitions need to engage with such governments at both national and local levels. On the other hand, previous chapters also provide vivid illustrations of some inherent tensions, including the potential tensions when community organisers move into government, as the chapter on Bolivia demonstrates (Geddes, chapter Six).

In the context of community trade union organising in Britain, party-political affiliations have proved a source of strength when politically experienced activists share their knowledge, skills and enthusiasm with others. Conversely, however, there have been examples of situations in which particular political parties and groups have pursued their own party-political agendas and/or prioritised recruitment to their own particular organisations over building effective joint campaigns. Such ways of operating have proved very destructive on occasion, alienating and demobilising others in the process.

There are issues relating to the Labour Party more specifically, too, given its historic emergence via the trade union movement in Britain. When the Labour Party has been in opposition, it was suggested, there has been considerable scope for identifying common ground in terms of shared support for the defence of public services such as the National Health Service (NHS). But there were also significant differences, such as to what extent to reject neoliberal austerity policies. Such differences have been especially marked among some of the younger community activists: many of whom are deeply suspicious of party politics in any case, favouring strategies involving direct action. As the Bolivian experience illustrates more generally, such differences and tensions could be expected to increase in the future if the Labour Party were to be directly involved in government again. The point to emphasise here, then, is simply that party politics have to be taken into account: for better or for worse. Community organisers therefore need to understand the varying ways in which party politics impact within and between trade unions at different levels: regionally and nationally.

In addition to these wider political factors, community organisers also drew attention to the vital roles played by individual activists and the varying ways in which these roles may be interpreted. Trade unions and community organisations both tend to attract particular types of activists to leadership positions, it was suggested. Dedication, determination and single-mindedness are key qualities for those who are going to make a difference; but charismatic leadership styles have their downsides as well as their advantages. Qualities such as dogged single-mindedness do not necessarily enhance the scope for alliance building and solidarity based upon mutual respect. Individuals with leadership qualities can and do bring different groups together, developing shared strategies in pursuit of their common interests; but particularly strong-minded individuals can also exacerbate conflicts, undermining relationships of mutual trust in the process.

Meanwhile, however, it is important to recall that trade union–community organising has placed particular emphasis on empowering those with little or no previous involvement. This has led to the development of new types of activists, who tend to have fewer of the aforementioned traits. Driven by very basic 'bread and butter' / 'bread if not also butter' necessity – such as defending their homes or protecting families and friends from extreme hardship – a new tranche of activists has been emerging, particularly female heads of households. And these activists tend to place more emphasis on collaborative than conflictual ways of working.

Summarising the lessons about what works in trade union community coalition building, Tattersall (2010) puts particular emphasis upon building trust: based on identifying the different partners' shared interests. This can provide the basis for developing strategies at both national and local levels, in her view, connecting the mutual self-interests of the participating parties with what she describes as a 'Sword of Justice' approach, underpinned with shared values for the longer term. This takes the discussion beyond immediate considerations, identifying potential partnerships around specific issues of common concern. While such one-off, ad-hoc alliances most definitely have their place, the development of longer-term alliances needs to also be based upon shared values, building support for social justice agendas for the future.

Wider implications: building effective and sustainable alliances for social justice

There seem to be a number of implications here for community development more generally. Officially sponsored community development initiatives have their own inbuilt tensions, even when policies and programmes are sponsored by generally progressive political parties (Craig, chapter Three; Hicks and Myeni, chapter Seven). Community development workers need to maintain a measure of distance even in these circumstances, taking account of the arguments in favour of working both 'In and Against the State' (LEWRG, 1980). While taking account of the inherent structural constraints, however, community development workers can still decide to explore the spaces within which to contribute to wider strategies to challenge inequalities relating to the workplace, as well as those that manifest themselves within community settings. Community workers can also enable communities to organise more effectively, building partnerships to address issues of immediate mutual interest or concern. But they can also go beyond this to contribute to the development of alliances and social movements, focussing upon the pursuit of social justice agendas for the longer term. Such alliances may also be strengthened when community development workers identify creative ways of building bridges across previous divides, including divides within and between workplaces and communities: whether these are communities of identity, interest or place.

But in order to contribute to such agendas – thereby enabling communities to acquire the knowledge, confidence and skills that they need in order to address the challenges involved – community development workers need clear understandings themselves, based upon critical analyses of the specific socioeconomic, political and cultural contexts in which they are working (points developed in previous chapters, including Bilon et al, chapter Nine; Newman, chapter Eleven; Shahid and Jha, chapter Eight; Fung, chapter Thirteen and Adhikari and Taylor, chapter Fourteen). They need to be able to work alongside communities to make power maps and to identify the spaces for effective collective action, taking account of political opportunity structures and making realistic appraisals of the underlying structural constraints. And they need to be able to develop links between 'top-down' and 'bottom-up' approaches – locally, nationally and beyond – building alliances with potential supporters inside and outside both the formal structures of the state and party-political organisations and groups.

As previous chapters and the preceding section on community trade unionism have also illustrated, such alliances need to be built upon mutual understanding and respect for diversity, taking account of different organisational structures and cultures within and between trade unions and communities (Barca and Leonardi, chapter Four; Martinez-Torres, chapter Ten). The search for this kind of mutual understanding can provide the basis for building trust, rooted in shared understandings of each partner's interests and values.

Most importantly, such understandings need to start from a clear analysis of the contested concepts of power (Newman, chapter Eleven) and social class (Fox Piven and Minnite, chapter Two). As previous chapters have demonstrated, a critical understanding of social class can provide the basis for identifying common interests between apparently disparate social groups with different experiences of organisational structures and cultures. For example, previous chapters have demonstrated the scope for building alliances between urban and rural workers and between trade unionists and community activists, including those from white-collar occupations as well as the blue-collar manual occupations that – in Weberian terms – have traditionally defined the working class.

In contrast, Marxist approaches – rooted as they are in exposing the underlying causes of exploitation and oppression – provide more analytical ways of identifying common class interests and offering ways of building alliances to tackle social inequalities, while continuing to be mindful and respectful of differences and diversities. There are potentially significant challenges here for dominant community development paradigms – as well as for training and professional support for community development workers – for the future.

References

Craig, G. (1998) 'Community development in a global context', *Community Development Journal*, 33(1): 2–17.

Della Porta, D. and Rucht, D. (2013) *Meeting democracy: Power and deliberation in global justice movements*, Cambridge: Cambridge University Press.

Dorling, D. (2014) *All that is solid: The great housing disaster*, London: Allen Lane.

Edwards, B. (1979) 'Organising the unemployed in the 1920s', in G. Craig, M. Mayo and N. Sharman (eds), *Jobs and community action*, London: Routledge and Kegan Paul, pp 27–32.

Hills, J. (2015) *Good times, bad times: The welfare myth of them and us*, Bristol: Policy Press.

Holgate, J. (2009) 'London citizens and the campaign for a living wage', in J. McBride and I. Greenwood (eds), *Community unions: A comparative analysis of concepts and contexts*, Basingstoke: Palgrave Macmillan, pp.49–74.

Holgate, J. (2015) *Community organising and the implications for union revitalisation*, ETUI Policy Brief, http://www.etui.org/content/download/20154/165291/file/Policy+Brief+2015.04+Holgate.pdf

Karamessini, M. and Rubery, J. (2014) *Women and austerity: The economic crisis and the future for gender equality*, London: Routledge.

Lapavitsas, C. (2013) *Profiting without producing: How finance exploits us all*, London: Verso.

LEWRG (London–Edinburgh Weekend Return Group) (1980) *In and against the state*, London: Pluto

Liddell, H. and Bryant, R. (1974) 'A local view of community work', in D. Jones and M. Mayo (eds), *Community Work One*, London: Routledge and Kegan Paul, pp 90–100.

Mayo, M. and Newman, I. (2014) *Tackling the housing crisis: Alternatives to declining standards, displacement and dispossession*, London: Centre for Labour and Social Studies.

Mundey, J. and Craig, G. (1978) 'Joint union–resident action', in P. Curno (ed), *Political issues and community work*, London: Routledge and Kegan Paul, pp 199–218.

Public Services International and the Transnational Institute (2014) *The tragedy of the private: The potential of the public*, Ferney-Voltaire and Amsterdam: Public Services International and the Transnational Institute.

Shaw, M. and Martin, I. (2008) 'Community work, citizenship and democracy: remaking the connections', in G. Craig, K. Popple and M. Shaw (eds) *Community development in theory and practice*, Nottingham: Spokesman, p.296–308.

Simms, M., Holgate, J. and Heery, E. (2013) *Union voices*, London: ILR Press.

Standing, G. (2011) *The precariat: The new dangerous class*, London: Bloomsbury Academic.

Stacey, M. (1969) 'The myth of community studies', *The British Journal of Sociology*, 20(2): 134–47.

Stewart, P., McBride, J., Greenwood, I., Stirling, J., Holgate, J., Tattersall, A., Stephenson, C. and Wray, D. (2009) 'Introduction', in J. McBride and I. Greenwood (eds), *Community unionism: A comparative analysis of concepts and contexts,* Basingstoke: Palgrave, pp 3–20.

Tattershall, A. (2010) *Power in coalition*, Ithaca and London: ILR Press.

Trades Union Congress (TUC) (2010) *Swords of justice and civic pillars*, London: Trades Union Congress.

Trades Union Congress (TUC) (2014) *Women and casualisation*, London: Trades Union Congress.

Weeks, J. (2014) *Economics of the 1%*, London: Anthem Press.

Wills, J. and Simms, M. (2004) 'Building reciprocal community unionism in the UK', *Capital and Class,* 28: 59–82.

Index